LAWRENCE AND THE NATURE TRADITION:
A Theme in English Fiction 1859–1914

LAWRENCE AND THE NATURE TRADITION:

A Theme in English Fiction 1859–1914

ROGER EBBATSON
Senior Lecturer in English,
University of Sokoto, Nigeria

HARVESTER PRESS . SUSSEX
HUMANITIES PRESS . NEW JERSEY

First published in Great Britain in 1980 by
THE HARVESTER PRESS LIMITED
Publishers: John Spiers and Margaret A. Boden
16 Ship Street, Brighton, Sussex
and in the USA by
HUMANITIES PRESS INC.,
Atlantic Highlands, New Jersey 07716

© Roger Ebbatson, 1980

British Library Cataloguing in Publication Data

Ebbatson, Roger
    Lawrence and the nature tradition.
    1. Nature in literature
    2. English fiction – History and criticism
    I. Title
    823'.8'0936   PR830.N36

    ISBN 0-85527-343-7

Humanities Press Inc.,

    ISBN 0–391–01884–1

Typeset by Inforum Ltd., Portsmouth
Printed in Great Britain by
Redwood Burn Limited, Trowbridge and Esher

For Rebecca

Contents

Preface

In a different form this study first took shape as a thesis submitted in the University of London. I am indebted to the staffs of many libraries for help in locating books, notably the University of London Library, Senate House, and the British Library. During the years I worked on this book I received much help and encouragement from Michael Rhodes and Frank Pinion. My deepest debt, however, is to Christopher Heywood, who has always been ready to share the findings of his own massive researches in the period under question. In preparing the typescript Peter Griggs rendered invaluable aid.

Reference to novels in the text is by abbreviated title (see Notes for full citation in the first instance) chapter (Roman numerals) and page (Arabic numerals).

ROGER EBBATSON
University of Sokoto, Nigeria
January 1980

Acknowledgements

The author and publishers are grateful to the following for permission to quote from copyright material:

King's College, Cambridge and The Society of Authors Ltd as the Literary Representatives of the Estate of E.M. Forster.

William Heinemann Ltd, Laurence Pollinger Ltd and the Estate of the late Mrs Frieda Lawrence Ravagli, and Viking Penguin Inc, New York as follows:

Aaron's Rod by D.H. Lawrence, copyright 1922 by Thos. Seltzer Inc, renewed 1950 by Mrs Frieda Lawrence, reprinted by permission of William Heinemann Ltd, Laurence Pollinger Ltd and the Estate of the late Mrs Frieda Lawrence Ravagli, and Viking Penguin Inc.

Collected Letters of D.H. Lawrence, ed. H.T. Moore. Copyright 1932 by the Estate of D.H. Lawrence and by Frieda Lawrence; copyright 1933, 1948, 1954 and subsequent years 1956–62 by A. Ravagli and C.M. Weekley. Reprinted by permission of William Heinemann Ltd, Laurence Pollinger Ltd and the Estate of the late Mrs Frieda Lawrence Ravagli, and Viking Penguin Inc.

Complete Poems of D.H. Lawrence, ed. V. de S. Pinto and W. Roberts. Copyright 1964, 1971 by A. Ravagli and C.M. Weekley, Executors of the Estate of the late Mrs Frieda Lawrence Ravagli. Reprinted by permission of William Heinemann Ltd, Laurence Pollinger Ltd and Viking Penguin Inc.

Kangaroo by D.H. Lawrence, copyright 1923 by Thomas Seltzer Inc, renewed 1951 by Frieda Lawrence. Reprinted by permission of William Heinemann Ltd, Laurence Pollinger and the Estate of the late Mrs Frieda Lawrence Ravagli, and Viking Penguin Inc.

Mornings in Mexico by D.H. Lawrence, copyright 1927 by Alfred A. Knopf. Reprinted by permission of William

Estate of the late Mrs Frieda Lawrence Ravagli, and Viking Penguin Inc.

The White Peacock by D.H. Lawrence. Copyright 1911, 1921 by D.H. Lawrence, and 1930 by Frieda Lawrence. Copyright 1966 by A. Ravagli and C.M. Weekley, executors of the Estate of the late Mrs Frieda Lawrence Ravagli. Reprinted by permission of William Heinemann Ltd, Laurence Pollinger Ltd and the Estate of the late Mrs Frieda Lawrence Ravagli, and Viking Penguin Inc.

Women in Love by D.H. Lawrence. Copyright 1920, 1922 by D.H. Lawrence, renewed 1948, 1950 by Frieda Lawrence. Reprinted by permission of William Heinemann Ltd, Laurence Pollinger Ltd and the Estate of the late Mrs Frieda Lawrence Ravagli, and Viking Penguin Inc.

1 Nature as ordeal and deliverance

I

'I call it a very fine country — the hills are steep, the woods seem full of fine timber, and the valley looks comfortable and snug — with rich meadows and several neat farm houses scattered here and there. It exactly answers my idea of a fine country, because it unites beauty with utility — and I dare say it is a picturesque one too, because you admire it; I can easily believe it to be full of rocks and promontories, grey moss and brush wood, but these are all lost on me. I know nothing of the picturesque.'

'I am afraid it is but too true,' said Marianne; 'but why should you boast of it?'

'I suspect,' said Elinor, 'that to avoid one kind of affectation, Edward here falls into another. Because he believes many people pretend to more admiration of the beauties of nature than they really feel, and is disgusted with such pretensions, he affects greater indifference and less discrimination in viewing them himself than he possesses. He is fastidious and will have an affectation of his own.'

'It is very true,' said Marianne, 'that admiration of landscape scenery is become a mere jargon. Everybody pretends to feel and tries to describe with the taste and elegance of him who first defined what picturesque beauty was. I detest jargon of every kind, and sometimes I have kept my feelings to myself, because I could find no language to describe them in but what was worn and hackneyed out of all sense and meaning.'

'I am convinced,' said Edward, 'that you really feel all the delight in a fine prospect which you profess to feel. But, in return, your sister must allow me to feel no more than I profess. I like a fine prospect, but not on picturesque principles. I do not like crooked, twisted, blasted trees. I admire them much more if they are tall, straight and flourishing. I do not like ruined, tattered cottages. I am not fond of nettles, or thistles, or heath blossoms. I have more pleasure in a snug farm-house than a watch-tower — and a troop of tidy, happy villagers please me better than the finest banditti in the world.'

(Jane Austen, *Sense and Sensibility*, Chapter XVIII)

'My temple as yet,' said Lancelot, 'is only the heaven and the earth; my church-music I can hear all day long, whenever I have the sense to be silent, and "hear my mother sing"; my priests and preachers are every bird and bee, every flower and cloud. Am I not well enough furnished? Do you want to reduce my circular infinite chapel to an oblong hundred-foot one? . . . my dreams of naiads and flower-fairies, and the blue-bells ringing God's praises . . . for the gross reality of naughty charity children, with their pockets full of

apples, bawling out Hebrew psalms of which they neither feel nor understand a word?'

(Charles Kingsley, *Yeast*, Chapter III)

To be! To live! To have an intense enjoyment in every inspiration of breath;
in every beat of the pulse; in every movement of the limbs; in every sense! . . .
Her whole existence was quivering with love; this intensity of life was love.
She was gathering from sunlight, azure sky and grassy fields, from dewy hills
and all the morning, an immense strength to love.

Richard Jefferies, *The Dewy Morn*, Chapter I)

In the seminal exchange between Marianne, Elinor and
Edward, with its backward glance to Gilpin, Burke and rampant Gothicism, Jane Austen economically dramatises what
was to become a crucial theme of nineteenth-century literature
— man's relation to Nature. Indeed, the evolution of this
concept in the literature of the period epitomised by the
movement of thought and response from Jane Austen,
through Kingsley, to Jefferies might be described as the victory
of Marianne over Edward. First in Romantic poetry, and later
in the novel, man's place in Nature came to be treated as a
matter of over-riding metaphysical importance, a theme which
was developed with increasing weight and urgency as a counterpoint to the encroachment of industrialisation.

1859 has been regarded as a cultural watershed. Whilst
dates are an arbitrary way of determining and defining literary
periods and genres, this date may stand as marking a new
movement in English fiction, a movement which was to have
the living force and potential of a tradition. The central concern of this tradition is man's place in Nature, and it was this
centrality which cut off the new novelists of the period from
their predecessors. Many novelists before Meredith had
delineated their characters in a natural setting in a manner
which showed how the ideas of Romanticism were percolating
into Victorian fiction. This is most profoundly true of the
Brontës, and specially of Emily Brontë, who seems to stand as
direct heir to Romanticism. Yet *Wuthering Heights*, with its
roots in the Gothic and in Byronism, should be read as the
termination of tradition, rather than as a growing-point. Later

fiction taking Nature as a central theme owes little to its example — Hardy, for instance, had never read it. If the Brontës remain a special case, their friend Mrs Gaskell also shows clearly the general tendency for the Romantic sensibility towards Nature to be gradually absorbed into the art of the novel. Her work abounds in minor figures like Mr Holbrook, 'who had spent so long a life in a secluded and not impressive country with ever-increasing delight in the daily and yearly change of season and beauty' (*Cranford*, Chapter IV). Such characters contribute importantly to the typical Gaskell atmosphere, and may be said to culminate in Dr Gibson, who is described as feeling:

the beauty of the seasons perhaps more than most men. He saw more of it by day, by night, in storm and sunshine, or in the still, soft cloudy weather. He never spoke about what he felt on the subject; indeed, he did not put his feelings into words, even to himself. But if his mood ever approached to the sentimental it was on such days as this

(*Wives and Daughters*, Chapter XXXIII).

Mrs Gaskell's novels are devoid of that sense of transcendent unity with Nature which was to mark the later Nature tradition — it is significant that Dr Gibson cannot communicate his feelings. Her work remains firmly anchored in a quiet realism, whereas the Nature novel tends towards the techniques of symbolism. Nonetheless certain areas of Mrs Gaskell's work, notably the Welsh scenes of *Ruth*, and the North-country scenes of *Sylvia's Lovers*, reveal her moving towards this new mode of presentation of character and theme.

Many Victorian novelists were masters of the technique of concealing their commentary by dramatising it as scenery, as Wayne Booth remarks in *The Rhetoric of Fiction*, though he goes on to observe how tiresome this trait can become when 'every bad turn in the plot is foreshadowed by a turn in the weather' — a device which Dickens himself often utilises. George Eliot employs such devices more subtly, and her early work is one of the chief sources of inspiration for the Nature novelists; her subdued Wordsworthian celebration of man's cultural connexions with the natural world was to be radically transformed by a new poetic immediacy of presentation.

The Nature tradition, which is the subject of this study, is to be seen as a coherent but contrasting body of work which radically extended the modes of English fiction. In each of its major exponents the social is subsumed within the natural. The novel, long regarded as the ideal form for the analysis of personal relations and social interconnexions, is developed into a form through which the larger theme of man's relation with Nature can be explored. The tradition which develops thus stands at the opposite pole to the contemporaneous Flaubertian tradition as perfected by James and his followers; it is a tradition which may claim Forster, Lawrence, the Powys brothers, Malcolm Lowry, Lawrence Durrell and William Golding as its modern heirs.

The development of a fiction centring in Nature draws upon a complex body of thought and feeling about Nature. The main elements may be identified as the Romantic treatment of Nature; New England Transcendentalism; the Victorian literature of the 'open road'; and the debate about evolution. Out of these elements a new synthesis was to be created which would alter the course of English fiction.

II

While it has been argued that the phrase 'the Romantic movement' conveys little to the literary historian, the Romantic concept of Nature, which was to be so crucial in the formation of the Victorian mind, can be seen as a coherent and dynamic body of thought, a doctrine of which *The Prelude*[1] is the text-book. The Romantic treatment of Nature might best be approached in the light of some words of Freud's:

Our present ego-feeling is, therefore, only a shrunken residue of a much more inclusive — indeed, an all-embracing — feeling which corresponded to a more intimate bond between the ego and the world about it. If we may assume that there are many people in whose mental life this primary ego-feeling has persisted to a greater or less degree, it would exist in them side by side with the narrower and more sharply demarcated ego-feeling of maturity, like a kind of counterpart to it. In that case, the ideational contents appropriate to it would be precisely those of limitlessness and of a bond with the universe — the same ideas with which my friend elucidated the 'oceanic' feeling.[2]

Exactly how this 'all-embracing' feeling of oneness with the Universe operated has been expounded in Lévy-Bruhl's examination of the primitive mind, which 'makes the direct transition from such-and-such a sense impression to such-and-such an invisible force': 'At the very moment when he perceives what is presented to his senses, the primitive represents to himself the mystic force which is manifesting itself thus'. Primitive man, therefore, — and in this he might be compared with the theoreticians of Romanticism — has 'implicit faith in the presence and agency of powers which are inaccessible to the senses, and this certainly equals, if it does not surpass, that afforded by the senses themselves'. In this state, the 'things which are unseen cannot be distinguished from the things which are seen'; it was a state as familiar to Wordsworth or Jefferies as to primitive man.[3] The vision of Nature, however variously presented by Romantic poetry and philosophy, is a vision of Freud's 'intimate bond' being rescued from the 'universe of death' bequeathed by the mechanistic thinking of Locke's Newtonian psychology. For a dualistic system of mind and inanimate Nature the Romantics substituted a monistic system. As Coleridge claimed in 'Religious Musings', 'There is one Mind, one omnipresent Mind, Omnific', and it is God 'Diffused through all, that doth make all one whole'. The Romantic movement was thus concerned with reconciling subject and object, man and Nature, consciousness and unconsciousness. Cartesian dualism, Hobbesian materialism, Hartleian mechanism, these became the identifiable *bêtes noires* of Romanticism from Blake onwards.

The Romantic *Naturphilosophie* is fundamentally an expression of an act of reintegration with the external world whereby the individual spirit regains its lost integrity. Through Nature man will be reconciled with his fellow men: *The Prelude* is eloquent testimony to the humanitarian tendency of Nature-worship. This was expressed philosophically in language, which echoed a now-discarded Christianity. Schelling, for example, posited an *Abfall* — a cosmic Fall which reaches its nadir, in the selfhood, the *Ichheit*, of man, a selfhood which entails the widest separation from God. The emergence of man into culture and civilisation is paradoxically often seen as a painful journey into self-division and etiolation of the spirit, a journey in which man's aspirations can find no adequate object. As Blake noted, 'The bounded is loathed by its possessor'. 'Our home', Wordsworth claimed, 'is with infinity'. This cataclysmic falling away from Nature, and the quest for deliverance from self-alienation, is a theme common to Romantic texts from *Songs of Innocence* to *Women in Love*. Deliverance and redemption are celebrated by Romantic pantheists as a marriage of mind and Nature — a 'prominent period metaphor' which M.H. Abrams, in his study of the question, relates to Christian theology.[4] In the *Fragments* Novalis claimed that the 'higher philosophy is concerned with the marriage of Nature and mind', and Hölderlin's *Hyperion* hailed this marriage as a regeneration of humanity:

Let all be changed from its Foundations! Let the new world spring from the root of humanity! . . . They will come, Nature, thy men. A rejuvenated people will make thee young again, too, and thou wilt be as its bride. . . . There will be only one beauty; and man and Nature will unite in one all-embracing divinity.

The typical Romantic consciousness, such as that of Wordsworth's Pedlar, discerned the intimate correspondence between the self and Nature:

In all shapes
He found a secret and mysterious soul,
A fragrance and a spirit of strange meaning.
('The Ruined Cottage')

This theology of redemption is expertly characterised by Abrams, who notes that the 'vision is that of the awesome depths and height of the human mind, and of the human mind as in itself adequate, by consummating a holy marriage with the external universe, to create out of the world of all of us, in a quotidian miracle, a new world which is the equivalent of paradise'.[5] This 'quotidian miracle' is a constant theme, emphasis being placed on the necessity, as Hölderlin expressed it, 'to return in blessed self-forgetfulness into the all of Nature'. In place of the Lockean *tabula rasa* Romantic ideology insisted upon the creative power of the mind, and its ability to merge with the universe — an ability exemplified by Wordsworth's Wanderer:

> All melted into him; they swallowed up
> His animal being; in them did he live,
> And by them did he live; they were his life.
> In such access of mind, in such high hour
> Of visitation from the living God,
> Thought was not; in enjoyment it expired . . .
> Such intercourse was his, and in this sort
> Was his existence oftentimes *possessed*.
> (*The Excursion*, i,208ff.)

The impact of pantheist theory upon Romanticism, and specifically upon Wordsworth and Coleridge, has been traced by H.W. Piper, who remarks that 'the crucial point in the history of English Romanticism came when the concept of the "active universe" met the developing theory of the Imagination. In its leading sense, Imagination meant full response to, and implication with, the living qualities of natural objects'. Piper shows how the Romantics reacted against Newtonian theory, postulating a belief in a type of evolution that saw spirit developing in Nature that derived from Diderot, Robinet and Priestley. Connexions with the Birmingham Lunar Society, whose members included Erasmus Darwin, Priestley, James Watt and Josiah Wedgwood, further reinforced this tendency.[6]

Piper summarises Coleridge's position in the mid-1790s thus:

It began with God who was 'Nature's vast ever-acting Energy', whose 'thoughts are acts' and whose acts, the appearances of Nature, are symbols designed to bring men to knowledge of him. In Nature, God acted through his 'component Monads', the forces of Nature, and through these forces Coleridge expected a decisive manifestation of God in history.

Wordsworth, similarly, is shown to have been in close contact with three groups in revolutionary Paris who espoused the new pantheism: the Unitarians; the Girondists, who were avid readers of d'Holbach's *Système de la Nature* and Volney's *Les Ruines des Empires*, and the salon of 'Walking' Stewart, a fiery adept of Nature-religion. Thus Piper amply demonstrates that by the time Wordsworth and Coleridge met, their pantheist theories were ripe for fertilisation, a process which the Coleridgean theory of the Imagination effected: 'Coleridge and Wordsworth were both seeking contact with the Divine in Nature, and for them, at this time, the Imagination was essentially a power of direct knowledge and understanding'.[7]

However, the Romantic *Pantheismusstreit* ultimately derived from Spinoza's *Ethics*,[8] the work which above all others gave serious philosophical credence to a monistic doctrine uniting man and Nature. In the crucial first part of the *Ethics*, Stuart Hampshire has explained, it is Spinoza's fundamental argument that 'there *can* be only *one* substance which is *causa sui*, and that this single substance must be identified with the universe conceived as a whole; this unique all-inclusive totality he therefore calls "God or Nature" '.[9] For Spinoza, 'God or a substance consisting of infinite attributes, each of which expresses eternal and infinite essence, necessarily exists' (Pt.1, Prop.XI). Apart from this, 'no substance can be granted or conceived' (Pt.1, Prop.XIV). This all-inclusive vision, Hampshire believes, derives from what Spinoza saw as 'the logical impossibility of conceiving the universe, as Descartes had conceived it, as consisting of *two* self-contained systems'.[10] Descartes' crucial distinction between extension and thought is annihilated by Spinoza: 'extension and thought are either attributes of God or modifications of attributes of God' (Pt.1, Prop.XIV, Cor.ii). The dichotomy between the perceiving mind and external 'reality', which is central to Cartesian philosophy, gives place to a view of mind as part of a unified whole: 'Whatever is, is in God, and nothing can exist or be conceived without God' (Pt.1. Prop.XV). The transcendent God of Christianity is replaced with logical ruthlessness: 'God is the indwelling, and not the transient cause of all things'

(Pt.1. Prop.XVIII), a cause, as Hampshire puts it, 'free in its self-creative activity'. God, or Nature, of which man is a part, is thus a single system infinite by definition, 'because if it were finite, there could be supposed something outside or other than it'.[11] This system is both creator and created, *Natura Naturans* and *Natura Naturata*. Hampshire justly remarks that Spinoza's philosophy, in its rigorous determinism, is far removed from the pantheist ecstasy of Romanticism; but this does not diminish the significance of the *Ethics* for the Romantic movement. The identification of man with Nature is Spinoza's chief bequest to the 'revolutionary climacteric'. This identification is strengthened by the Spinozan stress on the energy and fluidity of Nature, and of human life within Nature:

Human beings are finite modes within Nature, which, like all other particular things, persist and retain their identity only so long as a certain total distribution of motion and rest is preserved among the system of ultimate particles (*corpora simplicissima*) composing them; they constantly suffer changes of state or modifications of their nature in interactions with their environment; but, being relatively complex organisms, they can be changed in a great variety of different ways without their cohesion, or their 'actual essence' as particular things, being destroyed.[12]

Spinoza's God, as a *res extensa*, is clearly not the Christian deity. The reconciliation of mind and matter here postulated led Schelling to comment that Spinozism was a subject-object relationship in which the subject gets totally lost, and this is a pregnant observation, since the human mind is seen as part of Nature. As Matthew Arnold discerned in the *Essays in Criticism*, Spinoza's appeal was both philosophical and ethical, fortifying man's 'mobile, straining, passionate, poetic temperament by the moral lesson he draws from his view of Nature'. Romantic mythology is Spinozan and pantheistic: its major terms are mind and Nature, and the transactions between the two are conducted without the mediation of 'God'. The contemporary shuffling of terms such as 'panentheism' was indulged in by those who wished to secure a Christian gloss for the claims of Romanticism, and cannot obscure the main point. Coleridge, whose profound involvement with Spinoza and pantheism has been traced by Thomas McFarland, epitomised in his own career the clash of irreconcilables involved in adherence to both Christianity and pantheism. 'For a very long time', he confessed in *Biographia Literaria*, 'I could not reconcile personality with infinity; and my head was with Spinoza, though my whole heart remained with Paul and John'. Coleridge, in his synthesis of philosophical and romantic tendencies, personified the dichotomy in the *Naturphilosophie*. McFarland expresses it like this: 'Pantheism, the system of the "it is", exerted the strongest possible repulsion and the most extreme attraction upon Coleridge, and, while unfolding itself for him in its most coherent and consequent form as Spinozism, it was a crucial preoccupation throughout his career'.[13] Kant was careful to draw the distinction which he held as vital between the world as it is, which he believed we could never know, and the world as it appears to us, and this distinction sometimes colours the Romantic apprehension of Nature with its stress upon the sovereign creativity of the imagination:

> O Lady! we receive but what we give,
> And in our life alone does Nature live:
> Ours is her wedding garment, ours her shroud!

Even Wordsworth, who was far less 'subjective' than Coleridge, observed in a letter of 1816 that objects:

derive their influence not from the properties inherent in them, not from what they are actually in themselves, but from such as are bestowed upon them by the minds of those who are consonant with or affected by those objects. Thus the Poetry . . . proceeds whence it ought to do, from the soul of man, communicating its creative energies to the images of the external world.

The creative potency of the imagination is central Romantic dogma; but it seldom goes hand-in-hand with the image of such an 'inanimate cold world'. More normative is the image of the soul seeking out its mirror image in Nature, as Blake envisioned:

So man looks out in tree and herb and fish and bird and beast
Collecting up the scatter'd portions of his immortal body.
                                        ('The Four Zoas')

As Novalis remarked in the margin of F. Schlegel's *Ideen*:
'Do not animals, plants, stones, stars, and breezes also belong
with mankind, which is merely a central meeting point of
countless varied threads? Can mankind be understood divorced from Nature, and is it so very different from other manifestations of Nature?' Indeed, Coleridge himself had often
espoused the same doctrine, holding for instance in a letter of
1802 that 'a Poet's *Heart* and *Intellect* should be *combined,
intimately* combined and *unified* with the great appearances in
Nature — and not merely held in solution and loose mixture
with them, in the shape of formal similes'. The highest intuition of Romanticism is an awareness of monistic unity. As
Schelling wrote, 'Nature should be spirit made visible, spirit
Nature become invisible'. The identity of the creative mind
with Nature is the revelation given to Romantic adepts of
Nature, a revelation often accompanied by an elevation both
psychic and physical. Abrams has remarked on the ubiquity in
Romantic writing of a 'deeply significant experience in which
an instant of consciousness . . . suddenly blazes into revelation'.[14] 'The farther I ascend from animated Nature', wrote
Coleridge in 1803, 'from men, and cattle, and the common
birds of the woods, and fields, the greater becomes in me the
intensity of the feeling of life; Life seems to me then a universal
spirit, that neither has nor can have, an opposite'. These 'spots
of time', of which Wordsworth's ascent of Snowdon is the
locus classicus, are common property to the Romantic imagination from *The Prelude* to *The Story of My Heart*. Shelley's
'Mont Blanc' is a representative text:

> The everlasting universe of things
> Flows through the mind, and rolls its rapid waves,
> Now dark — now glittering — now reflecting gloom —
> Now lending splendour, where from secret springs
> The source of human thought its tribute brings
> Of waters, — with a sound but half its own,

This sense of transcendence typically urges man towards deeper fellowship and humanity, rather than to the solipsism of the mystic:

> Thou has a voice, great Mountain, to repeal
> Large codes of fraud and woe; not understood
> By all, but which the wise, and great, and good
> Interpret, or make felt, or deeply feel.

In such poems the deathly separation of that which is known from that which knows is obliterated, and spiritual deliverance granted. To characterise such a tense relationship as the pathetic fallacy is to misunderstand the quality and complexity of the experience described. The reciprocity of mind and Nature, in Romantic ideology, will save mankind from spiritual death.

It is this reciprocity, in all its changes, reversals, and illuminations, which *The Prelude* classically records. The growth of the poet's mind is an organic process of spiritual development, a *Bildungsgeschichte* of profound importance to the Victorian literary imagination. Hazlitt's joke that in Wordsworthian Nature poetry 'a puddle is filled with preternatural faces' contains an essential truth with regard to Nature's teachings. The poet must interpret 'whatso'er of Terror or of Love/Or Beauty, Nature's daily face put on' (III, 132–3; 1805 version). Indeed the first impression of the natural world upon the senses is one of the tutelage of fear; the boy's sensibility is formed by interaction with 'high-objects, with enduring things':

> With life and nature, purifying thus
> The elements of feeling and of thought,
> And sanctifying, by such discipline,
> Both pain and fear, until we recognise
> A grandeur in the beatings of the heart.
>
> (I, 437–41)

This reflection comes after the stealing of the boat; other seminal episodes further teach and refine the human spirit through fear: the trapping of the woodcocks, the birds' nesting, the scene at the gibbet, the encounter with the soldier, the

corpse in the lake, and the vision of a Druidic Stonehenge —
each illuminates the unknown modes of being which communion with Nature bestows. The apotheosis of this type of
experience of Nature occurs in crossing the Simplon Pass:

> The immeasurable height
> Of woods decaying, never to be decayed,
> The stationary blasts of waterfalls,
> And every where along the hollow rent
> Winds thwarting winds, bewildered and forlorn,
> The torrents shooting from the clear blue sky,
> The rocks that muttered close upon our ears,
> Black drizzling crags that spake by the wayside
> As if a voice were in them, the sick sight
> And giddy prospect of the raving stream,
> The unfettered clouds and region of the Heavens,
> Tumult and peace, the darkness and the light —
> Were all like workings of one mind, the features
> Of the same face, blossoms upon one tree;
> Characters of the great Apocalypse,
> The types and symbols of Eternity,
> Of first, and last, and midst, and without end.
>
> (VI, 556–72)

In this magnificent passage the ordeal of man faced with
wild untameable Nature is transmuted from the Augustan
distinction between beauty and sublimity into a revelation of
pantheistic monism which is capable of containing all
dualities. Abrams justly remarks of this episode that 'its anti-
thetic qualities of sublimity and beauty are seen as simultaneous expressions on the face of heaven and earth, declaring an
unrealised truth which the chiaroscuro of the scene articulates
for the prepared mind — a truth about the darkness and the
light, the terror and the peace, the ineluctable contraries which
make up our human existence'.[15]

So transcendent, indeed, is the potency of this revitalised
Nature, that even the city is experienced by analogy with
natural laws. Thus, on entering London, which was to become
the archetype for urban experience, the poet reflects:

> This did I feel, in that vast receptacle.
> The Spirit of Nature was upon me here;

> The soul of beauty and enduring Life
> Was present as a habit, and diffused,
> Through meagre lines and colours, and the press
> Of self-destroying, transitory things,
> Composure, and ennobling Harmony.
> (VII, 734–40)

The works of man, both physical and imaginative, are thus subsumed within this litany of Nature. The person who 'in his youth a wanderer among the woods and fields With living Nature hath been intimate' is able to receive 'enduring touches of deep joy From the great Nature that exists in works Of mighty poets' (V, 610 ff.). At only one critical point, after his disillusion over the French Revolution, is the poet shut off from the potency of Nature, judging it according to prescribed aesthetic rules, and thus imposing the human will upon the external world — an *impasse* which is resolved in the conclusion. The poet, Wordsworth writes elsewhere, is a 'chosen son':

> For hither I had come with holy powers
> And faculties, whether to work or feel:
> To apprehend all passions and all moods
> Which time and place and season do impress
> Upon the visible universe, and work
> Like changes there by force of my own mind.
> (III, 83–8)

The climactic ascent of Snowdon embraces all the elements of the poem in a final coherent vision of unity in multiplicity, and peace in energy:

> it appeared to me
> The perfect image of a mighty mind,
> Of one that feeds upon infinity,
> That is exalted by an underpresence,
> The sense of God, or whatso'er is dim
> Or vast in its own being, above all
> One function of such mind had Nature there
> Exhibited by putting forth, and that
> With circumstance most awful and sublime,
> That domination which she oftentimes
> Exerts upon the outward face of things,
> (XIII, 68–78)

Such moments recur in the Nature novel. Their value, for Wordsworth, lay not only in the intensity and transcendence of the vision, but in the humanising influence they exerted upon man's social intercourse. Love of Nature led axiomatically to love of mankind as the boy is led in the mountain solitudes to love and reverence the Shepherd, a 'solitary object and sublime':

> Thus was man
> Ennobled outwardly before mine eyes,
> And thus my heart at first was introduced
> To an unconscious love and reverence
> Of human nature; hence the human form
> To me was like an index of delight,
> Of grace and honour, power and worthiness.
>
> (VIII, 410–16)

This dual insight, of the primacy of Nature and the fellowship and community of man, is Wordsworth's legacy to the nineteenth century. It is repeated with variations throughout the period, gaining a new intensity against the perspective of an aggressive industrial democracy. Such figures as George Eliot, Matthew Arnold and Mill have long been recognised as disciples. But the percolation of Romantic *Naturphilosophie* goes much further, and finds expression in the Nature tradition in the novel, whose practitioners would concur in their apprehension of Wordsworthian presences:

> From this beloved Presence, there exists
> A virtue which irradiates and exalts
> All objects through all intercourse of sense.
> No outcast he, bewildered and depressed:
> Along his infant veins are interfused
> The gravitation and the filial bond
> Of Nature that connect him with the world.
> Emphatically such a Being lives,
> An inmate of this *active* universe;
> From Nature largely he receives; nor so
> Is satisfied, but largely gives again,
>
> (II, 258–68)

III

The exaltation which the Romantics carried away from Nature was transmitted, in an idealist form, by the American Transcendentalists, whose works were widely disseminated in Victorian England.[16] This idealist cast of thought leads to a view of the Universe as a type of cosmic psyche. The Transcendentalists' rebellion against Lockean epistemology, their Kantean distinction between the sacred Reason and empirical Understanding, and their indebtedness to Marsh's edition of Coleridge's *Aids to Reflection* — all this is well known. The transcendentalists denied that they were pantheists, seeing God as cause and the Universe as effect: yet the drift of their argument, with its appeal to the Universal Spirit, is frequently pantheistic in essence. Alcott, for instance, describes this Spirit in characteristic language:

that power which pulsates in all life, animates and builds all organisations, shall manifest itself as one universal deific energy, present alike at the outskirts and centre of the universe, whose centre and circumference are one: omniscient, omnipotent, self-subsisting, uncontained, yet containing all things in the unbroken synthesis of its being.

This 'unbroken synthesis' was epitomised by Nature. In the Concord woods Emerson once pointed out to Holmes 'all the waving branches of the trees, and all the flowers, and the field of corn yonder, and the singing brook, and the insect and the bird, — every living thing and things we call inanimate feel the same universal impulse while they join with us, and we with them, in the greeting which is the salutation of the Universal Spirit'. Following the Romantics, Emerson[17][18] claimed that it was the poet who 're-attaches things to nature and the Whole' ('The Poet'). Indeed, it is true to claim that the Transcendentalists reproduced, with variations, the full Romantic programme. Intuition, the 'inner light' which they took from their Puritan ancestors, is ahistorical: all 'inquiry into antiquity', Emerson held, 'is the desire to do away this wild, savage, and preposterous There or Then, and introduce in its place the Here and Now' ('History') — another version of the 'spots of time'. The intuitive mode of knowledge here urged by Emerson emancipates the individual from history. Through revelation man comes to the truth, revelation being 'an influx of the Divine Mind into our mind' ('The Over-Soul'). The heightened emotion, the deliverance from circumstance, the intuitive, revelatory powers of Nature, all these are common to Romantic and Transcendental thought. 'The way of life is wonderful', Emerson declared, 'it is by abandonment' ('Circles'). It was for this abandonment that Hawthorne characterised Emerson as a 'mystic, stretching his hand out of cloudland, in vain search for something real'. 'Nature is a mutable cloud, which is always and never the same', Emerson averred ('History'). But what Emerson is fundamentally concerned with is totality: 'Nature knows neither palm nor oak, but only vegetable life, which sprouts into forests' ('The Method of Nature'). In this Transcendental vision Nature is to be construed as a set of symbols to be understood by aid of the sovereign imagination. As Emerson says, 'The world of the senses is a world of shows; it does not exist for itself, but has a symbolic character' ('Prudence'). Thus Nature ministers to the soul of man — this is its chief function, since Nature 'is the opposite of the soul, answering to it part for part. One is seal and one is print' ('The American Scholar'). Though man is permitted by the senses to 'see the world piece by piece, as the sun, the moon, the animal, the tree', 'the whole, of which these are the shining parts, is the soul' ('The Over-Soul').

The key document in the dissemination of Transcendental Nature philosophy was Emerson's essay 'Nature' (1836 — the central statement of the movement, and one which enjoyed great popularity in England. Emerson opens his essay by proposing that the Universe is composed of Nature and Soul, the NOT ME being designated as Nature, whether it is artificial or natural. Almost immediately he recounts one of those mystical moments of rapport with the natural world which link him with both Wordsworth and Jefferies: 'Standing on the bare gound, — my head bathed by the blithe air, and uplifted into infinite space, — all mean egotism vanishes. I become a transparent eyeball; I am nothing, I see all; the currents of the Universal Being circulate through me; I am part or parcel of God.' The greatest delight of Nature lies in the suggestion of an 'occult relation' between man and the vegetable world, yet 'the power to produce this delight does not reside in nature, but in man, or in a harmony of both'. Emerson proceeds to classify the perception of Nature into three stages: first, simple delight in natural beauty; secondly, the detection of a spiritual element in this process; and thirdly, Nature's beauty, absorbed into the mind, acting as the source for new creative work. Art, therefore, is 'nature passed through the alembic of man'. Nature has furnished man with language and a system of symbols: 'man is an analogist, and studies relations in all objects'. Emerson was later to make it clear that Nature is permeated by a fundamental polarity when he wrote in 'Compensation' that 'An inevitable dualism bisects nature, so that each thing is a half, and suggests another thing to make it whole; as, spirit, matter; man, woman; odd, even; subjective, objective; in, out; upper, under; motion, rest; yea, nay.' As an image of motion and energy Nature may therefore be seen as 'a metaphor of the human mind' ('Nature'). Yet its power is also to impose a discipline on the mind, which it contains: 'The Supreme Critic on the errors of the past and the present, and the only prophet of that which must be, is that great nature in which we rest . . . that Unity, that Over-Soul, within which every man's particular being is contained and made one with all other' ('The Over-Soul'). Through apprehension of likeness, order and variety in the natural world, the mind is subjected to 'a discipline of the understanding in intellectual truths' ('Nature'), and in its variety, Emerson characteristically asserts, Nature 'shall hint or thunder to man the laws of right and wrong' (*ibid.*). In direct antithesis to the evolutionary theory which lay ahead, Emerson espouses the fundamental unity of life, each creature being seen as 'only a modification of the other': 'So intimate is this Unity, that, it is easily seen, it lies under the undermost garment of nature, and betrays its source in Universal Spirit' (*ibid.*). Yet within this all-embracing unity, there is a hierarchy of values, and the mind is granted supremacy. Emerson closes his essay by showing how thought distances man from Nature, speaking of the 'reverential withdrawing of nature before its God'. Indeed the essay in its closing pages becomes a paean to Idealism when he writes that 'Idealism sees the World in God. It beholds the whole circle of persons and things, of actions and events, of country and religion, not as painfully accumulated, atom after atom, act after act, in aged creeping Past, but as one vast picture which God paints on the instant eternity for the contemplation of the soul.' In this final stage of Romantic Idealism the concrete multiplicity of the world of natural phenomena dissolves into self-communion: 'the world is a divine dream, from which we may presently awake to the glories and certainties of day'.

IV

This 'divine dream' was vitally influential in the latter part of the century, and the novels of the Nature tradition stand in part as a notable expression of this influence. But the optimist thrust of both Romantic and Transcendentalist belief in a return to Nature, and in the deliverance of man through union with the cosmos, was undermined by the pessimism of the late Victorian period. Walter Houghton has remarked 'how terribly exposed the Victorians were to a constant succession of shattering developments', a succession which dictated that they had to live 'between two worlds, one dead or dying, one struggling to be born, in an age of doubt'. Even before the publication of *The Origin of Species*, German rationalism, Biblical criticism, geological and palaeontological theory, and utilitarian logic had chipped away at optimistic views of the Universe, whether Christian or Romantic. As this happened, Houghton notes in *The Victorian Frame of Mind*, there emerged 'the scientific picture of a vast mechanism of cause and effect, acting by physical laws that governed even man himself' — a picture exemplified by Huxley's 1868 lecture on

'The Physical Basis of Life', which argued that life was simply a combination of oxygen, hydrogen, nitrogen and carbon, and that the concept of the soul or spirit was a delusion. Two years earlier Kingsley had preached on the 'Meteor Shower' asking 'Are we only helpless particles, at best separate parts of the wheels of a vast machine, which will use us till it has worn us away, and ground us to powder? . . . Tell us not that the world is governed by universal law; the news is not comfortable, but simply horrible.' This 'horrible' news was what science every day seemed to confirm, and into the Victorian imagination percolated a cold awareness of mechanism which opposed itself to the Romantic concept of organic growth. Contemplation of the post-Darwinian world led to new concepts of the greatest relevance to the emergent novel of Nature. 'Where the loss of faith', Houghton writes, 'was accompanied, as it usually was . . . by the image of Nature ruling all things with blind indifference, another kind of isolation swept over the Victorians, with an emotional impact more painful than madness or bitterness — cosmic isolation and the terror of absolute solitude'. The dialectic between Romantic and Darwinian evaluations of Nature thus forms the ground-plan for this tradition of the novel. The Wordsworthian natural harmony is discomposed by the cries of suffering and struggle discerned by Tennyson.

One of the most influential pre-Darwinian statements of this anguish was Mill's essay on 'Nature',[19] written during the 1850s. Embedded in its calm logical reasoning is an awesome outline of Nature as essentially inimical to mankind, a view which must have gone a long way towards undermining the Romantic identification of Nature with divinity.

Mill begins by defining Nature as 'the sum of all phenomena, together with the causes which produce them'; thus the term 'Nature' suggests 'not so much the multitudinous detail of the phenomena, as the conception which might be formed of their manner of existence as a mental whole, by a mind possessing a complete knowledge of them'. Mill goes on to distinguish two usages of 'Nature': by one he understands 'all the powers existing in either the outer or the inner world and everything which takes place by means of those powers'; by the other, 'only what takes place without the agency, or without the voluntary and intentional agency, of man'. It is in reference to the latter conception that Mill argues that Nature's powers 'are often towards man in the position of enemies, from whom he must wrest, by force and ingenuity, what little he can for his own use'. Contrary to the doctrines of Romanticism or Transcendentalism, man should not set out to emulate or participate in the processes of Nature, with her 'vast forces', since Nature is characterised by a most 'supercilious disregard both of mercy and of justice, emptying her shafts upon the best and noblest indifferently with the meanest and worst'.

Mill, at the time of composition, was not familiar with the theory of evolution, though he readily accepted it upon publication of *The Origin of Species*. Thus it was possible for him to argue with conviction that 'No one, either religious or irreligious, believes that the harmful agencies of nature, considered as a whole, promote good purposes, in any other way than by inciting human rational creatures to rise up and struggle against them'. This is indeed part of the Creator's plan: God could not wholly subdue the forces of evil in the universe, but he endowed man with the capability 'of carrying on the fight with vigour and with progressively increasing success'. Condemning Romantic exaltation of instinct at the expense of reason as 'an aberration', Mill classifies the animal world into 'devourers and devoured'. His conclusions are consonant with the tenor of his argument; the responsibility for progress lies squarely upon man himself, and he believes that 'Whatsoever, in nature, gives indication of beneficent design, proves this beneficence to be armed only with limited power; and the duty of man is to co-operate with the beneficent power, not by imitating but by perpetually striving to amend the course of nature.'

To the Victorian reader familiar with Mill's essay the Darwinian revolution must have seemed inevitable. In his portrayal of the pressures of population upon food resources, in his treatment of random variation and heredity, and above all in his presentation of the struggle for existence and the consequent 'survival of the fittest', Darwin dismantled earlier versions of man's place in Nature. In 1856, contemporaneously with Mill's essay, he had exclaimed, 'What a book a devil's chaplain might write on the clumsy, wasteful, blundering, low and horribly cruel works of nature'. Darwin, indeed, recognised the pathos of his position. 'I cannot look at the universe', he once wrote, 'as the result of blind chance, yet I can see no evidence of beneficent design of any kind, in the details'.

Following the publication of *The Origin of Species* speculation about man's place in the natural world became a matter of universal concern. The fixed realm of Nature dissolved into what Loren Eiseley describes as the 'phantom' of an 'emergent world of change'. The transformation wrought by Darwin was of profound significance not only to biology; he was responsible for a psychic revolution, a process well summarised by Eiseley:

In penetrating the past of the organic realm, Darwin and Wallace had been forced to sacrifice existent nature, nineteenth-century nature, and indeed man himself, for a wilderness of subjective possibilities which, in turn, led out of the present into a world of 'indefinite departure'. Nature, the twentieth century was to discover, would no longer be the old visible 'lawful' nature of field and forest, the nature which many Victorians regarded as the direct expression of God's will. . . . The world beneath the atom did not follow the order of the macroscopic universe.[20]

This is not to assert that the pessimism accompanying a breakdown of faith is directly traceable to Darwin; such a formulation does not account for the complexity of the intellectual and cultural situation at this time of transition. As early as 1849 Arnold had warned:

> Nature is cruel, man is sick of blood;
> Nature is stubborn, man would fain adore;
>
> Nature is fickle, man hath need of rest;
> Nature forgives no debt, and fears no grave;
> Man would be mild, and with safe conscience blest.

Man must begin, know this, where Nature ends;
Nature and man can never be fast friends.
('In Harmony with Nature')

Browning gave a more extended expression of similar feelings and precepts in his 'Caliban upon Setebos' of 1864. Every variety of doubt was voiced in the pre-Darwinian period, but *The Origin of Species* focussed and intensified these doubts. In the 1880s and 1890s — indeed, as controversy raged around varieties of Social Darwinism as postulated by Spencer, Bagehot and others — the actual science of evolution ironically lost favour. The observations upon which evolution theory was based had been familiar for many years before the publication of Darwin's book, as Disraeli had amusingly revealed in the speech of a fashionable lady who has been reading Chambers's *Vestiges of Creation:*

"You know, all is development. The principle is perpetually going on. First, there was nothing, then there was something; then, I forget the next, I think there were shells, then fishes; then we came, let me see, did we come next? Never mind that, we came at last. And the next change there will be something very superior to us, something with wings. Ah! that's it; we were fishes, and I believe we shall be crows."

(*Tancred*, Bk.ii, Chapter IX)

The dissolution of old ways of thought and the new scientific conception of man combined to drive minds into depression and ennui, moods which may be detected in even a devoted Darwinian like Grant Allen. Allen's career illuminates the connexions between literature and biology at this time; by settling at Dorking he gained the friendship of Meredith, and at Edward Clodd's Aldeburgh symposia he got to know Hardy, Gissing and others. As a populariser of science he counted Darwin, Wallace, Huxley, Müller, Frazer and Spencer among his correspondents. The 'hill-top' novels were a conscious attempt to admit the larger world of Nature into contemporary fiction, as Allen explained in the preface to *The British Barbarians* (1895):

When I raise my eye from my sheet of foolscap it falls upon miles and miles of broad, open moorland. My window looks out upon unsullied nature.

Everything around is fresh, and pure, and wholesome . . . away below in the valley, as night draws on, a lurid glare reddens the north-eastern horizon. It marks the spot where the great wen of London heaves and festers.

As the author of a wide range of biological and nature studies it may be that in his fiction the organisation of the Universe, as Le Gallienne put it, distracted Allen 'from the human miracle'. Nevertheless, Allen betrays a symptomatic ambivalence towards Nature, most nakedly expressed in the collection of poems which he dedicated to Clodd, entitled *The Lower Slopes* (1894), where scientific optimism and personal pessimism coexist. Nature, Allen holds, must be studied with a dispassionate largeness of mind:

> who would read the whole
> Must scan it first from pole to pole,
> And not expect at once to find
> All worlds the mirror of his mind.
> ('Animalcular Theology')

It is for this quality that Spencer is praised:

> Ere thou hadst read the universal plan
> Our life was unto us a thing alone:
> On this side nature stood, on that side man,
> Irreconcilable, as twain, not one:
> Thy voice first told us man was nature's child,
> And in one common law proclaimed them reconciled.
> ('To Herbert Spencer')

That this breadth and insight cannot finally reconcile Allen to suffering in Nature is painfully revealed in his poem on the death of a moth:

> Why in the whole
> Wide Universe
> Should a single soul
> Feel that primal curse?
> Not all the throes
> Of mightiest mind,
> Nor the heaviest woes
> Of human kind,
> Are of deeper weight
> In the riddle of things

Then the insect's fate
With the mangled wings.
('Only An Insect')

'A Ballade of Evolution', noting the implications of Darwinism, 'For the fittest will always survive/While the weakliest go to the wall', does not hesitate to draw social conclusions, telling of how 'the wealthy in coaches can drive/ Whilst the needier go to the wall'.

This deepening pessimism marked Huxley himself, and in the 1893 Romanes Lecture he addressed himself to the problems of 'Evolution and Ethics'. Evolution, he now appreciated, gave no guidance upon moral questions:

Social progress means a checking of the cosmic process at every step and the substitution of it for another, which may be called the ethical process; the end of which is not the survival of those who are ethically the best. . . . The ethical progress of society depends, not on imitating the cosmic process, still less in running away from it, but in combatting it.

The new science here collides with the Romantic-Victorian theology of Nature, and it is a collision which reverberates through the period. That the adoption of Darwinism did not entail such pessimism axiomatically is exemplified by the diverse treatment of Meredith, Shaw and Wells; but the intellectual atmosphere of the time compelled writers to take up a position, with profound consequences for their work.

V

The generation of novelists after Dickens stood as direct heirs to both Romantic and scientific versions of Nature. Beginning with Meredith a clear line of development in the English novel, taking man and Nature as a central theme, is discernible; it was a line which could touch upon such diverse talents as Blackmore, Stevenson, Baring-Gould, Olive Schreiner and Eden Phillpotts, and which was to peter out in one direction through Sheila Kaye-Smith, Mary Webb and others, in the kitchen of Cold Comfort Farm. But the main line, a tradition capable of self-renewal, leads direct from Meredith to Lawrence; it is this line which may be seen as one vital tradition in the English fiction of the period.

The key Romantic doctrine concerning Nature and the creative imagination filtered into the mundane art of the novel over a long time-span, ultimately providing the germ for a new kind of novel. In this germination and expansion of sensibility Carlyle was probably a crucial mediating factor. This expansion was manifold in its results; but in the English novel, as opposed to the continentally inspired Jamesian school, it manifested itself in an enlargement of the fictional world to encompass man's place in Nature. The effort of the new school of novelists is to invent a sort of writing which will encompass both the vastness of natural process and the intricate workings of the human spirit, and a form for the novel which can accommodate this heuristic art.

The Nature tradition in the novel took the form of a synthesis of Romantic visions of Nature as revelation and deliverance and Darwinian pictures of man's ordeal in the natural world. It is a tradition of great variety and complexity, and it culminates in the work of D.H. Lawrence.

Notes

1 W. Wordsworth, *The Prelude* (ed., J.C. Maxwell), (Harmondsworth, Penguin Books, 1971).
2 S. Freud, *Civilisation and Its Discontents* (London, The Hogarth Press, p.5).
3 L. Lévy-Bruhl, *Primitive Mentality* (Boston, Beacon Press, 1966), pp.59–61.
4 M.H. Abrams, *Natural Supernaturalism* (London, Oxford University Press, 1971) passim.
5 *Ibid.*, p.28.
6 H.W. Piper, *The Active Universe* (London, The Athlone Press, 1962), p.2.
7 *Ibid.*, pp. 2, 58, 64 and 83.
8 B. Spinoza, *Ethics* (London, Dent, Everyman edn. 1938).
9 S.Hampshire, *Spinoza* (Harmondsworth, Penguin Books, 1970), p.36.
10 *Ibid.*, p.62.

11. *Ibid.*, p.38.
12 *Ibid.*, pp.121–2.
13 T. McFarland, *Coleridge and the Pantheist Tradition* (Oxford, The Clarendon Press, 1969), p.190.
14 Abrams, *op.cit.*, p.315.
15 *Ibid.*, p.107
16 In C. Gohdes, *American Literature in Nineteenth-Century England* (Carbondale, Ill., Southern Illinois University Press, 1944), the author notes that Emerson was 'the American author who probably exerted the greatest influence on the intellectuals of the British Isles'. The record includes Morley, Froude, Müller, Spencer, Clough, Arnold and George Eliot, who came to Emerson via the Hennells and John Chapman. Emerson's views were spread by his lecture tours. Thoreau was also widely admired later in the period: at least twenty editions or issues of volumes by Thoreau were published in England between 1880 and 1900; *op. cit.*, pp. 145 and 46).
17 R.W. Emerson, *Essays* (Oxford, Oxford University Press, World's Classic edn., 1927).
18 R.W. Emerson, *Nature, Addresses and Lectures* (London, Routledge & Sons, The Riverside edn., n.d.
19 J.S. Mill, *Three Essays on Religion* (London, Longman, Green Read & Dyer, 1874).
20 L. Eiseley, 'The Intellectual Antecedents of Darwinism', in B. Campbell (ed.), *Sexual Selection and the Descent of Man* (London, Heinemann, 1972), pp.9 and 14.

2 D.H. Lawrence

I

The keynote of Nature in Lawrence is energy and movement. 'I never admire the *strength* of mountains and fixed rocks', he wrote in 1908, 'but the strength of the sea that leaps and foams frantically and slips back in a lame underwash ... I am fascinated by that sort'.[1] Unlike Wordsworth, whom this early reference may glance at, Lawrence seeks 'unknown modes of being' in images of flux and dynamism. Nature images in its wider totality that flow and recoil which characterises Lawrence's dramatisation of human relations — a dialectic of passion which, in his analysis, has been stifled in the modern world. It is this very flow and recoil of Lawrence's own feelings and ideas, charted in the novels and poems, which renders definitions of his position in terms such as 'pantheist' or 'vitalist' inappropriate. 'The business of art', he came to hold, 'is to reveal the relation between man and his circumambient universe, at the living moment'.[2] This sense of the 'vivid relatedness between man and the living universe that surrounds him' (PH, 27), characterises all the writers of this tradition, and Lawrence rivals Jefferies in his rendition of the transcendent power of this relationship, whilst showing it as increasingly impossible.

Lawrence's contemporaries were agreed that he 'seemed to see things differently from other folk',[3] and Jessie Chambers recalled, 'The wood held a fascination for us. The shade, the murmur of the trees, the sense of adventure, the strong odour of the undergrowth, the sudden startled call of a pheasant, the whirr of a partridge's wings, were thrilling things'. Lawrence's view of Nature was 'a kind of immediate possession'.[4] He writes, as Edwin Muir once observed, 'like one whose whole being, whose blood, lusts, instincts, and senses are ecstatically sharing in the life of the thing described', as if he were 'a

mystical sharer in their being'. With the term 'mystical' Lawrence would perhaps have concurred. 'One thing Wells lacks',
he wrote in 1909 whilst revising *The White Peacock*, 'the
subtle soul of sympathy of a true artist. He rigidly scorns all
mysticism' (L, 51). Two years later, in an important declaration, he set out to reassure his sister: 'There still remains a God,
but not a personal God: a vast, shimmering impulse which
waves onwards towards some end. . . . When we die, like
raindrops falling back again into the sea, we fall back into the
big shimmering sea of unorganised life which we call God' (L,
76). Lawrence's early work is imbued with the potency of this
'vast, shimmering impulse'; God is conceived as the natural
order constantly evolving towards new modes of being. This
struggle is to become crucial in Lawrence's fiction, but he had
from the beginning, as Helen Corke reveals, a sense of this
larger pattern: 'The power of seizing upon subtle analogies, of
perceiving delicate relationships, of apprehending old and new
rhythms, of capturing truth in symbols, is his in very great
measure'.[5] The intuitive response to the natural world, and the
sense of man as part of a greater organism, illuminates Lawrence's study of other cultures, 'dying religions that have not
yet invented gods or goddesses, but live by the mystery of the
elemental powers in the Universe, the complex vitalities of
what we feebly call Nature'.[6] In these ancient religions
'everything was alive, not supernaturally but naturally alive.
There were only deeper and deeper streams of life, vibrations
of life more and more vast'.[7] All of Nature in Lawrence is an
impassioned unity. Lawrence, like the Romantics, and like
Meredith and Jefferies, rejected supernatural theism in favour
of natural pantheism: 'in the beginning was not a Word, but a
chirrup' (EP, 126). In Sicily, Australia, or Mexico Lawrence
felt closer to the pulsations of a natural world which industrialisation was throttling. This nexus of ideas was epitomised
for him by the Etruscans:

To the Etruscan all was alive; the whole universe lived; and the business of
man was himself to live amid it all. He had to draw life into himself, out of
the wandering huge vitalities of the world. The cosmos was alive, . . . and

had a great soul, or anima: and in spite of one great soul, there were myriad roving, lesser souls: every man, every creature and tree and lake and mountain and stream, was animate, and had its own peculiar consciousness. And has it today . . .

So it was. The universe, which was a single aliveness with a single soul, instantly changed, the moment you thought of it, and became a dual creature with two souls, fiery and watery, for ever mingling and rushing apart . . .

The old idea of the vitality of the universe was evolved long before history begins, and elaborated into a vast religion before we get a glimpse of it . . . It was the living cosmos itself, dazzlingly and gaspingly complex, which was divine.

(EP, 146–8)

Man's separation from, or renewed immersion in, this 'living cosmos' gives Lawrence his central theme: the image of the single soul which 'instantly changed the moment you thought of it and became a dual creature' is at the heart of his work, with its emphasis upon duality, unity, and separation. As Lawrence declared in *Apocalypse*:[8]

What man most passionately wants is his living wholeness and his living unison. . . . We ought to dance with rapture that we should be alive and in the flesh, and part of the living, incarnate cosmos. I am part of the sun as my eye is part of me. That I am part of the earth my feet know perfectly, and my blood is part of the sea.

(A, 125–6)

That is what Constance Chatterley comes to recognise after her sexual awakening:

the universe ceased to be the vast clockwork of circling planets and pivotal suns, which she had known. . . . Everything had its own anima. . . . The universe is all things that man knows or has known or ever will know. It is all there. We only need become aware.[9]

The cutting-off of man from Nature, whether wrought by Christianity, intellectual consciousness, industrialism and mechanisation, or by an insidious combination of all these forces, resulted in a civilisation based upon democracy and technology. This development may be traced in Lawrence's thought from the warmth of colliery life in *Sons and Lovers*[10] and the plays, through the portrayal of death of a culture in *Women in Love*,[11] to the redemption offered in *Lady Chatter-*

ley's Lover[12] — a development in which Nature is placed antithetically to mass humanity in a tradition harking back to the Romantics. Thus Kate, in *The Plumed Serpent*,[13] announces: ' "I like the world, the sky and the earth and the greater mystery beyond. But people — yes, they are all monkeys to me" ' (PS, XVII, 263). And Somers discerns in the Midlands:

a universal desire to take life and down it: these horrible machine people, these iron and coal people. They wanted to set their foot absolutely on life, grind it down, and be master. Masters, as they were of their foul machines. Masters of life, as they were masters of steam-power and electric power and above all, of money-power. Masters of money-power, with an obscene hatred of life, true spontaneous life.[14]

Lawrence told Louie Burrows in 1909, 'The town too is good, it has books, and people; it is not so desolating',[15] and many passages in the novels bear witness to the enchantment of London. Nonetheless, the agglomerations of urban man came ultimately to represent the deathly squalor of industrialism as it was made manifest in the mining towns of his home district. The thwarting of 'true spontaneous life' in this environment is drawn repeatedly in Lawrence's work, and its abiding presence in Nature is constantly stressed. Visiting London, Will Brangwen is 'frightened and awed' by 'the ponderous, massive, ugly superstructure of a world of man upon a world of nature'; it is 'extraneous to his own real life with Anna': 'Sweep away the whole monstrous superstructure of the world today, cities and industries and civilisation, leave only the bare earth with plants growing and water running'.[16] This aspect of the Lawrencean critique of Nature and industrialism was to culminate in *Lady Chatterley's Lover*, in which the debate is mythically dramatized, and the living potency of Nature given an objective correlative in terms of sexual love. A scene in the final version gets to the core of Lawrence's meaning:

'I consider this is really the heart of England,' said Clifford to Connie, as he sat there in the dim February sunshine.

'Do you?' she said, seating herself, in her blue knitted dress, on a stump by the path.

'I do! This is the old England, the heart of it; and I intend to keep it intact.'
'Oh yes!' said Connie. But, as she said it she heard the eleven o'clock hooters at Stacks Gate colliery. Clifford was too used to the sound to notice.

(LC,V, 44)

In a symbolic scene in the first version Parkin, the gamekeeper, lies 'with his back to Tevershall, indifferent to the whole of life as it lay outside. Somehow in the circle of his arms was the whole sky, the whole of another sort of life, the great living stillness. All he wanted now was to breathe the living stillness. He cared nothing about Tevershall and the days behind'.[17] Parkin's insouciance, his re-entry into the life of Nature, is mirrored by Connie's more complex redemption:

she thought again of Clifford's dictum: 'Nature is a settled routine of crude old laws. One has to go beyond nature, break beyond. And that is one's destiny that makes one break beyond the settled, arbitrary laws of nature'. She herself saw it differently. She couldn't feel the laws of nature so arbitrary. It was the laws of man that bothered her. She couldn't feel anything very arbitrary about the tossing daffodils, dipping now in shade. If only one could be simpler and more natural! If only one could be really simple! Men were so complicated and full of laws.

(FLC, 42)

The 'crude old laws' which dominate Clifford's views are those of evolution, and it is these which the versions of *Lady Chatterley* reject, transferring them to the ugly inhuman world of Tevershall, the world of labour and paternalistic mass exploitation. Clifford, ensconced in his mechanised wheel-chair, applies the law of survival of the fittest to his mines, whilst the keeper nurtures and preserves the free life of Nature on the estate.[18]

Lawrence had imbibed evolutionary dogma at an early age. Jessie Chambers records Lawrence's reading *The Origin of Species*,[19] Huxley's *Man's Place in Nature*,[20] and Haeckel's *The Riddle of the Universe*,[21] and comments that this 'rationalistic teaching impressed Lawrence deeply. He came upon it at a time of spiritual fog, when the lights of orthodox religion and morality were proving wholly inadequate, perplexed as he was by his own personal dilemma' (ET, 112).[22]

For Lawrence, as for Hardy at a similar point of crisis, reading in the literature of evolution was seminal. Huxley's triumphant assertion of unity may have pierced the mental 'fog':

in view of the intimate relations between Man and the rest of the living world; and between the forces exerted by the latter and all other forces, I can see no excuse for doubting that all are co-ordinated terms of Nature's great progression, from the formless to the formed — from the inorganic to the organic — from blind force to conscious intellect and will.[23]

In his paper on 'Art and the Individual', completed concurrently with the second version of *The White Peacock*,[24] in the spring of 1908 (L, 12) Lawrence discerned a similar purposive design:

when [man's sympathy] reverentially recognises the vast scope of the laws of nature, and discovers something of intelligibility and consistent purpose working through the whole natural world and human consciousness, the religious interest is developed and the individual loses for a time the sense of his own and his day's importance, feels the wonder and terror of eternity with its incomprehensible purposes. This, I hold it, is still a most useful and fruitful state.[25]

In Huxley, perhaps more than in Darwin, Lawrence discovered an exciting new vision of the interconnexion and animation of all Nature:

the whole of the vast array of living forms with which we are surrounded, constantly growing, increasing, decaying, and disappearing; the animal constantly attracting, modifying, and applying to its sustenance the matter of the vegetable kingdom, which derived its support from the absorption and conversion of inorganic matter. And so constant and universal is this absorption, waste, and reproduction, that it may be said with perfect certainty that there is left in no one of our bodies at the present moment a millionth part of the matter of which they were originally formed![26]

This conception is presented almost socialistically in Lawrence's lecture, as when he refers to a growing comprehension 'of the individual in the great social body whose interests are large beyond his personal feelings. He is a unit, working with others for a common welfare, like a cell in a complete body'.[27]

The general pattern of Lawrence's reaction to Darwinian thought is clear. First, the image of the struggle going on in all organic life, with its concomitant pattern of survival and extinction, reappears constantly in Lawrence, from George Saxton or the miner in 'Odour of Chrysanthemums' through Gerald Crich to the woman who rode away. Secondly, Huxley's account of the strenuous rivalry between an organic creature, its 'rivals' and 'direct opponents' is translated into direct sexual rivalry and subtly transmuted by Lawrence: the rivalry in *The White Peacock* over Emily and Lettie results in an underlying affirmation of male brotherhood; Cecil Byrne must fight against the ghost of Siegmund for possession of Helena in *The Trespasser*;[28] the struggle between Paul and Baxter Dawes over Clara in *Sons and Lovers* emanates in a drawing-together of the two men; the examples may be multiplied. Thirdly, the stress in evolution upon the organic connexion and interrelatedness of the whole of Nature is characteristically rewritten by Lawrence, in the 'Reflections on the Death of a Porcupine' of 1925:

The primary way, in our existence, to get vitality, is to absorb it from living creatures lower than ourselves. It is thus transformed into a new and higher creation. (There are many ways of absorbing: devouring food is one way, love is often another. The best way is a pure relationship, which includes the *being* on each side, and which allows the transfer to take place in a living flow, enhancing the life in both beings.)[29]

It was, however, through Haeckel's *The Riddle of the Universe*, which he knew well, that Lawrence's concept of Nature was most radically extended. Haeckel's work, as his translator and fellow Rationalist Press member Joseph McCabe remarked, is an admirable summary of 'the positions taken up by science and evacuated by theology'.[30] Haeckel was the chief Darwinian in Germany at the turn of the century and a prolific writer on evolutionary matters. He is perhaps the strictest of Darwin's disciples. In his view a single organism is in its developmental stages an epitome of form modifications experienced by successive ancestors: ontogeny, the development of the single organism, thus recapitulates phylogeny, the development of whole species. Haeckel divides all organisms into two categories, the unicellular, as protozoa, and the multicellular, as metazoa. *The Riddle of the Universe* was known by Lawrence as early as 1908. In it Haeckel expounds the view that the chemico-physical properties of carbon are the sole mechanical cause of these phenomena of movement which distinguish organic from inorganic substances. Every living cell possesses psychic properties, and the psychological life of multicellular organisms is simply the sum total of the psychic function of their cells. The highest human faculties have developed in this way, Haeckel argues, thus demolishing beliefs such as the immortality of the soul, the freedom of the will, or the existence of a personal God.

Haeckel begins with the proposition that life has a cellular basis. He recognises in the tiny cell 'the all-pervading "elementary organism" of whose social communities — the tissues — the body of every multicellular plant and animal . . . is composed'.[31] This is extended by analogy to the community at large: 'We can only arrive at a correct knowledge of the structure and life of the social body, the State, through a scientific knowledge of the structure and life of the individuals who compose it, and the cells of which they are in turn composed'.[32] This image is picked up by Lawrence in his Croydon paper, where he refers to the 'individual in the great social body' who is 'a unit, working with others for a common welfare, like a cell in a complete body'. Lawrence also adopts Haeckel's distinction between the sensations of the individual cell, which reveal themselves in 'the assertion of their individual independence' and the 'common sensation of the entire community of cells' — what Haeckel terms the 'mutually dependent "citizens" which constitute the community'.[33] The image of a shifting pattern of individual and communal cells is transformed in Lawrence's art into a vision of lines of movement, evolution and disintegration within a whole society — as in *Women in Love*.

Haeckel's work is founded in what he calls his monistic philosophy: the universe is definite and illimitable, and is composed of substance which 'fills infinite space, and is in eternal motion', a motion which sways between life and death,

evolution and devolution. Monism 'recognises one sole substance in the universe, which is at once "God and Nature";
body and spirit . . . it holds to be inseparable'.[34] This 'law of
substance' is a modernised version of Spinozan pantheism, as
Haeckel acknowledges; the universal substance exists in two
forms, matter (extended substance) and spirit (energy of
thought).[35] Pantheism is indeed, he asserts, 'the world-system
of the modern scientist',[36] and it is already a fundamental
principle of the Lawrencean system in the letter to his sister
already referred to, and in the natural worlds of *The White
Peacock* and *The Trespasser*.

According to the law of substance all mental phenomena are
dependent on a definite material substratum. The task of the
psychologist is to undertake a 'comparative study of the long
gradation by which man has slowly arisen through a vast series
of lower animal conditions' — that very 'struggle into being'
which is at the heart of *The White Peacock* or *The Rainbow*.[37]
Haeckel visualises that man may not be the final issue of
evolution; there may be other planets containing 'higher
beings' who 'far transcend us earthly men in intelligence'.[38]
This is commonplace in the neo-Darwinian thought of the
period; it informs much of the work of Wells, for instance.
Lawrence himself toys with it at certain points in his work, as
in Mellors's delight in the concept of evolution. ' "To contem-
plate the extermination of the human species and the long
pause that follows before some other species crops up, it calms
you more than anything else" ', he assures Connie (LC, XV,
227). No species can, according to Haeckel, achieve perfection; the 'gradual perfecting' of species, their *teleosis*, 'is the
inevitable result of selection, and not the outcome of a preconceived design', therefore no organism can be perfect, all are
subject to 'continuous adaptation' of the type experienced by
Lawrence's characters.[39] Haeckel postulates a universe whose
nature is both unified and dualistic. The bases of the will of
man are to be found in attraction and repulsion, which
operates like the 'tropism' in plants — the way they strive
'after light or darkness, heat or cold . . . positive and negative

electricity'. In man 'delight and disgust, . . . love and hatred' form the 'mainsprings' of civilisation.[40] But even the basic molecules are animated by this polarity and affinity,[41] and Haeckel constructs a somewhat Lawrencean table contrasting Ether and Mass — a duality upon which the entire universe is based.[42] 'The whole drama of nature', he observes, 'apparently consists in an alternation of movement and repose'[43] — a clear prefiguration of Lawrence's thesis of the Will-to-Motion and the Will-to-Inertia.

When Haeckel turns his attention to ethical matters his remarks are again germane to the student of the formation of Lawrence's thought. Like all social animals man has two sets of duties, to himself and to his society; he is therefore motivated by both egoism and altruism: egoism ensures the survival of the individual, just as Paul asserts his self-hood to gain release from his mother and his women; and altruism ensures the survival of the species.[44] Christianity, which over-emphasises altruism, had led not only to 'an extremely injurious isolation from our glorious mother nature', but also to contempt for all other organisms.[45] Related to this is Haeckel's view of sexual relations. 'The intimate sexual union, on which the preservation of the human race depends, is just as important on that account as the spiritual penetration of the two sexes'.[46] The pertinence of this to Lawrencean dogma needs no further remark.

In the 'Cathedral' chapter of *The Rainbow* Anna rejects Will's ecstatic response to the great enclosed womb of Lincoln Cathedral, feeling the freedom of the sky beyond and needing to 'get out of this fixed, leaping, forward-travelling movement' which the church represents, to get up into 'open space' (TR, VII, 202–3). In like manner Haeckel insists that the 'goddess of truth dwells in the temple of nature, in the green woods, on the blue sea . . . not in the gloom of the cloister'. The modern rationalist 'needs no special church, no narrow, enclosed portion of space', since 'his church is commensurate with the whole of glorious nature'[47] — a Nature, Haeckel finally grants, whose essence 'becomes more mysterious and enigmatic the deeper we penetrate into the knowledge of its attributes'.[48]

Haeckel's pantheist vision, founded in his great cosmic law of monism, his reintegration of matter and spirit, his cellular concept of the basis of organic and social life, and his unified approach to man and Nature combined to render *The Riddle of the Universe* a book pregnant with import to the young Lawrence. Its influence, readily discernible in *The White Peacock* or *The Trespasser*, went deep; it may be that in *The Rainbow* and *Women in Love* Lawrence was drawing upon this evolutionist primer. Certainly Birkin's final Alpine reflections are profoundly Haeckelian. 'Whatever the mystery which has brought forth man and the universe,' he observes, 'it is a non-human mystery, it has its own great ends, man is not the criterion'. If man failed, the 'eternal creative mystery could dispose' of him, 'and replace him with a finer created being':

The mystery of creation was fathomless, infallible, inexhaustible, for ever. Races came and went, species passed away, but ever new species arose, more lovely, or equally lovely, always surpassing wonder. The fountain-head was incorruptible and unsearchable. It had no limits. It could bring forth mirac-les, create utterly new races and new species in its own hour, new forms of consciousness, new forms of body, new units of being. To be man was as nothing compared to the possibilities of the creative mystery.

(WL, XXXI, 538)

Lawrence finally claimed to have rejected evolution as a rigorously determinist reading of Nature: 'I don't believe in evolution', he declared later in *Mornings in Mexico*,[49] 'like a long string hooked on to a First Cause, and being slowly twisted in unbroken continuity through the ages. I prefer to believe in what the Aztecs called Suns: that is, Worlds succes-sively created and destroyed'. And in the introduction to his paintings Lawrence wrote, 'After years of acceptance of the "laws" of evolution — rather desultory or "humble" acep-tance — now I realise that my vital imagination makes great reservations'.[50] These reservations centre upon the creativiey of man, his realisation of a self-hood which may be subdued to no mechanical law or cause and effect. The Haeckelian vision of the universe is subtly reformulated so as to retain this vital spark in the closure of *Sons and Lovers*, where Paul wanders out into the darkened countryside after his mother's death. Everywhere he finds 'the vastness and terror of the immense night which is roused and stirred for a brief while by the day, but which returns, and will remain at last eternal, holding everything in its silence and its living gloom'. In a sentence which echoes Haeckel, Paul reflects, 'There was no Time, only Space'. The dark silence seems 'pressing him . . . into extinction, and yet, almost nothing, he could not be extinct'. Paul's imagination reaches out into a universe recognisably evolutionary: 'Night, in which everything was lost, went reaching out, beyond stars and sun. Stars and sun, a few bright grains, went spinning round for terror'. This scenario is Haeckelian; *The Riddle of the Universe* spoke of the 'birth and death of countless heavenly bodies', and described the 'embryo of a new world' being formed from nebulae in one part of the universe, another condensed 'into a rotating sphere of liquid fire', a third casting-off rings at its equator, and 'frozen moons' falling on to the planets, and the planets on to their suns.[51] Yet Paul makes the great Lawrencean assertion against a world of dead matter, the heritage of rationalism: he is 'infinitesimal', writes Lawrence, 'yet not nothing' (SL, XV, 510). Yet with reference to human development the theory of evolution was seminal to Lawrence, as the 'struggles into being' in the novels from *The White Peacock* to *Women in Love* demonstrate.[52] Lawrence expounded on this in the 'Study of Thomas Hardy':

It seems as though one of the conditions of life is, that life shall continually and progressively differentiate itself, almost as though this differentiation were a Purpose. Life starts crude and unspecified, a great Mass. And it proceeds to evolve out of that mass ever more distinct and definite particular forms, an ever-multiplying number of separate species and orders, as if it were working always to the production of the infinite number of perfect individuals, the individual so thorough that he should have nothing in common with any other individual. It is as if all coagulation must be loosened, as if the elements must work themselves free and pure from the compound.

(STH, 43)

The idea of individuation and differentiation derives from another rationalist study of great import to the young Lawrence, Herbert Spencer's *First Principles*, which he knew by 1909 (ET, 113). Indeed *The Rainbow* and *Women in Love* offer us a magnificently actualised presentation of Spencer's principle of evolution and dissolution. Spencer believed there was a fundamental law of matter which he designated the law of persistence of force; the effect of this law was to bring about what he terms an 'Advance from the homogeneous to the heterogeneous'.[53] Evolution 'is a change from a less coherent form to a more coherent form, consequent on the dissipation of motion and integration of matter'.[54] The whole cosmos is subject to this 'vast transformation',[55] from the stars and planets down to the smallest organism, and including language, social institutions, industry and the arts. The 'more that I am driven from admixture', Lawrence notes in the 'Study of Thomas Hardy',[56] 'the more I am singled out into utter individuality, the more this intrinsic me rejoices'. He goes on to advance ideas which are pure Spencerean doctrine. In its origin life was 'uniform, a great, unmoved, utterly homogeneous infinity, a great not-being ... one motionless homogeneity'. Gradually this mass has 'stirred and resolved itself into many smaller, characteristic parts'; it has evolved, that is to say, from 'organic tissue' to invertebrates to mammals, finally 'from tribesman to me'. The naked doctrinal indebtedness here is of the utmost significance, when it is recalled that *The Rainbow* was being composed simultaneously with the Hardy essay. The Brangwens originate in primal homogeneity, and evolve over the three generations towards ever greater heterogeneity; Mrs Forbes, who inculcates Alfred Brangwen into Spencer's philosophy, is clearly one of the agents of this evolution (TR, 111, 90–1).

Spencer traces in his book profound movements of change; there is here no stasis. 'Absolute rest and permanence do not exist. Every object, no less than the aggregate of all objects, undergoes from instant to instant some alteration of state',[57] just as Lawrence warned Garnett not to look for 'the old stable ego of the character' in *The Rainbow*, the individual being seen as passing through 'allotropic states' of being.[58] These alterations of state are due to what Spencer terms the 'continuous adjustment of internal relations to external relations'.[59] The external forces have a tendency to 'bring the matter of which living bodies consist into that stable equilibrium shown by inorganic bodies; there are internal forces by which this tendency is constantly antagonised; and the unceasing changes which constitute Life, may be regarded as incidental to the maintenance of the antagonism'.[60] Lawrence told Garnett early in 1914 that *The Rainbow* had 'plenty of fire underneath, but, like bulbs in the ground, only shadowy flowers'. It was his 'transition stage' as an author, 'something deep evolving itself' in him. Garnett was not to look for the development of the novel to 'follow the lines of certain characters: the characters fall into the form of some other rhythmic form, as when one draws a fiddle-bow across a fine tray delicately sanded, the sand takes lines unknown' (SLC, 16–18). The 'antagonistic principle' to which Spencer refers as a law of existence is the result of his fundamental conception of rhythm pervading all existence. This concept was to be equally vital to Lawrence:

If each species of organism be regarded as a whole, it displays two kinds of rhythm. Life, as it exists in every member of such species, is an extremely complex kind of movement, more or less distinct from the kinds of movement which constitute life in other species. This extremely complex kind of movement begins, rises to its climax, declines, and ceases in death. And every individual in each generation thus exhibits a wave of that peculiar activity characterising the species as a whole.[61]

Life as successive waves: this was of paramount importance to Lawrence's conception of life. During longer epochs, Spencer observes, 'whole orders have thus arisen, culminated, and dwindled away'; thus life on earth 'has not progressed uniformly, but in immense undulations'.[62]

Turning his attention to society Spencer notes how 'while each individual is developing, the society of which he is an insignificant unit is developing too'[63] — the whole evolving towards what he calls 'increasing multiformity'. Man thus moves towards ever-larger aggregates whilst paradoxically evolving as an individual: 'From the lowest living forms upwards, the degree of development is marked by the degree in which the several parts constitute a co-operative assemblage — are integrated into a group of organs that live for and by one another'.[64] The 'co-operative assemblage' leads to constant modifications of man's institutions, 'alterations of structure in all those things which humanity creates'.[65]

Spencer's vision culminates, however, not in millennial grandeur but in dissolution, a bleak asseveration which helps to account for the role of Loerke in the icy disintegration of Gerald Crich, for instance. *First Principles* ends with an unanswered and unanswerable question: does evolution 'advance towards complete quiescence' — what Lawrence was to call 'the long journey towards oblivion' ('The Ship of Death')? Spencer contemplates, as the final outcome of all things, 'a boundless space holding here and there extinct suns, fated to remain for ever without further change'.[66]

The tragedy of George Saxton or Gerald Crich is the tragedy of individuation within this evolutionary process, in which the characters are uprooted from the reviving life of Nature and thrust into the 'advance post' of modern consciousness without the imaginative resources to occupy this exposed position. Thus, in Lawrence, does the inexhaustible fecundity and protean flux of Nature, often felt as good in itself, become a source of tragedy, the resultant dislocation, failure and blind struggle extending and deepening the similar plight of Henchard, Tess or Jude.

The Lawrencean process of individuation has been analysed by John Goode, who sees Lawrence's work developing 'in relation to a three-fold antithesis, industrial and rural, community and social aspirations, convention and idealism'. The old 'equilibrium between "inner" and "outer" being which is the basis of characterisation in the nineteenth century novel' is demolished by 'the Lawrencean affirmation of vitality':

There was no return to the dualistic "personality" of Jane Austen and George Eliot. The apart, inner self that their *modus vivendi* relies on ultimately takes refuge in mental consciousness, and this, Lawrence realised, was only destructive since it could only make of the "inner self" a mirror image of the social being from which it is withdrawn. The inner self might be the antithesis of social being, but this too is just another kind of reflection. The early short stories . . . affirm a different order of being which can make no compact with the social world which must either subvert that world or atrophy within it.

It is against, not a static background of social opinion, but a Haeckelian universe of ebb and flow, that Lawrence's characters are conceived, as Goode discerns: 'We are witnessing not the struggle of the emergent individual against the static group, but the inextricable involvement of the emergent individual with the *emergent* group — itself the medium of individual vitality'. This social dynamism is a key feature of *The White Peacock*, where Lawrence is utilising a medium of personal relationships 'to register forces which are beyond "personality" and which determine the development not merely of single individuals but also of the human group in which they have their being'. Cyril, Lettie, and supremely George, enact Goode's contention that 'awakening will mean separation from the landscape and growth will mean uprooting' — a life-process which was to be epically treated in *The Rainbow*.[67]

These Lawrencean characters are aware of their emergence and separation from organic life, but unaware of the goal to which this emergence tends. They reflect what had become a more generalised sense in Lawrence of the national spiritual crisis imaged in the Great War: 'When I drive across this country, with autumn falling and rustling to pieces, I am so sad, for my country. . . . So much beauty and pathos of old things passing away and no new things coming: this house of Ottoline's — it is England — my God, it breaks my soul — their England, these shattered windows, the elm-trees, the blue distance — the past, the great past, crumbling down' (L, 378).

Jessie Chambers concluded, with regard to Lawrence, that 'the suffering of self-division to its utmost limit was a lifetime's work'. This is a just, but partial verdict: it leaves out of account that almost hallucinatory oneness with Nature which characterises his greatest work, and that sense of natural process which may arbitrarily release or destroy the human psyche. If the process of individuation within Nature no longer corresponds to Meredith's optimistic investment in the blood–brain–spirit triumvirate, this must mark the encroachment of a psychic deathliness through which the natural life is suborned by spirituality, industrialism and egoism. 'Only when we fall into egoism', Lawrence held, 'do we lose all chance of blossoming'.[68] This is the tragedy of Clifford Chatterley: 'No breath entered him from any other living being or creature or thing. He was as it were cut off from the breathing contact of the living universe' (FLC, 55). Yet Lawrence in his finest moments always conveys the potency and liberation which man may find in Nature. In this, he is the great inheritor of the English Nature-tradition.

II

Proof of this lies in *The White Peacock* and in *The Trespasser*. A reading which places these novels directly in the line from Meredith onwards casts light on the development of Lawrence's art in the works which lie beyond the scope of this study.

The origins of *The White Peacock* are often traced to Lawrence's announcement to Jessie Chambers that the 'usual plan is to take two couples and develop their relationships'. ' I don't want a plot', Lawrence added (ET, 103). Thus George Eliot and Emily Brontë provided Lawrence with a starting-point in terms of familial connexions and permutations. In the first version, *Letitia*, written, as Lawrence said in 1908, 'during the year that I changed from boyhood to manhood' (L, 27), George Saxton was a 'noble young farmer who had married a Lettie who was beyond him socially; she had gone through a reductive process by letting a young man of even higher social standing seduce her'.[69] In *Nethermere*, the second version,

Lawrence remarked, Lettie 'responded, and that very weakly, to Leslie, only in the sex melody. It needed that the other chords of her nature, the finer, should be jangled in an agony of discord before she realised how much she was sacrificing' (L, 23). The resultant novel, in its third and final version, was characterised by the author as 'all about love — and rhapsodies on Spring scattered here and there — heroines galore — no plot — nine-tenths adjectives — every colour of the spectrum descanted upon — a poem or two — scraps of Latin and French — altogether a sloppy, spicy mess' (L, 5). Though there were 'some exquisite passages, such as I shall not write again' (L, 12), the faults of the early versions were too obtrusive, devaluing both characterisation and structure. Cyril, Lawrence conceded, is 'a young fool at the best of times, and a frightful bore at the worst' (L, 19). The structure, he told Jessie, would have disintegrated into 'a mosaic, a mosaic of moods'.

A number of factors contributed to a strengthening and unifying of the whole in the final version of 1910. First the 'sloppy, spicy mess' was moulded into coherence by the introduction of the powerful alien figure of Annable the gamekeeper, and through him Lawrence was able to orchestrate the theme of man and Nature. Whether or not he was modelled, as Moore suggests, upon Kingsley's voluble keeper, Tregarva,[70] Annable, as Lawrence assured Jessie, '*has* to be there' because he 'makes a sort of balance. Otherwise it's too much one thing, too much *me*' (ET, 117). This balance on the male side was countered by gains in the conception and presentation of Lettie, and of female psychology generally. This must be partly ascribed to Lawrence's wider experience of women by 1910 and to the events depicted in *Sons and Lovers*. But a specifically literary influence may also be detected in the relationship with the Scottish poetess, Rachel Annand Taylor. They first met in Hampstead in the spring of 1910. 'Her cultural sophistication, her Pre-Raphaelite beauty, and her romantic poetry so strongly impressed Lawrence that when, in the autumn, he was asked to give a paper on a living poet

before a Croydon literary group, he chose her as his subject'.[71]
Whilst Lawrence found that in *Rose and Vine* 'the full,
luscious buds of promise are fullblown', he complained that
she had become 'esoteric' in *The Hours of Fiammetta*, and
that 'Her symbols do not show what they stand for of themselves'. Yet this sequence, he went on, was 'as interesting, more
interesting far to trace than a psychological novel',[72] and his
letters of this period reveal that it was this sonnet-sequence
which occupied his imagination. In the preface to this volume
Mrs Taylor expounded the theory that there are 'two great
traditions of womanhood. One presents the Madonna
brooding over the mystery of motherhood; the other, more
confusedly, tells of the acolyte, the priestess, the clairvoyante
of the unknown gods' who 'troubles and quickens the soul of
man', just as Lettie troubles George, 'redeeming him from the
spiritual sloth which is more to be dreaded than any kind of
pain'.[73] In the novel Emily achieves fulfilment as a Madonna
figure, and Lettie finally succumbs to this mould, whilst still
hysterically playing the role of the 'priestess' of the arts. Both
archetypes exude a power before which the men are helpless as
Annable had been with Lady Crystabel, a power fundamentally sexual, as Mrs Taylor hinted in her sonnet 'Perils': 'the
myrrhs/And music of our beauty are mixed with shame' — a
mixture of sexual and excretory functions which prefigures
the appearance of the white peacock in the novel, and in the
sonnet called 'The Change':

> I spun my soul about with soft cocoons
> Of pleasure golden-pale. For me, for me
> Were precious things put forth by crescent moons,
> Of pearl and milky jade and ivory.
> Grave players on ethereal harpsichords,
> My senses wrought a music exquisite
> As patterned roses, all my life's accords
> Were richer, ghostlier than peacocks white.
> So in my paradise reserved and fair
> I grew as dreamlike as the Elysian dead;
> Until a passing Wizard smote me there,
> And suddenly my soul inherited

Some gorgeous terrible dukedom of desire
Like those in bright Andromeda's realm of fire.

Whereas Annable will falsify Nature in the name of his own atavism and feral rejection of womanhood, Lettie will emasculate Nature; she is the type of whom Mrs Taylor wrote, 'Estruscan mirrors are as dear to her as the daisies', and for whom Nature 'formed the swan and the peacock for decorative delight'.[74]

By synthesising the disparate elements of *Letitia* and *Nethermere* Lawrence was able to compose a novel in which, as Edward Garnett observed, 'an extraordinary intimacy with the feminine love instincts is blended with untrammelled psychological interest in the gamut of the passions'. What seems to have been originally conceived as a regional novel of manners is transformed into a work pulsating with a sense of universal life. This transformation might be expressed in purely literary terms: the genesis of *The White Peacock* charts a transfer of allegiance from the world of George Eliot to that of Jefferies and Hardy.

The opening paragraph of 'The People of Nethermere' adumbrates the concerns of the entire novel:

I stood watching the shadowy fish slide through the gloom of the mill-pond. They were grey, descendants of the silvery things that had darted away from the monks, in the young days when the valley was lusty. The whole place was gathered in the musing of old age. The thick-piled trees on the far shore were too dark and sober to dally with the sun; the woods stood crowded and motionless. Not even a little wind flickered the willows of the islets. The water lay softly, intensely still. Only the thin stream falling through the mill-race murmured to itself of the tumult of life which had once quickened the valley.

(i, I, 13)

The image is one of a secret prelapsarian idyll going into decline. The lustiness of the valley's 'young days' is displaced by the 'musing of old age', a quietism imaged by the dislimning of the 'tumult of life' to a murmurous stream. The movement of this paragraph is enacted not only historically but immediately, within the timespan of the novel, most specifically in the insidious degeneration of George Saxton from primal strength into premature alcoholic decrepitude. If Nethermere is conceived as a type of Eden, yet it is the decadence of Nethermere, ruled over by the 'head of an ancient, once even famous, but now decayed house' (i, VI, 82), which exerts the formative influence upon character. This was best explained years later by Lawrence himself, when he argued that 'the fatal change today is the collapse from the psychology of the free human individual into the psychology of the social being'. This collapse, which Lawrence came to see as universal, is due to the withering away of Nature from the human world:

> when the human being becomes too much divided between his subjective and objective consciousness, at last something splits in him and becomes a social being. . . . While a man remains a man, before he falls and becomes a social individual, he innocently feels himself altogether within the great continuum of the universe. He is not divided nor cut off.
>
> (SE, 219)

It is this split which the primitives, from Annable to Mellors, seek to repair. Lawrence's theological terminology is significant here: Lettie, with her invitation to George to join the circle of advanced thought, acts unwittingly as Eve. George, she alleges, is only 'half alive' (i, II, 31): ' "You are blind; you are only half-born" ', she instructs him, imagining him, in a cunning authorial reference to the opening paragraph, as 'a monk — a martyr, a Carthusian' (i, III, 46–7). George acknowledges this: ' "You have awakened my life" ', he tells Lettie, ' "I imagine things that I couldn't have done" ' (i, IX, 158). Against this, Lawrence opposes the creed of Annable that ' "When a man's more than nature he's a devil. Be a good animal, says I, whether it's man or woman" ' (ii, I, 178). George, whose muscular commonalty with the agricultural cycle is frequently stressed by Cyril, is dissatisfied with 'work and sleep and comfort — half a life' (ii, IV, 245). The novel thus takes the form of a dialogue between culture and primitivism, but it is a dialogue in which the characters are unwitting agents rather than conscious spokesmen.

This sense of cultural crisis derives from the awakening of

the characters, and their subsequent separation from the land-scape. Thus George is reduced from a natural force to a mere cipher. *The White Peacock* is in essence a novel about evolution. Huxley argued that 'there is no faculty whatever that is not capable of improvement; there is no faculty whatsoever which does not depend upon structure, and as structure tends to vary, it is capable of being improved'. [75] But this structure, Darwin stressed, 'is related, in the most essential yet often hidden manner, to that of all other organic beings, with which it comes into competition for food or residence, or from which it has to escape, or on which it preys'.[76] George, Cyril, Lettie and the others are competitors in the enclosed and dying pastoral confines of Nethermere, their careers a tragic instance of Darwin's words on evolution in a confined area, where 'new places in the natural economy of the country are left open for the old inhabitants to struggle for, and become adapted to'.[77] This struggle and adaptation takes a variety of forms, from George's thwarted social and intellectual aspirations, through Cyril's aestheticism and Annable's primitivism, to Lettie's entry into the landowning class. The isolation of the valley, however, bears out Darwin's thesis that 'fewness of individuals will greatly retard the production of new species through natural selection, by decreasing the chance of the appearance of favourable variations'.[78,79] Such favourable variation is denied the people of Nethermere, as it is to the denizens of Wessex.

George Saxton, who is culturally closest to an organic way of life, moves away under the pressure of modern life and consciousness. Annable's reversion to Nature which counteracts this movement, though powerfully articulated, is as willed and mechanical as Clym's return to the heath, a *modus vivendi* which must lead towards nihilism. Caught between these antitheses stand the other major figures, Cyril and Lettie. Both, in different ways are idealists who project their fantasy images upon Nature and society, like the squire's wife who 'had written a book filling these meadows and the mill precincts with pot-pourri romance' (ii, IX, 295). If George's heavy stooping towards the earth represents his roots in earth, the Beardsall children suffer from an excess of idealism which etherealises and displaces reality by wish-fulfilment. While Cyril turns to Nature to gain solace for his personal inadequacy but fails because he is self-engrossed, so to an ever more delusive degree does Lettie project her pathetic fallacies upon Nature. In praising Clausen to George she argues, 'he is a real realist, he makes common things beautiful, he sees the mystery and magnificence that envelops us even when we work menially' (i, III, 45). This illusory projection of the self into Nature in an attempt to fix the fluidity of the personality is epitomised in two seminal passages in which the identification of the human with the natural is vitiated by the human projection of self.

Lettie's vision of the woodland is thus highly personalised:

'Look!' she said, 'it's a palace, with the ash-trunks smooth like a girl's arm, and the elm-columns, ribbed and bossed and fretted, with the great steel shafts of beech, all rising up to hold an embroidered care-cloth over us; and every thread of the care-cloth vibrates with music for us, and the little broidered birds sing; and the hazel-bushes fling green spray round us, and the honeysuckle leans down to pour out scent over us. Look at the harvest of bluebells — ripened for us! Listen to the bee, sounding among all the organ-play — if he sounded exultant for us!'

(ii, VII, 281)

The second passage more subtly demonstrates how Cyril's reading of earth gives him, in its powerful natural imagery, that dream of ultimate rest which he seeks from life:

I was born in September, and love it best of all the months. There is no heat, no hurry, no thirst and weariness in corn harvest as there is in the hay. If the season is late, as is usual with us, then mid-September sees the corn still standing in stook. The mornings come slowly. The earth is like a woman married and fading; she does not leap up with a laugh for the first fresh kiss of dawn, but slowly, quietly, unexpectantly lies watching the waking of each new day. The blue mist, like memory in the eyes of the neglected wife, never goes from the wooded hill, and only at noon creeps from the near hedges. There is no bird to put a song in the throat of morning; only the crow's voice speaks during the day. Perhaps there is the regular breathing hush of the scythe — even the fretful jar of the mowing-machine. But next day, in the morning, all is still again. The lying corn is wet, and when you have bound it, and lift the heavy sheaf to make the stook, the tresses of oats wreathe round each other and droop mournfully.

(i, VI, 84)

Cyril constantly seeks sustenance from Nature for his second-hand imaginative life: 'I wished that in all the wild valley where cloud shadows were travelling like pilgrims, something would call me forth from my rooted loneliness. Through all the grandeur of the white and blue day, the poised cloud masses swung their slow flight, and left me unnoticed.' (ii, I, 171). This wish is granted in the 'Poem of Friendship' chapter, in which Cyril achieves his desire for 'someone to nestle against, someone who would come between me and the coldness and wetness of the surroundings' (ii, VIII, 289), a desire which also gets focussed upon Annable. The gamekeeper's 'magnificent physique, his great vigour and vitality, and his swarthy, gloomy face drew me', Cyril confesses (ii, II, 195). Cyril and Lettie are attracted by George's animalism, but their education causes them to destroy him — the point is to be made again in 'Snake'. They taint the young farmer with their own almost hysterical degree of consciousness, so that the final effect is of a Gabriel Oak transformed into a bibulous Jude Fawley, full of rustic *Weltschmertz*. This process is constantly dramatized in the novel, for example in the Theocritean picnic scene, 'Pastorals and Peonies' (ii, IX), with its uneasy conjunction of upper-class idyll and agrarian realism. The effect of this juxtaposition is that George and Lettie injure one another as Gudrun and Crich are to do more fatally. Neither of them is able to accommodate natural vitality to the social milieu. In Darwinian terms George's tragedy is that of a misfired attempt at adaptation.

Yet the total effect of *The White Peacock* is far from pessimistic, because the inner movement of the novel follows the seasons and the pulsations of the greater world of Nature. In its presentation of the multiplicity and dynamism of the natural world *The White Peacock* relates directly to *The Ordeal of Richard Feverel, Tess* and *The Dewy Morn*. It is not so much that there is a conflict between the emergent social world of the characters and the circumambient world of farm and woodland; rather, that the characters are dwarfed by the intensity of the realisation of the life of Nature. George, Lettie, Cyril and the others, in their complex interrelationships, are not sufficiently individuated; unlike Cathy and Heathcliff, for instance, they are swamped by their environment, and the novel inevitably culminates in the disintegration of Nethermere as a social organism. The characters remain figures in a landscape, a small part of an overwhelming totality. In this conception Lawrence may well have been influenced by traditions of landscape painting in Poussin, Lorrain and Salvator Rosa; there can be little doubt, however, that the novel is primarily an expression of Lawrence's concern with Romanticism, the Transcendentalists, Darwin, and the fiction of Meredith, Hardy and Jefferies. It is against a background of amoral Nature that the characters contend, but their puny struggles ultimately become a withdrawal from organic Nature; just as Angel Clare cannot seize upon the true potential of the Vale of the Great Dairies and accept the fecundity of Nature, so the people of Nethermere, burdened by twentieth-century consciousness, are guilty of a similar poverty of response. In *The Trespasser* Lawrence was to show the protagonists grappling with this connexion with Nature; in *The White Peacock* the final note is one of retreat and failure. The novel indeed suggests that some key to life has been lost, dooming the characters to a life of struggle and failure. Sex, which is to become Lawrence's 'objective correlative' for the deep flow of Nature, is here a source of frustrated longing, as Mrs Taylor's decadent poems had suggested it would be. If the impulse to be in physical contact with Nature permeates the book it is an impulse which is thwarted by disruptive psychic and cultural forces, processes of dissolution which were to preoccupy Lawrence up to *Lady Chatterley's Lover*.[80]

This is not to say that the images of Nature deployed so densely throughout the novel are consistently optimistic in tone. On the contrary Lawrence scrupulously emphasises

Darwinian struggle from the outset, in premonitory anticipation of George's career, for instance, when he pulls off the bees' wings (i, I, 14). Even Lettie, who 'had sought the bright notes in everything' (i, V, 66), is brought to acknowledge that ' "If we move the blood rises in our heel-prints" '. (i, II, 28). At her engagement party there is a significant exchange between Cyril and Marie Tempest:

'People must be ill when they write like Maxim Gorky.' 'They live in town,' said I. 'Yes — but then look at Hardy — life seems so terrible — it isn't, is it?'
(i, IX, 148)

The Hardyesque version of Nature is a persistent undertone; and equally persistent is the parallelism between human and natural worlds. Thus when the unknown father is discovered asleep on a log, 'Suddenly through the gloom of the twilight-haunted woods came the scream of a rabbit caught by a weasel' (i, III, 39) — a moment which recalls the proposal in *Under the Greenwood Tree*. The trapping and drowning of Mrs Nickie Ben, the hunting down of the rabbits and mice, the depredations of the wild dog amongst the sheep, and its strangulation by Emily in the quarry, the burning of Mrs Saxton's chick — all illuminate the struggle for existence in both natural and human worlds. Indeed *The White Peacock*, and especially the chapter entitled 'The Scent of Blood', might be read as a gloss on *The Origin of Species:*

We behold the face of nature bright with gladness, we often see superabundance of food; we do not see, or we forget, that the birds which are idly singing round us mostly live on insects or seeds, and are thus constantly destroying life; or we forget how largely these songsters, or their eggs, or their nestlings, are destroyed by birds and beasts of prey;[81]

Paradoxically it is Lettie who is compelled to notice 'the cruel pitiful crying of a hedgehog caught in a gin . . . the traps for the fierce little murderers . . . baited with guts of a killed rabbit' (i, V, 66).[82] This ruthless struggle is equally located in the human world, and Lawrence reinforces his point with the subtly understated images of domestic squalor in Annable's cottage, and of the miners trapped by the pit at Selsby.

The White Peacock is neither pastoral nor anti-pastoral. Lawrence surrounds his characters by a Nature whose chief feature is its 'eternal incomprehensibility', and places 'the little human morality play' within this context. Thus does the 'terrific action of unfathomed nature' both place and frame all human action.

This sense of the transcendence of Nature may be illustrated by an examination of two climactic scenes, since Lawrence is already working towards the symbolist technique which he perfected in *Women in Love.* Lawrence's chief motifs — conflict between mind and instinct, paganism, female-dominated idealism — may be clearly discerned in both 'A Shadow in Spring' and 'A Poem of Friendship', sustained and amplified by Lawrence's vision of Nature.

With the eruption of Annable into the placidity of Nethermere 'like some malicious Pan' (ii, I, 176), a new element enters the novel, an element which is to persist in Lawrence's work. Annable is the man who opts for Rousseauistic simplicity, raising his children as 'natural as weasels' according to his creed that ' "One's more a man here in th'wood, though, than in my lady's parlour" ' (ii, I, 177). Believing that 'all civilisation was the painted fungus of rottenness' (ii, II, 196), Annable sets his face against society, his life becoming the epitome of vitality and brute indifference. Yet it is perhaps an unconscious irony that, as gamekeeper, Annable's role is to curb and restrain Nature, subtly altering the balance of survival in favour of his game. He is an outcast from society, a 'devil of the woods' to the villagers and miners who swear vengeance on him (ii, II, 195), contriving to lead an amoral and animalistic life. A 'thorough materialist', he is drawn to Cyril when he comes upon the young man watching maggots at work in a dead rabbit, and he proceeds to expound his motto, 'Be a good animal, true to your animal instinct' (ii, II, 196). Yet this naturalism is essentially perverse, an act of will motivated by his early marital experience.

This experience is rehearsed in the extraordinary scene in the Hall churchyard, with the abandoned church looming 'black and melancholy', prey to birds and beasts within. In the churchyard overlooking the Hall Cyril encounters the keeper. The atmosphere, recalling that of *Maud,*[83] is redolent with decay and suffering. A peacock from the Hall perches on the neck of 'an old bowed angel' and Annable apostrophises it: ' "The proud fool! — look at it! Perched on an angel, too, as if it were a pedestal for vanity. That's the soul of a woman — or it's the devil" '. When Annable flings a sod at it the bird flaps away: ' "Just look!" ' he said, "the miserable brute has dirtied that angel. A woman to the end, I tell you, all vanity and screech and defilement" ' (ii, II, 198).[84] This inability to accept the natural functions of the woman underlines the falsity and deathliness of Annable's reversion to Nature, a retreat which he goes on to justify by telling Cyril of his marriage to Lady Crystabel. Like Coleridge's heroine this lady is an unwitting agent of evil who destroys Annable by viewing him 'in an aesthetic light' (ii, II, 200), as Lettie is to view George. When Crystabel affected Pre-Raphaelitism Annable abandoned his 'white peacock' and she died. Lawrence's obsession with the rich lady–poor young man situation, with its origin in his domestic and literary background, clearly recurs in the later work.

After this confessional scene it is as if Annable is propelled by his nihilism towards death. Returning to animalism has rendered him non-human, so that he lacks the organic connexion with the natural habitat, acquired through useful work, which is George's natural birthright. The Freudian associations of the quarry in which he meets his death need not be over-stressed; nonetheless Lawrence beautifully dramatizes, in Cyril's exploration of the place, with the boy's attempts to resuscitate his father, the horror of the ambience, a horror which surely echoes *Maud*:

> I hate the dreadful hollow behind the little wood,
> Its lips in the field above are dabbled with blood-red heath,
> The red-ribb'd ledges drip with a silent horror of blood,
> And Echo there, whatever is ask'd her, answers 'Death'.

For there in the ghastly pit long since a body was found,
His who had given me life — O father! O God! was it well? —
Mangled, and flatten'd, and crushed, and dinted into the ground:
There yet lies the rock that fell with him when he fell.

(Maud, Pt. I, i-ii)

This sense of Gothic *Schrecklichkeit* is common to Tennyson and Lawrence,[85] and it is reinforced by Cyril's acknowledgement that Annable 'treated me as an affectionate father treats a delicate son' (ii, II, 196). The inquest brings in 'death by misadventure' but 'vague rumours' of revenge circulate in the village: as the narrator of *Maud* demands, 'Did he fling himself down? who knows?' This action is the most violent expression of the Darwinian view in the novel, which coalesces Romantic pantheism with Victorian fatalism in uneasy conjunction:

For nature is one with rapine, a harm no preacher can heal;
The Mayfly is torn by the swallow, the sparrow spear'd by the shrike,
And the whole little wood where I sit is a world of plunder and prey.

(Maud, Pt. I, iv, IV)

The fine evocation of Annable's funeral day, with its exuberant plasticity of language and sensuous immediacy, acts as a collocation of the pantheistic and Darwinian views of Nature, held up as complementary visions:

It was a magnificent morning in early spring when I watched among the trees to see the procession come down the hillside. The upper air was woven with the music of the larks, and my whole world thrilled with the conception of summer. The young pale wind-flowers had arisen by the wood-gale, and under the hazels, when perchance the hot sun pushed his way, new little suns dawned, and blazed with real light. There was a certain thrill and quickening everywhere. . . . Birds called and flashed on every hand; they made off exultant with streaming strands of grass, or wisps of fleece, plunging into the dark spaces of the wood, and out again into the blue.

(ii, II, 206–7)

The burial is in a sense the burial of the dark tragic side of Nature, and a rebirth of pantheist ecstasy, the counterpoint between the swirling new life of spring and the slow human procession of death being beautifully caught in Lawrence's writing.

In the funeral scene the Darwinian image of Nature as dominated by bestial predators is transcended by vitalist pantheism, a romantic affirmation which is acted out by the 'Poem of Friendship' chapter. In a bitter and wet May, during which the 'tender-budded trees shuddered and moaned', 'the cattle crouched among the gorse, distressed by the cold, while the long-billed snipe flickered round high overhead, round and round in great circles' (ii, VIII, 286), Cyril goes potato-picking with George. In the drenched grass he uncovers a lark's nest occupied by two fledglings, 'their tiny bodies rising and falling in quick unison'. He envies them their warmth and safety, his heart 'heavy with vague longing': 'It seemed as if I were always wandering, looking for something which they had found even before the light broke into their shell'. 'What did I want that I turned thus from one thing to another?' he demands (ii, VIII, 289). At the outset of June the weather becomes warm, and haymaking begins in an atmosphere of natural benediction:

Little, early birds — I had not heard the lark — fluttered in and out of the foamy meadow-sea, plunging under the surf of flowers washed high in one corner, swinging out again, dashing past the crimson sorrel cresset. Under the froth of flowers were the purple vetch-clumps, yellow milk vetches, and the scattered pink of the wood-betony, and the floating stars of marguerites. There was a weight of honeysuckle on the hedges, where pink roses were waking up for their broad-spread flight through the day.

(ii, VIII, 290)

In the early morning Cyril comes upon George bathing in the mill-pond, and strips off to join him. Like the equivalent scenes in *Richard Feverel, The Dewy Morn, A Room with a View* and *Maurice*, the action here proposes immersion as baptism or initiation into intimate companionship under the tutelary influence of Nature. The icy water momentarily deprives Cyril of his senses, but soon he is sensible of 'nothing but the vigorous poetry of action', and specifically of the poetry of George's body:[86] 'he knew not I admired the noble, white fruitfulness of his form. As I watched him, he stood in white relief against the mass of green'. At this moment, significantly,

Cyril recalls the history of Annable, as if both these strong men act as father-substitutes. George rubs Cyril down as if he were 'a woman he loved and did not fear': 'the sweetness of the touch of our naked bodies one against the other was superb', 'our love was perfect for a moment, more perfect than any love I have known since', Cyril concluded, 'either for man or woman'. This love gets expressed by the comradeship of scything, when the 'cool, moist fragrance of the morning, the intentional stillness of everything, of the tall bluish trees, of the wet, frank flowers, of the trustful moths folded and unfolded in the fallen swaths, was a perfect medium of sympathy' (ii, VIII, 291–2). Despite the note of wistfulness in George's recognition of ephemerality in human affairs the scene is invested with an interfusing sense of the joy of Nature: 'Life was full of glamour for us both'. It is this pantheist affirmation of beauty, rather than the homoerotic anticipations of *Blut-brüderschaft*, which holds the key to the episode and relates it to similar scenes in Meredith, Jefferies and Forster. Nature here is a sacrament and communion with it endows man with a new dimension of being.

The third section of the novel reproduces a slow decline, the inability of the human to find a purpose in Nature or society leading the characters into mental dissolution. The valley is now seen as a lost paradise: 'It was time for us all to go, to leave the valley of Nethermere whose waters and whose woods were distilled in the essence of our veins. We were the children of the valley of Nethermere, a small nation with language and blood of our own, and to cast ourselves each one into separate exile was painful to us' (iii, I, 309).[87] Lawrence's technique changed correspondingly, the tone modulating into grey realism. The uprooting from the 'happy valley' is painful and ultimately disintegrates the psyche, as George comes to realise. ' "I dread above all things" ', he confesses, ' "this slow crumbling away from my foundations by which I free myself at last" ' (iii, I, 309). Freedom is achieved, but the price is too great and the decay imaged in the opening paragraph of the novel, and echoed in Mr Saxton's feeling of stagnation (iii, III,

339), overwhelms the children of Nethermere. A type of culture-shock reduces George to a drunken horse-dealer and, like Jude, he mistakenly marries a sensual girl who cannot appreciate his dilemma. On the day of the wedding his coat is smeared with bird-droppings, a recollection of the white peacock which reinforces the image of enslavement to woman (iii, I, 311). Though Cyril suffers 'acutely the sickness of exile' in London (iii, III, 336), he comes to love the urban scene 'for its movement of men and women, the soft, fascinating flow of the limbs of men and women' (iii, III, 341), 'with all the subtle grace and mystery of their moving, shapely bodies' (iii, V, 368). Cyril thus reduces the life of the city to the same question of Pre-Raphaelite aesthetics as swamps his experience of Nature. By comparison with the metropolis, with its bustling movement, Cyril recognises on his return to Nethermere that it is 'a small, insignificant valley lost in the spaces of the earth' (iii, III, 344). This draining of significance from life is for-mulated in the chapter entitled 'The Dominant Motif of Suf-fering', in which George is shown some London social outcasts and contrasts them with Lettie's pretentious dinner party. Lettie as a mother has determined 'to ignore her own self, to empty her own potentialities into the vessel of another or others, and to live her life at second hand' (iii, V, 365). This abnegation signals her own falling away just as starkly as George's dependence on whisky. She justifies it, in the face of George's new socialist dogma, in evolutionary terms: ' "It is a question of life and the development of the human race" ' (iii, VI, 379). Similarly, Leslie Tempest, a pale precursor of Crich and Chatterley, embraces Social Darwinism, becoming an 'advocate of machinery which will do the work of men' (iii, VI, 381).

The final movement of the novel, with Cyril 'cast out' from Nethermere and losing Emily to a local farmer, and George drunkenly dominated by his wife and daughter, completes the pattern of dissolution. This larger pattern is exemplified in the fate of Alice Gall, most iconoclastic of the Beardsall circle. Alice marries a pious clerk and lives near the iron foundries, 'in a dirty little place', 'all her little crackling fires were sodden down with the sods of British respectability' (iii, VIII, 405). The final 'Prospect Among the Marshes of Lethe', in which Cyril recognises his 'pale, erratic fragility' beside the agricultural solidity of Swineshed Farm (iii, VIII, 409), expresses in terms of natural imagery the culminating sense of inexorable deterioration. Thus George, waveringly recuperating from delirium tremens, is seen by Cyril as 'a tree that is falling, going soft and pale and rotten, clammy with small fungi' (III, VIII, 415) — an image which recalls Darwin's simile of evolution as a tree from which 'many a limb and branch has decayed and dropped off'.[88] In Cyril's journey through the autumnal lanes to visit a George who is virtually unrecognisable, Lawrence movingly encapsulates the heuristic movement of the novel away from a vivifying Nature towards an imprisoning industrialism. As Lawrence was to write at the end of his life 'The industrial England blots out the agricultural England. One meaning blots out another. The new England blots out the old England. And the continuity is not organic, but mechanical' (LC, XI, 163). Where *The White Peacock* ends, *Sons and Lovers* begins: 'I rode slowly on, the plants dying around me, the berries leaning their heavy ruddy mouths, and languishing for the birds, the men imprisoned underground below me, the brown birds dashing in haste along the hedges' (iii, VIII, 407).

The Trespasser, though a lesser work, in its celebration of a sensual pantheism, may be read as an extended exploration of the 'Poem of Friendship' chapter. Written, as Jessie Chambers testified, 'in feverish haste between the Whitsuntide and Midsummer of 1910', Lawrence soon came to reject the novel. Its 'florid, luscious quality', he felt, made it 'too *chargé*, too emotional' (L, 93, 88). The hothouse atmosphere derives from the origins of the work in Helen Corke's affair with Herbert MacCartney of the Carl Rosa Opera, his subsequent suicide, and Lawrence's own involvement with Helen Corke at Croydon.[89] Helen Corke's final judgement is that the book 'was too nearly life, and life upon that plane of superhuman perception which is charged with danger'.[96] Nonetheless, it should be recognised that Lawrence worked on *The Trespasser* very carefully, and paid close attention to its form. The story of the lovers' idyll on the island is scrupulously placed by the framing scenes between Helena and Cecil Byrne, and by the calculated realism of the domestic scenes, so that the frenetic quality of the affair is neither wholly endorsed nor rejected. Also, the urgent but oblique sexual-psychological complexes of the lovers are taken as illustrative of the life-giving power of Nature. Indeed despite the wealth of artistic and mythic allusion it is the treatment of man's relation with Nature which dominates the novel and imparts a tonal coherence to the narrative. The novel may be construed as a reply to the 'Prospect Among the Marshes of Lethe'. The lovers, during their island sojourn, inhabit a world not unlike that of Talbothays, a world of throbbing pantheist ecstasy which manifests itself both through Nature-worship and sexual passion, the latter being simply an element within the boundless energy of Nature as it is here conceived. This is not to overlook the tensions inherent in the relationship, tensions which are to lead finally to suicide. But the overriding impression of the Isle of Wight section is of the unbounded fertility of the natural world, and of the quest of the human beings to connect themselves with this fertility. If the affirmation ends in domestic tragedy this reflects upon the inadequacy of the human response to the redemptive potentialities revealed on the island. In a sense Siegmund trespasses against the laws of his own being;[91] but this statement fails to do justice to the multiple possibilities, the symbolic resonance of Nature in the novel, that sense of the mysterious teeming life to which the sexual passions give man access. *The Trespasser* proposes nothing less than a reunification of man, woman and Nature. It was to be Lawrence's life work to bring this theme to a resolution. The paradoxes and difficulties of *The Trespasser* indicate the task ahead.

The opening chapters lay bare the thematic threads. In a suburban room 'foreign to the trams and to the sound of the London traffic' (T, 5), Helena and Louisa play Mozart, whilst

Cecil Byrne tries unsuccessfully to rouse Helena from the
memory of her love-affair with Siegmund. Helena is one of
Rachel Annand Taylor's 'dreaming women', and in her withdrawal from the world she is likened to a beech tree or a sulky
animal.[92] The Buddha which stands in the room, 'locked in his
renunciation' (T, I, 6), epitomises that emotional paralysis
which Byrne will release in the final return to Nature in the
closing scene. In the next chapter Lawrence reverts to the
beginning of the narrative proper, delineating Siegmund at the
opera house, his unhappy married life with Beatrice and the
children, and the imbroglio with Helena, a lover of 'beautiful
things and of dreams' (T, II, 16). The protagonists are thus
classified: Siegmund inhabits an operatic world of primary
passions and exaltation, whilst Helena is a member of 'that
class of "dreaming women" with whom passion exhausts
itself at the mouth', her dreams 'abstract, and full of fantasy'
(T, IV, 30). The sense of sexual struggle is occasionally overwhelmed by passion and joy; as soon as Siegmund nears the
island he is 'mated with joy':

He felt the sea heaving below him. He looked round, and the sea was blue as
a periwinkle flower, while gold and white and blood-red sails lit here and
there upon the blueness. Standing on the deck, he gave himself to the breeze
and to the sea, feeling like one of the ruddy sails — as if he were part of it all.
All his body radiated amid the large, magnificent sea-moon like a piece of
colour.   (T, III, 20-1)

The mist which encloses the lovers on the downs, the *Tristan*
note of the foghorn,[93] serve to isolate the intense union, an
intensity from which Helena repeatedly draws away: 'She had
not the man's brightness and vividness of blood' (T, IV, 30).
Even when Helena 'seemed to be offering him herself to sacrifice', there is 'a good deal of sorrow in his joy' (T, V, 35).

The deepest relationship into which Siegmund is initiated is
not with Helena but with the effulgent natural world of the
island, the earth seemingly replacing woman as the love-
object. This act of communion is fraught with danger, and
Siegmund gets injured in the leg and arm:[94] 'I am a fool to
think myself one with [the elements]', 'It was an illusion' (T,

V I, 40; T, XVII, 112). *The Trespasser* debates this judgement; and the novel is indeed Wordsworthian in its grasp of the theme of man, woman and Nature. When Siegmund is near to Helena he loses 'the yearning towards something': 'She seemed to connect him with the beauty of things, as if she were the nerve through which he received intelligence of the sun, and wind, and sea, and of the moon and the darkness. Beauty she never felt herself came to him through her' (T, V I, 44). Yet Lawrence also places this pantheism within a cosmic framework, and the lovers' individual relations are transformed in a memorable vision:

There was a shelving beach of warm white sand, bleached soft as velvet. A sounding of gulls filled the dark recesses of the headland; a low chatter of shingle came from where the easy water was breaking; the confused, shell-like murmur of the sea between the folded cliffs. Siegmund and Helena lay side by side upon the dry sand, small as two resting birds, while thousands of gulls whirled in a white-flaked storm above them, and the great cliffs towered beyond, and high up over the cliffs the multitudinous clouds were travelling, a vast caravan *en route*. Amidst the journeyings of oceans and clouds and the circling flight of heavy spheres, lost to sight in the sky, Siegmund and Helena, two grains of life in the vast movement, were travelling a moment side by side.[95]   (T, V I, 46)

The human is necessarily a fragile and ephemeral part of this great design, human survival being as fortuitous as that of the light bulb on the beach. From this struggle for survival, even in the ecstatic idyll of love, Siegmund turns away: 'He could never take part in the great battle of action. It was beyond him' (T, V II, 51). This is the result of that 'civilisation' of which he is a fine flower. As Helena observes, artists 'are supremely unfortunate persons' (T, IX, 61). This aestheticism makes Siegmund's relation to Nature ultimately too frenzied. He cleaves to the warm sand, 'the warm body of the sea-bay'. But in the end 'he found the cold mystery of the deep sand also thrilling' — a suggestion that the otherness of death will finally tempt him, a slipping away into the 'relentless mass of cold beneath — the mass of life which has no sympathy with the individual, no cognisance of him' (T, V III, 58; X, 64). Yet on the Island Siegmund is indeed, in his 'purification', 'a happy priest of the sun' (VIII, 59). In *The Trespasser*, as more outspokenly in the later 'Sun', Lawrence connects fertility with the sun as a means of rebirth.[96]

The cathartic central experience on the downs at night dramatizes with poetic economy the incompatibility of the lovers. As Hampson later diagnoses, in a diatribe worthy of Annable, it is the 'dreaming woman' who suppresses the 'gross and animal' and degrades and castrates Nature: ' "We, as natural men, are more or less degrading to them and to their love of us; therefore they destroy the natural man in us — that is, us altogether" ' (T, XIII, 84). The lovers wandering lost on the downs project, under deep emotional stress, their own images upon Nature. For Helena the vision is one of a universe of nerveless sentiment: 'gorse and the stars and the sea and the trees, are all kissing, Siegmund. The sea has its mouth on the earth, and the gorse and the trees press together, and they all look up at the moon, they put up their faces in a kiss, my darling' (T, XI, 73). Siegmund, by contrast, sees the earth as a mother into whose womb he can withdraw: 'This woman, tall and pale, drooping with the strength of her compassion, seemed stable, immortal, not a fragile human being, but a personification of the great motherhood of women' (T, XI, 74). Later he is to reflect that 'a man needs a mother all his life' (T, XXIII, 159). Under the moonlight, 'wandering in another — a glamorous, primordial world' (T, XII, 77), the lovers traverse the graveyard of the Catholic chapel, and Siegmund is wracked by the futility of his existence. His critical ordeal, though accompanied by sun-worship, is his dissociation from natural instinctive life, a life symbolised in the novel by farming: watching the sheep-dipping Siegmund finds 'a passion for farming at the bottom of his blood', but recognises the impossibility of this dream of continuity and community, the labourers appearing 'more than twenty centuries' from the pair (T, XIV, 90–1); later, as the train runs through the Sussex downs, it seems to Siegmund that the earth 'is always kind; it loves us, and would foster us like a nurse'. Seeing a farm, 'he wondered what fortunate folk were there, nourished and quiet' (T, XXI, 142), and he dreams of farming in Canada (T, XXIII, 161). In these moments, and in Byrne and Helena's walk near the woodland sheep-pen at the end, the hectically solipsist Nature-worship of Siegmund is placed against a perspective of a genuine communal working life rooted in the cycles of Nature.

The spiritual climax of the novel is significantly acted out near a tumulus in the twilight. Against this reminder of prehistory, Siegmund, modern spiritualised man, seeks to flee back to the womb of earth:

He lay down flat on the ground, pressing his face into the wiry turf, trying to hide. Quite stunned, with a death taking place in his soul, he lay still, pressed against the earth. He held his breath for a long time before letting it go, then again he held it. He could scarcely bear, even by breathing, to betray himself. His consciousness was dark. (T, XV, 101)

This immolation recurs in one of the poems:

Why, dear,
Are you letting me go, and hiding your face to the ground!
Siegmund, dear, what are you doing, lying with your face on the turf,
Lying rigid and silent with your face on the short sea turf?
('A Love Passage')[97]

From this deathly communion with the earth, like Rickie at Cadbury Rings, Siegmund emerges with a new and sacramental vision:

He looked up at the nave of the night, where the sky came down on the sea-like arches, and he watched the stars catch fire. At least it was all sacred, whatever the God might be. Helena herself, the bitter bread, was stuff of the ceremony, which he touched with his lips as part of the service.
(T, XV, 102–3)

The value of life lies in the apprehension of such moments, which in their intensity annihilate time.

With the return to the city Lawrence swiftly dissolves the romantic ecstasy. His portrait of Beatrice and the family circle, of Siegmund's bewilderment and suicide, and the discovery of the body by the window-cleaner, all this is characterised by a new note of realism. Yet Lawrence's fundamental concern in

The Trespasser, as elsewhere, is with the passional self in its emergent struggle with the circumambient universe. *The Trespasser*, in its boldly erotic style, anatomises man's cutting-off of himself from the earth and his subsequent entombment. Unlike Forster's Maurice, Siegmund cannot deliver himself from this entombment. That quest for deliverance was to be the burden of Lawrence's mature work.

However, the purpose of this study is not to trace yet again the fundamental themes of Lawrence's major work; rather, it is to lay bare the sources of Lawrence's art in the treatment accorded to the Nature-theme in the novels of his most immediate predecessors. These novels formed a clear tradition upon which the younger generation, and notably Lawrence and Forster, were able to draw, and they marked the culmination of a long artistic debate upon man's place in Nature.

Notes

1 D.H. Lawrence, *The Collected Letters of D. H. Lawrence* (ed. H.T. Moore) (London, Heinemann, 1962, hereafter cited as L.), p. 34.

2 D.H. Lawrence, *Phoenix* (ed. E.D. McDonald) (London, Heinemann, 1961, hereafter cited as PH), p. 527.

3 W.E. Hopkin, quoted in H.T. Moore, *The Priest of Love* (London, Heinemann, 1974), p. 69.

4 'E.T.' [Jessie Chambers], *D.H. Lawrence, A Personal Record* (ed. J.D. Chambers) (London, Cass, 1965, hereafter cited as ET), pp. 33 and 39.

5 H. Corke, *D.H. Lawrence: The Croydon Years* (Austin, University of Texas Press, 1965), p. 7.

6 D.H. Lawrence, *Etruscan Places* (1932) (Harmondsworth, Penguin Books, 1973, hereafter cited as EP), p. 17.

7 D.H. Lawrence, *Selected Essays* (Harmondsworth, Penguin Books, 1960, hereafter SE), p. 187.

8 D.H. Lawrence, *Apocalyse* (1931) (Harmondsworth, Penguin Books, 1974, hereafter cited as A).

9 D.H. Lawrence, *John Thomas and Lady Jane* (1972) (Harmondsworth, Penguin Books, 1973, hereafter cited as JT), p. 176.

10 D.H. Lawrence, *Sons and Lovers* (1913) (Harmondsworth, Penguin Books, 1964, hereafter cited as SL).

11 D.H. Lawrence, *Women in Love* (1921) (Harmondsworth, Penguin Books, 1961, hereafter cited as WL).

12 D.H. Lawrence, *Lady Chatterley's Lover* (1928) (Harmondsworth, Penguin Books, 1960, hereafter cited as LC).

13 D.H. Lawrence, *The Plumed Serpent* (1926) (Harmondsworth, Penguin Books, 1970, hereafter cited as PS).

14 D.H. Lawrence, *Kangaroo* (1923) (Harmondsworth, Penguin Books, 1971, hereafter cited as K), Chapter XII, p. 284.

15 Letter of 28 February 1909, in J.T. Boulton (ed.), *Lawrence in Love* (Nottingham, Nottingham University Press, 1968), p. 29.

16 D.H. Lawrence, *The Rainbow* (1915) (Harmondsworth, Penguin Books, 1961, hereafter cited as TR), Chapter VI, p. 193.

17 D.H. Lawrence, *The First Lady Chatterley* (1944) (Harmondsworth, Penguin Books, 1973, hereafter cited as FLC), p. 176.

18 Though it is worthy of note that Mellors himself is an evolutionist of sorts.

19 C. Darwin, *The Origin of Species* (ed. J. Burrow) (Harmondsworth, Penguin Books, 1970).

20 T.H. Huxley, *Man's Place in Nature and Other Essays* (London, Dent, Everyman edn., n.d.).

21 E. Haeckel, *The Riddle of the Universe* (trans. J. McCabe) (London, Watts, 1929).

22 As a student Lawrence planned to challenge a local minister 'to define his position' with regard to J.M. Robertson, Huxley and Haeckel (ET, 84). Jessie's sister recalled Mrs Chambers saying 'she never thought to see under her roof' volumes such as these (*ibid.*, p. 241).

23 T.H. Huxley, *op. cit.*, p. 101.

24 D.H. Lawrence, *The White Peacock* (1911) (Harmondsworth, Penguin Books, hereafter cited as WP).

25 D.H. Lawrence, 'Art and the Individual' (1908), in A. Clarke and S. Gelder, *Young Lorenzo* (Florence, Orioli, 1931), p. 254.

26 T.H. Huxley, *op. cit.*, p. 167.

27 'Art and the Individual', p. 253.

28 D.H. Lawrence, *The Trespasser* (1912) (Harmondsworth, Penguin Books, 1971), hereafter cited as T).

29 A.H.H. Inglis (ed.), *D.H. Lawrence, A Selection from Phoenix* (Harmondsworth, Penguin Books, 1971, hereafter cited as PH Sel.)

30 This translation was probably the one known to the Lawrence circle.

31 Haeckel, *op.cit.*, p. 2.

32 *Ibid.*, p. 6.

33 *Ibid.*, pp. 127–8.

34 *Ibid.*, pp. 11 and 16.

35 *Ibid.*, pp. 176–7.

36 *Ibid.*, p. 236.

37 *Ibid.*, p. 88.

38 *Ibid.*, p. 303.

39　*Ibid.*, p. 218.
40　*Ibid.*, pp. 103–4.
41　*Ibid.*, p. 184.
42　*Ibid.*, p. 188.
43　*Ibid.*, p. 189.
44　*Ibid.*, pp. 285–6.
45　*Ibid.*, p. 289.
46　*Ibid.*, pp. 291–2.
47　*Ibid.*, pp. 275 and 281–2.
48　*Ibid.*, pp. 310.
49　D.H. Lawrence, *Mornings in Mexico* (1927) (Harmondsworth, Penguin Books, 1967, hereafter cited as MM), p. 12.
50　SE, p. 335.
51　Haeckel, *op. cit.*, p. 304.
52　Constance Chatterley, immersed in her own struggle into being, recalls reading that ' "inside nature there is a spark which sometimes flies into consciousness and causes the shrivelling of old feelings and the kindling of new ones, and displaces old habits and makes a little creative chaos out of which a new nature of man emerges" ' (FLC, 138).
53　H. Spencer, *First Principles* (London, Williams & Norgate, 1910).
54　*Ibid.*, p. 262.
55　*Ibid.*, p. 220.
56　D.H. Lawrence, *Study of Thomas Hardy and Introduction to these Paintings* (ed. J.V. Davies) (London, Heinemann Educational, 1973, hereafter cited as STH), p. 44.
57　Spencer, *op. cit.*, pp. 220–1.
58　D.H. Lawrence, *Selected Literary Criticism* (ed. A. Beal) (London, Mercury Books, 1964, hereafter cited as SLC), p. 18.
59　Spencer, *op. cit.*, pp. 61.
60　*Ibid.*, p. 60.
61　*Ibid.*, p. 209.
62　*Ibid.*, p. 210.
63　*Ibid.*, p. 439.
64　*Ibid.*, p. 263.
65　*Ibid.*, p. 256.
66　*Ibid.*, pp. 423–4.
67　J. Goode, 'D.H. Lawrence', in B. Bergonzi (ed.), *The Twentieth Century* (London, Sphere Books, 1970), pp. 109 ff.
68　D.H. Lawrence, *Phoenix II* (ed. W. Roberts and H.T. Moore) (London, Heinemann, 1968, hereafter cited as PH II), p. 393.
69　Moore, *op. cit.*, pp. 77–8.
70　*Ibid.*, p. 78. Lawrence may have been familiar with other fictional keepers such as the one in Eden Phillpotts's *The River* (1902). In J.S. Fletcher's *At the Gate of the Fold* (1896) a miller and keeper are rivals

for the heroine. Annable, like other characters, also had local foundations, being modelled on a keeper called Naylor; see B. Pugh, *The
Country of My Heart* (Nottingham, Notts Local History Council,
1974), p. 22. George may be identified with Alan Chambers, Emily with
Jessie, Lettie with Ada Lawrence, and Cyril with the author, whilst
Tempest probably owes something to the Barbers, the local mine-
owners.

71 M. Ewing, *Eight Letters to R.A. Taylor* (Pasadena, Castle Press, 1956),
unpaged.

72 'Rachel Annand Taylor' (1910), *Young Lorenzo*, pp. 234, 238, 241 and
243.

73 R.A. Taylor, *The Hours of Fiammetta* (London, Elkin Matthews,
1910), p. 5.

74 *The Hours of Fiammetta*, p. 7. Lawrence's title may also appropriately
echo the poised eroticism of Tennyson's 'Now sleeps the crimson petal':
'Now droops the milkwhite peacock like a ghost,/And like a ghost she
glimmers on to me'. In *The Trespasser* Tennyson was to be criticised as a
writer who 'did belittle great things': 'Not peacocks and princesses, but
the bigger things' (T, VI, 45).

75 Huxley, *op. cit.*, p. 260.

76 Darwin, *op. cit.*, p. 127.

77 *Ibid.*, pp. 149–50.

78 *Ibid.*, p. 150.

79 See Tom Brangwen's verdict upon himself as a man 'put apart with those
whose life has no more developments' (TR, IV, 128).

80 See the seminal scene where Birkin, fighting the 'river of dissolution' he
discerns in Hermione, returns naked to the earth: 'Nothing else would
do, nothing else would satisfy, except this coolness and subtlety of
vegetation travelling into one's blood'. He is 'weary of the old ethic, of
the human being, and of humanity', and longs to 'love the vegetation and
be quite happy and unquestioned' (WL, VIII, 119 ff).

81 Darwin *op. cit.*, p. 116.

82 By the time he wrote *Lady Chatterley* Lawrence was able to utilise this
theme to dramatize the psychic life of his characters; in the second
version, for example, if Clifford 'heard a rabbit scream, caught by a
weasel or caught in a trap, his heart would stand still for a second, then
he would think: 'There's another one gone to death! Another one! And
I'm not gone!'' And he exulted curiously' (JT, I, 14).

83 See 'Birds in the high Hall-garden/When twilight was falling' (*Maud*,
XIII, i), and 'the grace that, bright and light as the crest/Of a peacock,
sits on her shining head' (XVI, i). Lawrence was especially fond of
Maud, and Jessie Chambers noted that the passage on the birds 'evoked
memories of our own wood' (ET, 95). Cyril may be named after the
protagonist of Tennyson's *The Princess*. Also see the description of

Anna Brangwen leaving church, 'a vain white peacock of a bride perching herself on the top of the wall' displaying 'the vanity of her white, slim, daintily-stepping feet, and her arched neck' (TR, V, 136). This complex scene may also owe something to Darwin's sketch of the operation of sexual selection amongst peacocks (Darwin, *op. cit.*, p. 137); to Mrs Poyser's denigration of Hetty Sorrel as ' "a peacock, as 'ud strut about on the wall and spread its tail when the sun shone if all the folks i' the parish was dying" ' (*Adam Bede*, XV); to Felix Holt's initial judgement of Esther Lyon as 'a nice-stepping, long-necked peacock' (*Felix Holt*, V); and to Herod's 'beautiful white peacocks' in Wilde's *Salome*.

84　The original text was stronger: ' "Just look!" he said, "the dirty devil's run her muck over that angel. A woman to the end, I tell you, all vanity and screech [and] defilement" '. See M. Bruccoli, 'A note on the text', *The White Peacock* (Carbondale, Ill., Southern Illinois University Press, 1961), p.356.

85　The image of the quarry returns in Lawrence's last fragment, 'A dream of Life', in which withdrawal to the womb, and terror, are curiously mingled: 'The quarry was a haunt of mine, as a boy. I loved it because, in the open part, it seemed so sunny and dry and warm. . . . And then the old part, the deep part, was such a fearsome place. It was always dark — you had to crawl under bushes. . . . I started, hearing a sudden rush and clatter of falling earth. Some part of the quarry must be giving way' (*The Princess*, Harmondsworth, Penguin Books, 1972), 164–5. Later in the fragment Newthorpe (Eastwood) is apotheosised into a temple of the Lawrencean *vita nuova*. Lawrence's vitalist poem, 'The Wild Common', offers a similar sensation:

Oh but the water loves me and folds me,
Plays with me, sways me, lifts me and sinks me, murmurs:
　Oh marvellous stuff!
No longer shadow — and it holds me
Close, and it rolls me, enfolds me, touches me, as if it never could touch
　　　　　　　　　　　　　　　　　　　　me enough.

87　Jessie Chambers wrote of the time Lawrence left for Croydon: 'He had sometimes hinted that he feared the world would drag him away its whole width from the valley he loved so deeply. . . . His first letters were full of the anguish of the loss of the old life' (ET, 242).

88　Darwin, *op. cit.*, p. 171.

89　The inspiration for *The Trespasser* was the five days' diary subsequently expanded into the later part of Helen Corke's novel *Neutral Ground*, to which Lawrence added sketches of his colleagues at Davidson Road School: see Moore, *op. cit.*, 134; and H. Corke, 'The writing of *The Trespasser*', *D.H. Lawrence Review*, VII (1974), 227–39, and *In Our*

Infancy (Cambridge, Cambridge University Press, 1975), passim.

90 Quoted in Moore, *op. cit.*, p. 134.

91 Nonetheless, Lawrence may be using 'trespass' in a different sense, as he does in describing the ecstasy of Tom and Lydia, 'beyond all conceiving good, it was so good, that it was almost like a passing-away, a trespass' (T, I, 46).

92 See Hampson's description of Siegmund: ' "You're like a tree that'll flower till it kills itself" ' (TR, XIII, 84).

93 The dominant Wagnerian overtones may derive from Moore's *Evelyn Innes*, which mediated the *fin de siècle* cult of Wagner in the English novel. See W.F. Blissett, 'George Moore and literary Wagnerism', in Graham Owens (ed.), *George Moore's Mind and Art* (Edinburgh, Oliver & Boyd, 1968), pp. 53–76.

94 See Siegmund's reflection on parting from Helena: 'This bruise on my mind will never get better' (T, XXI, 140); and Helena's reaction on hearing of the suicide: 'She felt bruised . . . she could not get rid of the bruised sense of disaster' (T, XXIX, 196).

95 See the Hardyesque picture of the lovers 'like two insects in the niche of a hot hearth as they toiled along the deep road' (T, IX, 61).

96 *The Trespasser* reflects Haeckel's conviction that the 'whole marvellous panorama of life that spreads over the surface of our globe is, in the last analysis, transformed sunlight'. Sun-worship, Haeckel held, was 'the best of all forms of theism, and the one which may be most easily reconciled with modern monism' (Haeckel, *op. cit.*, pp. 75 and 99).

97 The conflation of sex and Nature imagery is a typical Romantic trait, see Novalis's *Die Lehrlinge zu Sais* (1799), with its description of a Nature-initiate: 'Love voluptuousness expands within him like a powerful, all-dissolving vapour and, trembling in sweet terror, he sinks into the dark, alluring womb of nature, his poor individuality consumes itself in the overwhelming waves of desire, and nothing remains but a focus of immeasurable creative force, an engulfing whirlpool in the mighty ocean' (*Schriften*, I, 100). Novalis's conception of the Isis mysteries here may have influenced *The Man Who Died*.

3 George Meredith

I

Meredith's friend John Morley once averred that for human fulfilment it was necessary to 'Exist in every day communion with Nature'. 'Nature bids you take all', he added cryptically, 'only be sure you learn how to do without'. This might stand as a motto for Meredith himself. His everyday communion with Nature is recorded in the poems and novels. The influence which such communion exerts upon the mind of man is a recurrent theme. In seeking to formulate his relationship with the natural world Meredith was led to experiment in poetry and prose; what he had to say was new and demanded new forms. His perennial struggle with the shaping of fiction aptly demonstrates that no work of genius dare want its appropriate form. The tradition of the Nature-novel begins with Meredith as its only begetter.

II

In his own lifetime Meredith was famed for his communion with Nature in the Surrey countryside. His contemporaries came to view him almost as a force of Nature, a kind of intellectual maelstrom. His sentences were 'thrown out with lavish opulence', H.W. Nevinson noted, 'the careless opulence of Nature at her kindest'.[1] This note of energy is fundamental to any appraisal of Meredith's ideas on Nature. It is the antithesis to his view of Society, which he held was 'kept in animation by the customary, in the first place, and secondly by sentiment'. Thus society, the 'natural' subject for the novel, 'has little love of Earth (or Nature)' (L).[2] Meredith's poetry[3] therefore tends to be asocial in the romantic tradition; but the novels endeavour to effect a 'bridge' between the life of Nature and the life of society, between natural permanence and human temporality.

Meredith's Nature is not that of Wordsworth. Rather is he the poet of Nature in action. In Wordsworth Nature is a visible sign of a spiritual order; in Meredith Nature possesses its own intrinsic value. Man and Nature are not dichotomised in the typical Victorian fashion; rather are they elements within a single process:

> For him the woods were a home and gave him the key
> Of knowledge, thirst for their treasures in herbs and flowers.
> The secrets held by the creatures nearer than we
> To earth he sought, and the link of their life with ours:
> And where alike we are, unlike where, and the veined
> Division, veined parallel, of a blood that flows
> In them, in us, from the source by man unattained
> Save marks he well what the mystical woods disclose.
>
> ('Melampus')

Man is one active participant in universal processes. This momentum places Meredith at odds with the bulk of his contemporaries, who took either Wordsworthian or Darwinian positions. Meredith reads Darwin differently, as Norman Kelvin explains, seeing Nature 'as an active and benevolent principle that reveals to man his kinship with the rest of creation and that teaches him to order his private, public, and political life'.[4] The Darwinian struggle may have come to replace the drama of a defunct Christianity, but it was struggle with a joyful outcome in Meredith. His characters thus experience change as a type of organic growth, their development metaphorically echoing natural processes. Through the evolutionary force the spiritual power embedded in the earth is set free.

The source of this view may be traced to Meredith's education. As a schoolboy the Moravians had inculcated him with their idealistic, Nature-loving ethos. The term 'pagan' recurs significantly in discussions of Meredith. 'Paganism no doubt deserved the ascetic reproof', he wrote to F.A. Maxse, 'but Christianity failed to supply much that it destroyed' (L, 140). On another occasion he told Maxse, 'Our great error has been

. . . to raise a spiritual system in antagonism to Nature' (L, 93). Yet it would be wrong simply to attribute Meredith's Nature-philosophy to the animus against Christianity which becomes familiar during the *fin de siècle*. On the contrary Meredith's paganism emerged fully fledged early in his life. His love of Nature enabled him to solve to his own satisfaction the body- —spirit dualism which bedevilled Christian thought: 'I hold that to be rightly materialist — to understand and take Nature as she is — is to get on the true divine highroad' (L, 247). Nevertheless, the Meredithian adept of Nature need not deny the rapacity of the animal kingdom:

> Hawk or shrike has done this deed
> Of downy feathers: rueful sight!
> Sweet sentimentalist, invite
> Your bosom's power to intercede.
>
> So hard it seems that one must bleed
> Because another needs will bite!
> All round we find cold Nature slight
> The feelings of the totter-knee'd.
> ('Whimper of Sympathy')

Without the survival of the fittest, and the struggle which that entails, Nature would atrophy. As Meredith expresses it in 'Hard Weather', 'Contention is the vital force, Whence pluck they brain, her prize of gifts'. Only the sentimentalist, that typical Meredithian butt, would require of Nature the smooth charm of human society. It is in this sense that Nature in Meredith acts as a moral agent, exposing the artificial and the sham in mankind, and framing moral questions relativisti-cally. The concept of Nature as a sanative force is frequent in the novels and poems. In 'The Woods of Westermain', for instance, Nature is shown to enlarge man's potentialities:

> Drink the sense the notes infuse,
> You a larger self will find:
> Sweetest fellowship ensues
> With the creatures of your kind.

It is just this 'sweetest fellowship' that is blighted by the egoism that Meredith delineates so memorably in his fiction.

Although he warns Leslie Stephen that there is 'no irony in Nature', Meredith also holds that 'Nature abhors precociousness, and has the habit of punishing it' (L, 1491 and 1497). The ideal state, in antithesis to the egoism which cripples so many Meredith characters, is that 'self-forgetfulness divine' rapturously hymned in 'The Lark Ascending', the ineffable potency emanating from Nature. In this state of exaltation Meredith adumbrates his own types of pantheism:

> ... natures at interflow
> With all of their past and the now,
> Are chords to the Nature without,
> Orbs to the greater whole:
> First then, nor utterly then
> Till our lord of sensations at war,
> The rebel, the heart, yields place
> To brain, each prompting the soul.
> Thus our dear Earth we embrace
> For the milk, her strength to men.
> ('A Faith on Trial')

These lines introduce the famous Meredithian trio of blood, brain and spirit. This tripartite division should be seen as evolutionary, that is to say, in movement, a vital concept for Meredith, to whom Nature is a living force. The domination of primal or instinctual man by blood is not viewed by Meredith, as it is by ascetic thought, as wholly bad; on the contrary, blood links man with the cosmos. The clash between instinct and thought leads to the evolution of brain, with its connotations of social order, law, self-control and human fellowship. The duality invoked here furnishes Meredith with much of his comedy, but it may be resolved through the efficacy of the spirit, which expresses itself in ethical idealism and selfless struggle. The interrelation of Man and Nature, to which industrial society is inimical, is resumed in the key scenes in the novels where human law makes way for the law of Nature. If blood, brain and spirit are not in accord man's wholeness breaks down — a process almost universal in a commercial society underpinned by denaturing technology:

> Each of each in sequent birth,
> Blood and brain and spirit, three
> (Say the deepest gnomes of Earth),
> Join for true felicity.
> Are they parted, then expect
> Someone sailing will be wrecked:
> Separate hunting are they sped,
> Scan the morsel coveted.
> Earth that Triad is: she hides
> Joy from him who that divides,
> Showers it when the three are one
> Glassing her in union.
> ('The Woods of Westermain')

The blood–brain–spirit hypothesis is therefore Meredith's programme of psychic integration, an integration which man can daily observe in Nature. 'The Woods of Westermain' presents this triad in an optimistic vision of social Lamarckism, in which qualities acquired through inculcation become transmissable. Man is the highest expression of Nature. The tragedy (or comedy) of advanced society is that its members divorce themselves from the primal forces of Nature, with tragic (or comic) results. Meredith's lifelong devotion to the heaths of Surrey was founded upon philosophical postulates of a vitally different order from the enervated Romanticism of much mid-Victorian Nature poetry. The complex aim of his work, the combination of passion and corrective satire, may be incapable of perfect realisation; the complexities of the later work suggest that this is so.

Thus Meredith's Nature is both an agent of the Cosmic Spirit and an active inspirational force. There is never in Meredith that desolation in the face of an indifferent universe which we encounter in Hardy; Meredith does not feel a sense of tragedy in landscape, nor does he see man subsisting within a hostile universe.[5] Intellect and reverence must clash, he says in *One of Our Conquerors*,[5] 'if we persist in regarding the Spirit of Life as a remote Externe, who plays the human figures . . . instead of being beside us, within us, our breath' (OC, XVI, 143). On the contrary, the contact between man and the landscape is felt to be fruitful:

O but hear it! 'tis the mind;
Mind that with deep Earth unites,
Round the solid trunk to wind
Rings of clasping parasites.
Music have you there to feed
Simplest and most soaring need.
('The Woods of Westermain')

Any attempt to encapsulate Meredith's thought on Nature is fraught with difficulties. His insights and discoveries, shifts of tone and emphasis, are the natural concomitants of so determinedly heuristic a writer, one who uses the term 'Nature' in a protean fashion. Nonetheless, it is possible to discern the main features of a coherent doctrine in the mass of his writing, and to define its terminology with some degree of exactitude.

First, Meredith sees 'God' as part of Nature; not as *all* Nature, as in the strict definition of pantheism, but as an immanent force for good which man must realise in his own active life. God is a kind of ethical progress which man must willingly undertake as 'a creature matched with strife to meet it as a bride' ('The Test of Manhood'). From primeval chaos evolution has developed mind and spirit, in this way idealising natural evolution. Religious and scientific ideas form interwoven strands of Meredith's philosophy. A life in accordance with Nature (that is, encompassing blood, brain and spirit in equal measure) is a life in accord with the laws of the Universe. This, for Meredith, emphatically did not entail the free play of sexual passion. Man should rather be:

Obedient to Nature, not her slave;
Her lord, if to her rigid laws he bows,
Her dust, if with his conscience he plays knave,
And bids the Passions on the Pleasures browse.
('The Test of Manhood')

The centrality of Meredith's doctrine of Nature lies in its human application. He replaces the potentially solipsist exaltation of pantheism by a belief in social progress wrought by acknowledging our kinship with earth:

> For love we Earth, then serve we all;
> Her mystic secret then is ours:
> We fall, or view our treasures fall,
> Unclouded, as beholds her flowers.
>   ('The Thrush in February')

Many of Meredith's heroes and heroines have painfully to
learn what he told Maxse: 'While you lovers are acting Nature
you are ignorant of her; and she has to cure you of your
idealistic mists, by running the sharp thorn of Reality into your
quivering flesh' (L, 129). This does not mean that in Meredith
there is no sense of the uplifting effect of mighty natural
objects; the Alps are his archetypal image of transcendence,
but more innately Meredithian is his close kinship with
growth, decay and rebirth. It is Meredith's obsession with
man's relationship with natural things which furnishes him
with his richest insights into the *sanctum sanctorum* of the
universe. Meredith's final position may be summarised as
acceptance of the necessity of evolution, and an assertion of
joy in the face of life. Joyful acceptance is indeed the corner-
stone of Meredith's work: a yea-saying in the face of man and
Nature. Meredith once told Richard Garnett that Emerson
'struck a tap-root of a forest-tree into our Mother Earth, and
had consequently the unfailing flow of her sap through him to
the end' (L, 885). It is this 'unfailing flow of sap' which gives
his own best work its fresh and living quality, imbued as it is
with a sense of transformation and renewal:

> Earth, the mother of all,
> Moves on her steadfast way,
> Gathering, flinging, sowing,
> Mortals, we live in her day,
> She in her children is growing.
>   ('Ode to the Spirit of Earth in Autumn')

III

Meredith's novels have no antecedents. He stands at the fron-
tier between Victorian and modern fiction, creating new forms

to contain wholly new matter. Whatever their faults his novels are totally underivative. In the finest of them he unifies his concepts of Nature and society to produce poetic narrative. The novel of Nature begins with Meredith, though it was to reach fulfilment in the work of his successors. Through a passional interaction with the fructifying agencies of Nature the protagonists are regenerated or their pretensions are ruthlessly exposed. The later novels, whose structural and linguistic complexities produce diminishing returns, make less of the Nature-theme, and devote themselves too exclusively to analysis of social and behavioural patterns. The frenzied creativity of late Meredith marks a falling-off of his powers; the conjunction of poetry and narrative was now in the hands of younger men.

Meredith's rejection of the tenets of High Victorian values is most explicit in the novels, where fluid poetics and free-flowing sensibility replace the novel of society on the Dickensian or Trollopian model. The stable ego of character is transposed in ways which were to be instructive to Lawrence. Meredith, requiring those qualities of a novel which he requires of a poem, makes no arbitrary division between fiction and poetry: they are both profoundly representative of his nature. All the novelists writing of Nature show a pervasive Idealist tendency which expresses dissatisfaction with available fictional modes, whether English or continental. In *Sandra Belloni* Meredith makes Barrett explain that 'in prose also we owe everything to the license our poets have taken in the teeth of critics' (SB, VIII, 51), and this defines Meredith's position. Complaining to a correspondent that 'in Smollett conduct is never *accounted* for', Meredith explains that his own principle is 'to show the events flowing from evident causes'. He adds, significantly, 'To *naturalise* them to the mind of the reader, I have many temptations to incident which I reject because they seem to me out of Nature' (L, 57). Meredith's failure with the reading public, except for 'that acute and honourable minority which consents to be thwacked with aphorisms and sentences and a fantastic delivery of the verities' (SB, LI, 426), owed much to his rejection of accepted fictional procedures. Even in 1900, when he enjoyed great prestige, we find him telling Lady Ulrica Duncombe, 'I have no pleasure in the present day English novel' (L, 1374). His idealism equally discounted the products of Naturalism — a reaction common to the novelists of Nature. He memorably described a book by Mendès as 'the monsterisation of Zolaism . . . sheer Realism, breeder at least of the dung-fly!', and concluded that 'Cloacina sits upon such productions' (L, 889). Meredith accounted himself a Realist, but his definition is revealing: 'Men to whom I bow my head (Shakespeare, Göthe; and in their way Molière, Cervantes) are Realist *au fond*. But they have the broad arms of Idealism at command. They give us Earth; but it is Earth with an atmosphere' (L, 161). Meredith's quarrel with Naturalism lies in its inability to penetrate beneath the surface of the material world in its interpretation of objective phenomena — Virginia Woolf was to make much the same point against Wells and Bennett. Since, as Meredith told Morley 'in this life there is no life save in spirit', the rest being 'an aching and a rotting' (L, 557), it follows that the Realists' obsession with the physical blinds them to the underlying reality.

The strangeness of Meredith's conception of what the novel should be has led modern commentators to query his artistic capacity. Certainly the creation of a new kind of fiction, a re-ordering of reality, was a formidable task which Meredith attempted single-handed. His failures are failures of ambition, rather than concessions to artistic limitation. The novel is to become an instrument of the Comic Spirit, having at its centre a proposed renewal of man's relation with Nature which is to restore man to wholeness and harmony. If this renewal proves impossible, that may explain the excessive dislocation of the later novels, and the increasingly private communings of the poetry. Meredith's work charts a major shift in sensibility: in a very real sense Lawrence could not have existed without Meredith.

It has often been remarked that *The Ordeal of Richard*

Feverel[1] begins as comedy and ends as tragedy. This gravitation from one mode to its antithesis has been a subject of debate since the novel's publication, and a general consensus as to the broken-backed effect has been arrived at. The pathos of the ending, it is held, violates the comic effect previously set up as the norm; a related point may be made in relation to the developmental failure of Adrian Harley, who represents the Comic Spirit and thus becomes superfluous to the narrative. This line of approach, however, scarcely does justice to the interpenetration and organic continuity of Meredith's themes, which are treated to a constantly transformatory reappraisal. In this novel it is the themes rather than the characters which truly develop. It has often been noted that despite his ordeal Richard does not grow, but simply repeats himself. Indeed the Feverels are subjected to an ordeal in each generation: Richard's problem is that he is as heavily encased in the carapace of egoism as Sir Austin; the humanising and liberalising powers of Nature are felt but go unheeded at the nodal point of the book, and disaster axiomatically ensues. There is little wonder that Meredith warned Katherine Vulliamy that *The Ordeal of Richard Feverel* dealt with 'certain problems of life' and was 'not of a milky quality' — a warning which might be pondered by those who find the ending a falsification of a comic drama. Notwithstanding Meredith's painful revisions, the structural interconnexions between the two parts are effortlessly made, and the novel is unified by the Nature-theme.

At the outset it is amply demonstrated that Sir Austin's inert perfectibilist theory is divorced from Nature, though he does not hesitate to claim her support, holding that 'Sin is an alien element in our blood. 'Tis the Apple-Disease with which Nature has striven since Adam. To treat Youth as naturally sinful, is, therefore, false and bad' (ORC, I, 11). The Great Shaddock Dogma prescribes a scientific education 'hedging round the Youth for corruptness' (ORC, I, 12), and thus in fact fatally corrupting him. Perfectibility, and its educational application, had rarely been dealt with in the novel before

Meredith. For the baronet, as for Condorcet and the *philosophes* generally, the world is potentially paradisiacal. The laws of human growth are empirically discoverable and practically applicable under a system whose severity is only increased by the baronet's own failed marriage. Thus the Shaddock Dogma centres its strictures upon a right marriage, and it is by a supreme irony that Richard marries badly, though his love-affair is endorsed by Nature. Adrian, who is careful not to contract himself in wedlock, utters a panegyric upon the institution, 'the solemn deed of Life, the culminating act of our existence', as he calls it. Sexuality is to be ruthlessly controlled under the Dogma, and those who 'anticipate' marriage are faced with 'Retribution rather than Absolution' (ORF, IV, 31). Thus does the baronet's ethos replace the moribund code of Christianity with a system equally distorted by nay-saying. That the Feverel system is more than an ironic deployment of perfectibility, that it is in effect a satire on current educational theory, is an interesting possibility. It is certainly clear that Sir Austin's aphoristic style neatly symbolises the tendency of the scientific temperament, that temperament which created Coleridge's 'universe of death'. Its failing lies not only in its overtly theoretical bias, but also in its treatment of the human personality as an automaton, to be encapsulated and sealed away from all natural forces, human and non-human. In this sense Meredith takes science as the antithesis of Nature; no synthesis is possible in the terms of the characters' lives, and tragedy ensues. To complain of the author's misjudgement is to misread Meredith's intention, just as the ploughman and tinker, with their theories of supra-mundane dominance in sublunary matters, misread the universe in their 'Magian Conflict' (ORF, VI). This conflict between good and evil is writ large in the two protagonists, father and son, whose characters are like a battleground for the forces which contend there.

The rebellious episodes of Richard's youth, such as the rick-burning, are eruptions of Nature, which kick against the pricks of the System. Yet they do not deter Sir Austin's wish, as

Adrian phrases it, 'to be Providence to his son' (ORF, VII, 68). Indeed, after the 'Preliminary Ordeal' with Farmer Blaize, the baronet reads in Nature a clear mandate for his plans: 'The solemn gladness of his heart gave Nature a tongue'. Sir Austin discerns 'intelligible signs of the beneficent order of the universe', and is confirmed in his belief 'in the ultimate Victory of Good within us, without which Nature has neither music, nor meaning, and is rock, stone, tree, and nothing more' (ORF, XIII, 111). This wilful imposition of bland optimism upon the evolutionary turbulence of Nature inspires Sir Austin to an aphorism, that characteristic mode of utterance in which living meaning may be embalmed. But it is when Richard reaches the adolescent 'Magnetic Age' that the clash between science and Nature is firmly articulated. Indeed, in the famous 'Ferdinand and Miranda' chapter Meredith releases the pent-up romanticism which has been stifled by the System and its concomitant social comedy. As Richard rows towards Lucy in close proximity to the thundering weir Nature grows 'Stiller and stiller', 'as at the meeting of two electric clouds' (ORF, XVIII, 149).[8] The restoration to Nature is Edenic, and the scene becomes a mimetic critique of the Shaddock Dogma. Richard's ducking in search of Lucy's book (his poems) is a symbolic immersion into the currents of sexual passion which are to smash the System and sunder him from his father. This social encounter with Nature transforms the youth and his vision of earth: 'it was no more the world of yesterday. The marvellous splendours had sown seeds in him, ready to spring up and bloom at her gaze' (ORF, XVIII, 159), so that his heart 'will build a temple here'. We may note the Freudian hints here, with Nature felt as soft and womb-like, as if taking the place of the mother Richard never knew, and opposing itself to the authoritarian father who has dominated his upbringing. The scene is pervaded by a genial sense of escape into a freer, regenerative atmosphere, a zone forever closed to the inmates of Bayham Abbey. These love-scenes also shatter the detachment of the author's tone. Meredith's empathy with Nature and with those who commune with Nature, breaks the satiric mask. Meredith here moves towards a statement of purpose: human life is something other than a complex of cause and effect, and this 'otherness' is exemplified by the link between the growth of love and natural processes. The organic connexions between the human and the natural are made here. Nature acts as catalyst, pre-empting the claims of kinship, the conformity institutionalised at Bayham Abbey. Indeed the code which Sir Austin erects is in essence a monolithic expression of his own egoism, utterly opposed to the polymorphous nature of the Universe, an egoism which cuts him off from both Nature and his fellow-men. Nature is not merely a static register of values alien to society; it may promote a spiritual palingenesis. However, Meredith's mind is sufficiently protean to save him from imposing a didactic pattern upon a novel of kaleidoscopic effect. This experimental audacity is exemplified by the 'Unmasking of Ripton Thompson' which follows the love-idyll, an ironic scene in which Sir Austin fastidiously reiterates that 'Man is a self-acting machine' who may 'lose the powers of self-guidance' through the pressure of his 'very vitalities' (ORF, XIX, 162). Thus the luckless Ripton's unmasking, revealing his clandestine adolescent eroticism, is made to endorse the System from Sir Austin's viewpoint, but from the reader's, to undercut the baronet's certitude.

The positives to which Meredith subscribes are stated in the brief chapter XXIII, where Richard and Lucy again rendezvous in the lap of Nature in a sunset scene which derives its impetus from the poetry. Although this is a 'Diversion played on a Penny Whistle', the tune conjures up Pan and his mythical variants; as in Forster, the pagan world contextualises the Christian, and this regression reveals the vapidity of closed moral systems. In Sir Austin's pantheon Nature is acceptable only when denatured, 'Cherished, trained, and purified' (ORF, XXVI, 240). Nature's vengeance upon the ideological martinet, and upon the moribund sophistication of Victorian society, is wrought through the marriage-plot and its attendant humours, presided over by the Shakespearian Mrs Berry, whose submerged passion is finally legitimised through the ieroic couple. Meredith cleverly mirrors the ruin of Sir Austin's lifework in the pliable compromises of Mrs Doria's plans for Clare, in her reflections that children's 'exercise of . . volition we construe as revolt,' and her comparison of the shifts of familial love with the birds, whose 'unsentimental acts' 'never wander from Nature' (ORF, XXXIII, 341). The poison endemic in the System taints the marriage, enacted under the shadow of a 'man of science in Life, who was bound to be surprised by nothing in Nature' (ORF, XXXVII, 388). By choosing a mate in accord with the dictates of passion Richard adheres to Nature; in undergoing a long period of separation from her, and in dallying with the 'dangerous Belona', he succumbs to social pressure and struggles with blood, brain and spirit. The honeymoon in the Isle of Wight irradiates the marriage briefly with intimations of a new order of life consonant with Nature. With the west 'all a burning rose round the one star', Richard exclaims ' "How can men see such sights as those, and live idle?" ' (ORF, XXXVIII, 413). But the renewal adumbrated here is stifled as Richard effectively reneges upon his marriage vows and abandons Lucy. In these later reaches of the book, encompassing Lucy's loveless marriage and subsequent death, Richard's 'seduction', and the baronet's alienation from the world, Meredith's tone darkens and prepares for the tragic *dénouement*. Society, in so ordering and structuring the free play of emotion and intellect, mummifies Nature and forces men and women into its mould. The living quick of Nature offers man an authentic model, a model adventurously examined in the poems. But in Meredith's evolutionary perspective the time is not ripe, and his protagonists smash their lives.

The great chapter in which 'Nature Speaks' offers a paradigm of the new type of Nature-novel, in which the characters are lifted out of society and placed in direct contact with universal forces. Richard's own growth is triadic, conforming to blood, blood and brain, and blood, brain and spirit, but the spiritual enlightenment comes too late to save him. The knightly ordeals which he undergoes offer solutions to the

Feverel *impasse*, and the final ordeal in the German forest is thrillingly realised by Meredith.[9] As in *The Waste Land* the 'thunder spoke' to Richard: the lightning seems like 'the eye of Heaven, and the thunder as the tongue of Heaven, each alternately addressing him'. The hero, 'sole human creature among the grandeurs and mysteries of storm', witnesses here the transcendence of Nature over society and its consequent redemptive power for impotent man, which is to predominate in the Nature novel. Richard's subsequent discovery of the leveret and prayer in the empty chapel restore him to full humanity, overwhelmed by 'a sense of purification so sweet he shuddered again and again' (ORF, XLVI, 556, 558). Yet this *aufklärung* collapses at the end of the book. The central opposition between Science and Nature is responsible for the conclusion; Lucy's deathbed scene is not simply Meredithian variation on Victorian cliché, it enacts the meaning of the book in human terms. Man may one day be regenerated through harmonisation with the natural order, but that day is far off.

Whilst Meredith gained in traditional novelistic qualities such as social verisimilitude and structural control, the unifying imaginative passion which informs *The Ordeal of Richard Feverel* erupts only fitfully in its successors. The immanence of Nature in man's world, orchestrated into a radically new mode of fiction in the novel, is suggested throughout the oeuvre; yet never again was it accorded the centrality of treatment which it demands. In the later novels, whose 'profundities and tortuosities' so enraged James, it is as if Meredith deliberately immerses himself in the subtle complexities of the upper strata of urban society, reserving his inmost feelings about Nature for his poetry. The reasons for the retreat from his deepest concerns must remain conjectural; there is no doubt that the difficulty *vis à vis* his audience, and the emotional drain of his marriage to a semi-invalid, led Meredith (like Mark Twain) into barren fictional areas. It is also true that the insatiable theoretician is given free rein in the later work, the novels moving away from the mimetic towards the didactic. Meredith's famous caveat to Stevenson *à propos*

The Egoist,[10] 'It is a Comedy, with only half of me in it', could stand for many of the later novels in which the social dominates the natural. Nonetheless, if in the later works Meredith's will dwarfs his imagination, the potency of Nature remained his ultimate touchstone. The worth of these social organisms, his analysis implies, is relative and contingent; Nature is absolute and *a priori*:

> For she the laws of growth most deeply knows,
> Whose hands bear, here, a seed-bag — there, an urn.
> ('Modern Love', st.XIII)

A survey of the later novels reveals the variable pattern of Meredith's response to Nature in his fiction, and his quixotic deployment of the theme of transcendence. In electing to follow *The Ordeal of Richard Feverel* by the covertly auto-biographical *Evan Harrington*[11] Meredith largely eschewed wider philosophical questions. The gain in manipulative effect, characterisation, and social nuance is undeniable; but the autonomous power of Nature is abandoned in favour of invertebrate landscape-painting whose schematic purpose is amusingly betrayed by the Countess. The narrator goes so far as to instruct his readers that Evan is a 'noble youth, for whom storms specially travel to tell [him] that [his] mistress makes faces in the looking-glass' (EH, XVIII, 191). However, in the specifically rural tale of *Rhoda Fleming*[12] which followed, Meredith introduces a more serious and sustained treatment of man and Nature, though his addiction to the cliché of the seduction plot rules out any extended treatment of metaphysics. Rhoda, we note, is conceived in terms of natural imagery, and the contrast with her urbanised sister Dahlia is implied at the outset when the money-grubbing uncle, Anthony Hackbut, representative here of the cash-nexus, priases Rhoda's 'sweet blackbirdy voice' (RF, III, 19). This resonance is deepened, and Meredith's range extended, by the rustic chorus of Master Gammon and Mrs Sumfit, whose comic expressions of natural piety must have impressed Hardy. This living closeness to Nature in its unromantic actuality is weighed against the city-bred vapourings of Algernon, who strolls through London comparing it 'with his visionary free dream of the glorious prairies, where his other life was', and where Nature would not 'shut up her pocket and demand innumerable things of him, as civilisation did' (RF, XII, 90). Thus the dream of this 'other life', revealed through and lived in Nature, is transposed from the idealism of *The Ordeal of Richard Feverel* into an agency of the Comic Spirit, puncturing the pretensions of the upper-class *poseur*. The goodness and sanity of a genuinely rural life, as opposed to the foppish dreams of Algernon's class, is projected in the figure of Jonathan Eccles, that 'Yeoman of the Old Breed', who sees the ruin of England epitomised in his scapegrace son. Foreseeing the market dominance of the United States in the wheat sales, Eccles looks to a time when there will be 'No more green pastures' or 'yellow harvests', 'but huge chimney-pots everywhere; black earth under black vapour, and smoke-begrimed faces' (RF, XVII, 128). Whilst Meredith does not develop this theme, becoming preoccupied with the seduction plot, the positives for which Eccles, Mrs Sumfit and Master Gammon stand, living as they do 'in harmony with universal nature' (RF, XXXIII, 305), provide a frame of reference to which all the characters more-or-less consciously refer. When, for instance, Hackbut suggests that the family leave the farm, the 'great good place' of the novel, Dahlia reiterates its values of home and tradition as passionately as any George Eliot heroine (RF, XXV, 222). These values are transformed at the crisis of the novel when Rhoda, gazing raptly on the 'green corn-tracts and the pastures by the river', 'the slow-footed cows' and 'far-away sheep', the 'white hawthorn bushes, and deep hedge-ways bursting out of the trimness of the earlier season', becomes conscious of a 'quick new impulse of affection for her old home', and for Robert, who through his labour sustains it. A longing comes upon her 'to go and handle butter'; like a Jane Austen protagonist she finally learns the value of her true lover, and accepts her ordained role in this rustic community (RF, XLIII, 384–5). If *The Ordeal of*

Richard Feverel expresses in its passionate sweep the transcendence of Nature in man's affairs, *Rhoda Fleming*, despite its unevenness, gives authentic expression to Meredith's feeling for Nature in its homelier aspect.

With *Sandra Belloni* Meredith returned to the higher social echelons which he adopted as his prerogative. The contrast between the Pole sisters sedulously cultivating their Fine Feelings, and the passionate Emilia, is beautifully executed; and in the baleful presence of Mr Pericles the dead hand of international finance is aptly suggested. Emilia's experience of the antithesis between urban and rural validates the substance of the novel. Indeed London is envisioned as a type of hell in the striking chapter in which Emilia 'Tastes Despair'. Wandering through the fog 'she fancied she had dropped into an underground kingdom, among a mysterious people' who traverse 'endless labyrinths': 'Up and down the groping city went muffled men, few women' (SB, XL, 352). Throughout her childhood in this maze-like conurbation Emilia longed for a day in the country, 'that was always one of my dreams as I watched the clouds flying over London' (SB, VI, 38). The imagery of the urban prison, which links Meredith with a whole tradition from Dickens and James Thomson to Eliot, is here explicitly set against the boundlessness and beauty of Nature, when Emilia and Wilfrid Pole meet by Wilming Weir (SB, XX). This love-scene, to which the emotions expand under the plenitude of Nature, is a more mature re-enactment of the Richard–Lucy scene. But Meredith is no longer content to explore the ecstasies of young love. In the last movement of the novel the comically atrophied Pole sisters are abandoned, and the political reunification of Italy introduces a new note of patriotism and commitment. The theme of the *risorgimento*, which here places the triviality of English society, receives full consideration in *Vittoria*,[13] where the libertarian sentiments of Vittoria's song, the female equivalent of male warfare, find echoes in Nature: when she sings the 'Addio' from *Hagar*, 'her voice possessed the mountain-shadowed lake' (V, XXXVIII, 417).

The nature-theme, which is submerged in the political furore in *Vittoria*, is absent from *The Adventures of Harry Richmond*,[14] where even the penetration of the German forest (HR, XV) yields a largely comic dividend. This subordination is equally severe in the ambitiously panoramic *Beauchamp's Career*,[15] in other respects one of Meredith's finest achievements. Beauchamp represents that 'glorified self-love' which needs to be subdued by a 'reading of the heavens, the earth too', indeed Meredith adds, 'earth foremost' (BC, XXIV, 207). His career is characterised by the gradual chastening of his headlong romanticism into an ideal of social service, and this is mirrored in Nature. Thus his passion for Renée is enacted against a Wagnerian landscape in the Adriatic, with 'shadows on the snow-fields' where 'You might imagine Gods to sit', towering over the sea 'like wings traversing infinity' (BC, IX, 67). Beauchamp's courtship of Cecilia Halkett in England is conversely marked by a new sobriety. He visits her 'on a November afternoon when the woods glowed, and no sun', with cobwebs 'chill in the feeble light', and a carpeting of dead leaves (BC, XXVIII, 257). The sobering effects of the electoral campaign, and the emotional altruism of the relationship, is faithfully rendered imagistically, and the way prepared for the personal and political seriousness of the later chapters in which 'spirit' predominates. Beauchamp's Comtean altruism, whilst tragically failing to fulfil itself, marks the end of Meredith's first phase, in which Nature develops from a supra-mundane force into an agency for human redemption.

Altruism is replaced by a sublime egoism in Meredith's next protagonist, Sir Willoughby Patterne. In this portrait Nature is treated antithetically as the oppositional equivalent of the corrosive power of human egoism. Clara reflects that 'If Willoughby would open his heart to nature, he would be relieved of his wretched opinion of the world' (TE, XIX, 229). The communion with Nature is essential if humanity is to escape the exploitive forms of social organisation. Clara comes to learn this, cogitating upon Laetitia's 'modest enthusiasm for rural pleasures, for this place especially, with its rich foliage and peeps of scenic peace'. This 'sincerity of feeling' 'gave her root in our earth' (TE, XIX, 228), a root which Willoughby signally lacks. As his name implies he exists by hubristically patterning the lives of those around him, especially the women, in accordance with his monstrous self-regard. When he is jilted he seeks to compensate through sexual domination, imposing his will upon his circle — again his name is significantly chosen. The elaborate social structuring which he delights in is essentially hermetic; whilst his egoism, according to Meredithian theory, is to be dissolved through irony, and exposure to the attacks of the comic spirit, the humane balance of an integrated personality is imaged through Nature. *The Egoist* may contain only half of Meredith — the architect of ironic fabrication and social comedy — but the other side of his psyche, his poetic sensibility and commitment to freedom and ideals of liberality, is here economically symbolised by Nature. It is this dialectic between society and Nature which gives the book its satisfying intellectual beauty, since Meredith counterpoises the drawing-room of Patterne Hall with open-air scenes. Indeed Clara's original dissatisfaction with the 'flat land' tamed by 'hedges and palings' (TE, XVI, 199) is a visceral rejection of Willoughby's attempted domination through will. Equally, her passion for the Alps transforms them into an emblem of 'intellectual freedom', and we are reminded of similar landscape-connotations in *Sense and Sensibility*. The presentation of Clara in terms of the poetry of Nature involves a transference effect: Laetitia, the amateur poetess, becomes hard-headedly practical while Clara moves nearer to the life and flow of Nature. These multiple meanings are fused in the image of the wild cherry tree beneath which Clara discovers the sleeping Vernon Whitford. Craning her neck to discern the title of his abandoned book she turns her face 'to where the load of virginal blossom . . . showered and dropped and clustered so thick as to claim colour and seem, like higher Alpine snows in noon-sunlight, a flush of white'. She experiences profound wonder, followed by mundane reflection on Vernon's goodness. The wonder 'was like soaring into homes of angel-crowded space, sweeping through folded and on to folded white fountain-bows of wings'; the moral reflection which replaces it, though 'poor by comparison', has the effect of 'conferring something' on Whitford (TE, XI, 154–5). This is a crucial episode in Meredith: the divine afflatus man experiences in Nature, though transitory, leaves behind it a revelation of commonalty and consequent humane understanding. If the Nature theme is given its most rhapsodic treatment in *The Ordeal of Richard Feverel*, in *The Egoist* Meredith loads every rift with ore with an elliptical new power, and the linear narrative gives way to a series of set-pieces in a new *symboliste* manner. The egoist, by excluding Nature, excludes life itself.

The origins of *Diana of the Crossways*[16] in the Caroline Norton affair have led critics to read the novel as a document of the New Woman question. The treatment of the emancipated female is indeed important to the substance of the book, and one which contributed largely to its success with the reading public. No one, however, was more prone to 'the fascination of what's difficult' than Meredith, who here grafts this topical subject onto the Nature theme. Thus whilst Diana is created in terms of a specific social stratum, and is seen as a rebel against repressive class mores, she is also viewed as an avatar of Nature. Indeed she defines herself in terms of the natural forces around her, forces which offer a silent critique of her high-society milieu. Without toppling into absurdity Meredith contrives to suggest something of the Nature-goddess about his heroine. She is often visualised as a solitary figure in a landscape. In her climb above Lake Lugano for instance, she enacts her highest aspirations for the future of her sex; feeling as if she has 'risen from the dead' in her Ibsenesque abandonment of the shallow life presented to her, through the 'influences of nature's beauty and grandeur' she gains 'a revelation of our human powers' which leaves her free of the past and compassionate towards her fellow men: 'Freedom to breathe, gaze, climb, grow with the grasses, fly with the clouds, to muse, to sing, to be an unclaimed self . . . that radiation — she craved no more' (DC, XV, 145–6). Despite the disclaimer, it is clear that Diana's ambitions are huge: to release herself through Nature, so that she realises her 'unclaimed self' in an enlarged sense of life. This apprehension of the numinous, with its attendant mystical glow, brings Diana momentarily close to the heroines of Jefferies. Indeed the semi-mythological treatment of Felise is paralleled here by Dacier's mountain glimpse of Diana. Coming upon a secret pool he conjures up 'classic visions of the pudency of the Goddess irate or unsighted' which are soon dispersed by the mortal woman (DC, XVI, 151). But Diana is just as much at home riding across the downs; indeed she is so inspired by the immense views that she exclaims' "I should like to build a hut on this point, and wait for such a day to return" ' (DC, XIX, 179). This role as votary of Nature fortifies her in her later tribulations, and Meredith comments that her 'love of nature saved her from . . . dire mischance during a two months' residence at Copsley'. Her 'fall' brings her 'renovatingly to earth', and her spiritual rescue is effected through Nature. Nor is Diana simply prone to Nature mysticism. Her enquiries into 'shells and stones and weeds' bring her into intimate contact with the created world, a contact made easier by the tutelage of Redworth (DC, XXXIX, 363–4). The resolution of the novel, with the long-delayed union of Diana and Redworth, is effected through the agency of Nature. They walk together at sunset, and Diana expresses her love of 'Sol'. The suggestions inherent in Redworth's name cannot be lost on the reader, since Meredith explicitly makes the transference: Diana 'put Sol for Redworth, Redworth for Sol' (DC, XLII, 395). The implication is that the protagonists have access to universal sources of energy and life, and they are finally united by a storm, descending 'upon great surges of wind piping and driving every light surface-atom as foam' in this 'sheer blissful instant' (DC, XLIII, 405). Meredith's belief in the energising power of Nature is realised through these lovers of his maturity, whose marriage is to work a 'singular transformation of

Old England', in Emma's final prophecy of a 'union of our human conditions with the ethereal and psychically divined' (DC, XLIII, 414).

The evolutionary aspect of love is neglected in *The Tragic Comedians*,[17] with its disturbing image of the heroine as 'Half a woman, half a tree' (TC, XIV, 126), and its titanic hero Alvan, who inspires himself by contemplating the mighty Alpine masses. However, in Meredith's strangest novel, *One of Our Conquerors*, he once again turns to the contrasts between Nature and society. Although Victor Radnor claims, 'I get back to primal innocence in the country' (OC, III, 19), his compromised past and the implacable power of the city which is so strikingly rendered in the stream-of-consciousness opening, ensures that the rural idyll is now hopelessly flawed. The possibilities of renewal through Nature are withdrawn from the characters in this dark vision, in which Meredith seems to synthesise the laws of Nature with those of society. His import is pessimistic, since active participation in the processes of Nature in no way averts the fate which Radnor's early life brings upon him, the ineluctable stripping away of his layers of social respectability being shown with grim power. Yet in each of these late novels it is hard to escape the conclusion that Meredith has lost his way artistically and is compensating through an increasingly convoluted syntax. *Lord Ormont and his Aminta*,[18] with its characteristic ending invoking an ideal of simultaneous withdrawal from and action in the world, is notable primarily for its sexual interpretation of natural impulse, an interpretation made openly by the Augustan Lady Charlotte: 'she saw [sex] as the animation of nature, senselessly stigmatised, hypocritically concealed, active in our thoughts where not in our deeds' (LOA, III, 49). This sexuality is made overt in the bathing scene, 'A Marine Duet' (LOA, XXVII), in which the passion of the lovers is dramatized in the natural setting with an almost Lawrencean force.

But of the late novels it is *The Amazing Marriage*[19] in which Meredith gives his final sustained treatment of the Nature theme. The central pivot of the novel is the clash in the mode of life of the protagonists. Carinthia, born in the mountains and envisioned as part of the natural scene in a Wordsworthian sense at her farewell to the old home (AM, IV, 40), stands over against the artifice of Lord Fleetwood. The pretence and egoism of Fleetwood are nowhere more stringently exposed than in his transparent pose as a Nature worshipper. As Chillon comments, 'it seems odd for an English nobleman to be raving about Nature' (AM, VI, 66): this *engouement* is in truth 'a pretence at sensibility' which masks his nullity. The denaturing effects of adherence to the norms of social intercourse are fully worked out in the portrayal of Fleetwood and his fatal marriage to Carinthia, as if Meredith now despairs of any *rapprochement* between Nature and society. Whilst Fleetwood as an egoist axiomatically fails to develop, Carinthia is gradually transformed into a type of earth-goddess, her Nature worship leading to good works and an ideal commitment to political liberty. Whilst Carinthia is soon immersed in her 'amazing marriage' and its implications for the position of woman, the denial of mass culture, class and commercial exploitation is given a more articulate spokesman in the symbolically named Gower Woodseer, a character partially based on Stevenson. At his first encounter with Carinthia and Chillon in the mountains Woodseer expounds his ideal: ' "I care for open air, colour, flowers, weeds, birds, insects, mountains. There's a world behind the mask. I call this life; and the town's a boiling pot, intolerably stuffy. My one ambition is to be out of it" ' (AM, VI, 64). This 'son of the mountains' (AM, XIX, 212) has educated himself in Nature, his college fellows being 'hawkers, tinkers, tramps and ploughmen' (AM, VIII, 82). He teaches the simple doctrine, 'Love Nature, she makes you a lord of her boundless, off any ten square feet of common earth' (AM, XXVII, 301). But the corollary, which goes to the heart of Meredith, is this: ' "Women and Nature are close. If it is rather general to hate Nature and maltreat women, we begin to see why the world is a mad world" ' (AM, XXXV, 392). Fleetwood's enclosed egoism is representative of the human condition, each man locked away from his fellows. His ludicrous adoption of the role of Nature's acolyte is a deluded sham, as Woodseer divines: ' "You hate Nature unless you have it served on a dish by your own cook" ' (AM, XXXI, 352). The encounter between Fleetwood and Carinthia, 'a noble daughter of the woods' (AM, XI, 130), and her subsequent enslavement, is a parable of the subordination of the natural and intuitional to the intellect and the will. It subsumes all of Meredith's work, and though the struggle is intense the outcome is one of muted hope: Fleetwood, abandoned at last, 'could not be satisfied with Nature', and enters a mountain monastery, whilst Carinthia enlists in the Carlist cause. Only through a reversion to the primary sources of Nature will man regain his lost humanity. Beyond this, in old age, Meredith could not go. The living connexion between man and Nature so tellingly proposed in his greatest novels and poems fades to an afterglow in *Celt and Saxon*.[20] Yet James's reflections in the closing pages of this final novel might stand for all: 'the strong flow of poetic imagination is wanted to hallow a passionate devotion to the inanimate; for this evokes the spiritual' (CS, XIX, 295). It is the function of Nature in Meredith that it 'evokes the spiritual', and raises man to a new intensity of being:

> For the road to her soul is the Real:
> The root of the growth of man:
> And the senses must traverse it fresh
> With a love that no scourge shall abate,
> To reach the lone heights where we scan
> In the mind's rarer vision this flesh;
> In the charge of the Mother our fate;
> Her law as the one common weal.
> ('A Faith on Trial')

Notes

1   Quoted in L. Stevenson, *The Ordeal of George Meredith* (London, Peter Owen, 1954), p. 339.

2 C.L. Cline (ed.), *The Collected Letters of George Meredith* (London, Oxford University Press, 1970, hereafter cited as L), p. 1618.

3 G. Meredith, *Poems*, 2 vols (London, Constable, 1903).

4 N. Kelvin, *A Troubled Eden* (London, Oliver & Boyd, 1961), p. 3.

5 Meredith remarks of Purcell Barrett, 'The reproaching of Providence by a man of full growth, comes to some extent from his meanness, and chiefly from his pride'; see G. Meredith, *Sandra Belloni* (1889, published as *Emilia in England*, 1864) (London, Constable, 1909, hereafter cited as SB), p. 448.

6 G. Meredith, *One of Our Conquerors* (1891) (London, Chapman & Hall, 1892, hereafter cited as OC).

7 G. Meredith, *The Ordeal of Richard Feverel* (1859) (New York, Random House, Modern Library edn., 1927, hereafter cited as ORF).

8 The image of running water, with its connotations of headlong sexual passion, is pervasive in early Meredith. In *Farina*, the eponymous hero 'could not restrain his tears' at the sight of the Rhine pouring on to 'the great marriage of waters'; see G. Meredith, *Short Stories* (London, Constable, 1902, hereafter cited as S), p. 190; in *Sandra Belloni* the lovers unite at a weir.

9 The place is significant, since the episode mirrors many such incidents in German romantic poetry; the closest parallel, however, is the storm-scene in *Childe Harold's Pilgrimage*, (canto III, stanzas xcii–xcvii).

10 G. Meredith, *The Egoist* (1879) (Harmondsworth, Penguin Books, 1968, hereafter cited as TE).

11 G. Meredith, *Evan Harrington* (1861) (London, Constable, 1909, hereafter cited as EH).

12 G. Meredith, *Rhoda Fleming* (1865) (London, Constable, 1907, hereafter cited as RF).

13 G. Meredith, *Vittoria* (1867) (London, Constable, 1909, hereafter cited as V).

14 G. Meredith, *The Adventures of Harry Richmond* (1871) (London, Constable, 1906, hereafter cited as HR).

15 G. Meredith, *Beauchamp's Career* (1876) (London, Constable, 1907, hereafter cited as BC).

16 G. Meredith, *Diana of the Crossways* (1885) (London, Constable, 1915, hereafter cited as DC).

17 G. Meredith, *The Tragic Comedians* (1880) (London, Constable, 1904, hereafter cited as TC).

18 G. Meredith, *Lord Ormont and his Aminta* (1894) (London, Constable, 1902, hereafter cited as LOA).

19 G. Meredith, *The Amazing Marriage* (1895) (London, Constable, 1906, hereafter cited as AM).

20 G. Meredith, *Celt and Saxon* (1910) (London, Constable, 1910, hereafter cited as CS).

4　Thomas Hardy

I

A guest at a meeting of the Omar Khayyam Club in 1895 percipiently recorded the differences between two of the luminaries at the dinner. Hardy's features, he wrote, 'gave the impression of many thought-worn eves and morrows', whilst the senior novelist 'looked as if he had met and mastered life'. Meredith enjoyed Hardy's visits to Box Hill, but afterwards found himself 'afflicted by [Hardy's] twilight view of life'.[1] The history of the relations between the two men, which began with Meredith's rejection of *The Poor Man and the Lady* for Chapman & Hall and his advice as regards more complex plotting, are well known. Hardy was deeply indebted to Meredith in *Desperate Remedies*,[2] and in the high society scenes of a novel like *The Hand of Ethelberta*;[3] but as a mature artist Hardy became more critical. In 1909 he told Mrs Henniker that 'the difficulty of reading — or at least enjoying — some of Meredith's books arises entirely (as I think) from his errors of method. Why he was so perverse as to infringe the first rules of narrative art I cannot tell, when what he had to say was of the very highest, and what he discerned in life was more than almost any novelist had discerned before'.[4] The discernment which Hardy praises lay in Meredith's central treatment of man and Nature, and in his examination of passion struggling to free itself from the trammels of social orthodoxy. Hardy may well have modelled his own dual career of poet-novelist upon the example of Meredith, and valued the older man for his links with Shelley and the Romantic circle. In both cases after a false start — Meredith with *The Shaving of Shagpat*, and Hardy with *Desperate Remedies* — each writer found himself in a work of romantic individuality — *The Ordeal of Richard Feverel* and *Under the Greenwood Tree*.[5] Each man renounced Christianity, Meredith with cheerful poise, Hardy with painful reluctance, and each endeavoured to forge a new post-Darwinian faith based in Nature. The crucial difference was one of temperament.

The simplistic label of 'pessimist' annoyed Hardy, and he was often at pains to counter it; but the term may stand as expressing his divergence from Meredith. It was in man's relation to Nature and to his fellow beings that Hardy found cause for gloom, though not for despair, and his 'evolutionary meliorism' was more sombre than Meredith's belief in blood, brain and spirit working in evolutionary harmony. Both men wrought a dynamic change in the possibilities of the novel. In this sense the common ground between them is more significant than their temperamental differences.

II

'Nature is played out as a Beauty, but not as a Mystery'. Thus wrote Hardy in 1887.[6] The unknowableness of the Universe must remain at the conclusion of any study of Hardy's ideas on Nature, founded as they are upon Spencer's First Cause. At the same time the novels should not be processed into a philosophical schema of belief: Hardy warned that writings extended over forty years must not be expected to exhibit 'a coherent scientific view of the universe'[7] — they are rather a series of 'seemings', or as he put it, 'mere impressions that frequently change'. Nevertheless, Hardy's work stands at the centre of a tradition, his novels constantly stressing man's closeness to, or alienation from Nature — and as he develops the note of alienation becomes more insistent.

Hardy recalled his father 'going alone into the woods or on the heath', like Clym, lying 'on a bank of thyme or camomile with the grasshoppers leaping over him' (*Life*, 21). In Hardy this homely familiarity is married to a larger, cosmic view of Nature in which man is ineluctably caught up. That this view is fundamentally pessimistic is a commonplace; a comparison between Meredith's 'The Woods of Westermain' and Hardy's 'In a Wood' is instructive in this respect. Meredith hymns a union of self with all created life:

> Drink the sense the notes infuse,
> You a larger self will find:
> Sweetest fellowship ensues
> With the creatures of your kind.

In Hardy man and Nature are equally blighted:

> Heart-halt and spirit-lame,
>   City-oprest,
> Unto this wood I came
>   As to a nest. . . .
>
> Sycamore shoulders oak,
> Bines the slim sapling yoke,
> Ivy-spun halters choke
>   Elms stout and tall.

Union with Nature is flawed by universal and personal tragedy, as Hardy says in 'The Rambler':

> Some say each songster, tree, and mead —
> All eloquent of love divine —
> Receives their constant careful heed:
> Such keen appraisement is not mine.
>
> The tones around me that I hear,
> The aspects, meanings, shapes I see,
> Are those far back ones missed when near,
> And now perceived too late by me!

The critical disagreement about Hardy's meaning is in essence a debate about his treatment of Nature. John Holloway sees Hardyesque Nature as an organic living whole, unified on a large scale in time and space, ruled by rigid and undeviating law. Due to this law 'human life, and indeed human consciousness itself, is wholly subject to the control of Nature': this is illustrated by Hardy's hauntingly lone figures in the landscape.[8] Roy Morrell quarrels suggestively with this, showing how Mill's 'Nature', which Hardy knew well, holds out the possibility of man's participating in natural processes. Mill saw Nature as inimical to man, but felt that his 'duty' was one of co-operation and amendment of Nature. This leads to a greater emphasis on man's free choice which makes a just *caveat* to Holloway's otherwise valid reading.[9] The ideas of a primal Cause immanent in the Universe, and of the emergent consciousness, probably derived from Spencer, are pervasive in Hardy's work, which presents us with what is, in the last analysis, an inscrutable universe, unreadable to man, who suffers accordingly:

> Crass Casualty obstructs the sun and rain,
> And dicing Time for gladness casts a moan. . . .
> These purblind Doomsters had as readily strown
> Blisses about my pilgrimage as pain.
>
> ('Hap')

Within this framework of blind determinism Hardy often came to feel that the earth 'does not supply the materials for happiness to higher existences' (*Life*, 218):

> The Cognisance ye mourn, Life's doom to feel,
> If I report it meetly, came unmeant,
> Emerging with blind gropes from impercipience
> By listless sequence — luckless, tragic Chance,
> In your more human tongue.
>
> ('Shade of the Earth', *The Dynasts*)

Human beings have, in this vision, reached 'a degree of intelligence which Nature never contemplated when forming her laws, and for which she consequently has provided no adequate satisfactions' (*Life*, 163) — this is the tragedy of Clym or Jude. Hardy's obsessive use of chance and coincidence is intended to ramify this world view: 'The more we know of the laws and nature of the universe the more ghastly a business one perceives it all to be — and the non-necessity of it', he once complained to Edward Clodd. This is not a question of man struggling against a conceit such as 'Fate', but of his being caught up in vast processes which are essentially non-human in their inevitability, as Spencer had explained. The unwitting separation of man from natural processes may be grounds for satire, a sense of comic absurdity at human plans and desires in the face of inscrutable processes. At any rate, the connexion of man and Nature in Hardy has the effect of placing the social milieu in a vast perspective of space and time, a perspective beautifully realised by Lawrence: 'The vast, unexplored morality of life itself, what we call the immorality of nature, surrounds us in its eternal incomprehensibility, and in its midst goes on the little human morality play, with its queer frame of morality and its mechanised movement'.[10] Yet we may baulk at this 'mechanised movement': frequently Hardy's characters endeavour to struggle free of this determinism. What critics refer to as 'fate', 'destiny', or 'the President of the Immortals', is seen at least partly to be within human control: Eustacia's errors, Henchard's decline, Jude's blindness, these result from acts of decision, or indecision.

Sometimes Hardy suggests that no connexion exists between man and Nature. He writes in *The Academy* in 1902, 'Pain has been, and pain is: no new sort of morals in Nature can remove pain from the past and make it pleasure for those who are its infallible estimators, the bearers thereof . . . to model our conduct on Nature's apparent conduct, as Nietzsche would have taught, can only bring disaster to humanity' (*Life*, 315). Yet the element of choice, and more important, of adaptability, is illustrated by many of Hardy's 'good' characters, such as Gabriel Oak, Diggory Venn, Marty South and Giles; significantly, the adaptability fails to save these later figures, however. A man like Oak wrests a living from Nature by study, adaptation and ingenuity, and is fitter to survive than the more overtly heroic figures. In the conceptualisation of such character changes Hardy seems to be hankering after a kind of fictional Lamarckism — Venn, for instance, can 'will' his own adaptability from obsolescent reddleman to successful dairy farmer. The transmission of acquired characteristics, Darwin had shown, was an illicit premise; but it enters in a muddled way into Hardy's thinking here.

The sense of an impersonal unthinking energy is the crucial difference between Hardy and the pantheism of Coleridge, Ruskin or Hopkins, and largely derives from the seminal influence of Darwinian thought. The sense Hardy had that, as he put it, the Cause 'is neither moral nor immoral, but *un*moral' is consonant with the sources of Hardy's philosophy in rationalism.[11] Rebuking an admirer who was insisting on his debt to Schopenhauer, Hardy wrote, 'My pages show harmony of view with Darwin, Huxley, Spencer, Hume, Mill, and others'. If Darwinian thought filled Hardy with a sense of waste and anguish it also enabled him to formulate a tenable theory of life from the debris of his religious faith. Hardy was a convinced Darwinian.[12]

The Darwinian hypothesis that all species were produced by development of varieties from common stocks, and that new species emerged by a process of natural selection which was effected by the struggle for existence, marks all of Hardy's work. That boyhood closeness to Nature was radically altered by the new intellectual view of Nature which Horace Moule was placing before him. From *The Origin of Species*[13] Hardy may have specially noted the ecological sections, in which Darwin demonstrates such matters as the delicate balance between flies and cattle; heathland trees, cattle and insectiverous birds, and so forth. Many of the novels portray such intricate relations within a rural community, and the threats and disturbances from outside which may disrupt it. The image of Nature as a battleground is the kernel of the mutability theory of the development of species, and Hardy's view of life is only to be fully understood within the context of such a passage as this from *The Origin of Species*:

Battle within battle must ever be recurring with varying success; and yet in the long-run the forces are so nicely balanced, that the face of nature remains uniform for long periods of time, though assuredly the merest trifle would often give the victory to one organic being over another. Nevertheless so profound is our ignorance, and so high our presumption, that we marvel when we hear of the extinction of an organic being.[14]

This passage, with its underlying emphasis on evolutionary struggle, and the role of chance in which the 'merest trifle' decides the fate of a species, is crucial to an understanding of the Wessex novels. The whole conception of 'Wessex' also owes something to Darwin's words on isolation as a factor in evolution: 'fewness of individuals will greatly retard the production of new species through natural selection . . . the new forms produced on large areas, which have already been victorious over many competitors'[15] — these will be the ones which succeed. Thus Hardy's 'Mephistophelaen visitants', his disturbers of the rural order, may be seen in biological terms. With this in mind Huxley's account of the struggle for existence is also relevant, giving a curious epitome of the general lines of movement in many Hardy novels where the law which determines survival operates without regard for human criteria of fitness:

> there are organic beings, which operate as *opponents*, and there are organic beings which operate as *helpers* to any given organic creature. The opponents may be of two kinds: there are the *indirect opponents*, which are what we may call *rivals*; and there are the *direct opponents*, those which strive to destroy the creature; and these we call *enemies*.[16]

Hardy's men and women interact in a highly Darwinian way. Darwin had shown how reproductive selection operates through inter-male competition, with its concomitant promotion of bird display and plumage, special weapons and generally combative behaviour. Huxley's account here illuminates both the direct and indirect sexual opponents in Hardy's novels — from Dick Dewy, Mr Shiner and Parson Maybold, through Oak, Boldwood and Troy, or Clym and Wildeve, to Jude and Phillotson. Continual struggle is part of the evolutionary process, and Nature is thus in perpetual ferment: 'spontaneous change is the rule, rest the exception — the anomaly to be accounted for. Living things have no inertia and tend to no equilibrium'.[17] Yet this absence of stasis, and the momentum of variabilility, does not preclude the possibility of unmodified species; according to Huxley evolution is not everywhere and always progressive or directional:

> there are particular kinds of animals and plants which have existed throughout vast epochs, sometimes through the whole range of recorded time, with very little change. By reason of this persistency, the typical form of such a kind might be called a 'persistent type', in contradistinction to those types which have appeared for but a short time in the course of the world's history.[18]

Huxley's 'persistent types' represent the third category of sub-process in modern biology, which distinguishes first, *cladogenesis*, the tendency towards ever greater diversity in organisms; secondly, *anagenesis*, the tendency towards more efficient internal and external organisation; and thirdly, *stasigenesis*, the long-lasting stabilisation of types. All these processes are humanly observable in Hardy, where Huxley's sense of 'vast epochs' and 'persistent types' gets translated into artistic terms. The unchanging rustic chorus so often remarked upon takes on a new perspective in relation to Huxley: for instance, in *The Return of the Native*[19] the rustics who have persisted from ancient times are carefully distinguished from the short-lived 'dynamic' types such as Clym and Eustacia, to provide the dialectic of the narrative.

Another feature of Nature in Hardy's novels, its multiplicity, interrelatedness and unity, is especially stressed in evolution:

The animal eats the plant and appropriates the nutritious portions to its own sustenance, rejects and gets rid of the useless matters; and, finally, the animal itself dies, and its whole body is decomposed and returned into the inorganic world. There is thus a constant circulation from one to the other, a continual formation of organic life from inorganic matters, and as constant a return of the matter of living bodies to the inorganic world; so that the materials of which our bodies are composed are largely, in all probability, the substances which constituted the matter of long extinct creations, but which have in the interval constituted a part of the inorganic world.[20]

This striking notion exerts a deep fascination on Hardy. In one of his favourite locales, a graveyard, he reflects upon the dead:

> So, they are not underground,
> But as nerves and veins abound
> In the growths of upper air,
> And they feel the sun and rain,
> And the energy again
> That made them what they were!
> ('Transformations')

Similarly at Talbothays an 'instalment of flowers, leaves, nightingales, thrushes, finches, and such ephemeral creatures, took up their positions where only a year ago others had stood in their place when these were nothing more than germs and inorganic particles'.[21]

Huxley does not hesitate to draw a moral from the evolutionary picture, and his conclusion has a stoically Hardyesque ring: 'I cannot but think that he who finds a certain proportion of pain and evil inseparably woven up in the life of the very worms, will bear his own share with more courage and submission'.[22] Elsewhere, Huxley points out how 'plague, pestilence, and famine are admitted, by all but fools, to be the natural result of causes for the most part fully within human control, and not the unavoidable tortures inflicted by wrathful Omnipotence upon his helpless handiwork'.[23] Hardy, *pace* many of his critics, would have concurred: the storm scene in *Far From the Madding Crowd* [24] is a symbolic enactment of this concept.

Hardy learns from Darwinian thought both of the unity of man and Nature — something more optimistically stressed in his beloved Shelley, and the Romantics generally — and of the struggle for survival. This ambiguity in the face of Nature lies at the heart of the great novels, and accounts for their rich, confusing power. As a metaphysician, Lawrence held, Hardy 'makes a poor show': 'His feeling, his instinct, his sensuous understanding is, apart from his metaphysic, very great and deep, deeper than that, perhaps, of any other English novelist. Putting aside his metaphysic, which must always obtrude when he thinks of people, and turning to the earth, to landscape, then he is true to himself' (STH, 92). Nature's unknowable mystery; its neutrality, which the humanist pathetic fallacy may interpret as hostility; sexual rivalry; the relative insignificance of man within the great natural processes, counterbalanced by the heroic ingenuity and adaptability of man in accommodating himself to the environment: these are the main features of Nature in the novels. Hardy's protagonists always act within a landscape of which they are a vital part, unwitting agents of organic processes of evolutionary change.

This account ignores the social and human features of Wessex. Hardy held that an 'object or mark raised or made by man on a scene is worth ten times any such formed by unconscious Nature. Hence clouds, mists, and mountains are unimportant beside the wear on a threshold, or the print of a hand' (*Life*, 116). The emphasis on work and custom is vital to Hardy. The impersonality of the view from above in those telling 'aerial' shots in the novels quickly gives way to the intimate view from within: the movement, in *Under the Greenwood Tree*, from the dark woodland into the tranter's cottage. This type of pastoral realism is defined by agricultural skills and activities, and the social relations which depend upon them. The reading of Nature which such a life entails is exemplified by many of the unequivocally 'good' characters — Oak, Winterborne, Marty South — and the life which is envisaged has a ballad quality in its stress upon seasons, fate and chance. The quality of this life is not romanticised; Hardy did claim, however, in 'The Dorsetshire Labourer', that 'a pure atmosphere and a pastoral environment are a very appreciable portion of the sustenance which tends to produce the sound mind and body, and thus much sustenance is, at least, the labourer's birthright' (PW, 171). This was a birthright threatened by inexorable socio-economic forces, and no doubt some of Hardy's sense of tragedy does derive from a sense of the doom of the old order. The unsettlement of tenants and copyholders and the resultant peregrinations symbolise the inevitable alienation from Nature accompanied by a shiftless, denaturing sense of obsolescence typified by old South or 'Sir John' Durbeyfield. But Hardy faces this squarely in the essay, and without too much wringing of hands.[25] Elsewhere he wrote hopefully enough of the 'modern Wessex of railways, the penny post, sowing and reaping machines, union workhouses, Lucifer matches, labourers who could read and write, and National school-children'.[26] The result of 'this increasing nomadic habit of the labourer is naturally a less intimate and kindly relation with the land he tills', Hardy reflects; but he concludes that 'it is too much to expect them to remain stagnant and old-fashioned for the pleasure of romantic spectators' (PW, 181).

The final impression of Hardy's world is of the intimate connexion of man and natural processes, a connexion which has the effect of placing the social and human within an immense perspective of space and time; this shows itself repeatedly in the openings of the novels, and is perhaps Hardy's unique contribution to fiction.

Under the Greenwood Tree pre-figures to a remarkable extent Hardy's mature handling of the relation of man and Nature. The interconnexion of the rural craftsman with his surroundings is beautifully handled, and the individual 'humours' of the characters are contained within the cycle of the seasons. There is no disturber of the rustic community (if we except Mr Maybold), and the reader is made aware of human labour close to Nature. Yet there is already present here something susceptible of a more tragic interpretation, though this is necessarily a matter of isolating a few features of the novel. Whilst the characters are in harmony with Nature, as is perfectly illustrated at the opening, with its subtle movement from the sound of the trees to their appearance, and then the gradual emergence of the (representative) human types — yet there are hints that this harmony masks a more sombre vision. In Maybold, Dick and Shiner Hardy experiments with an early version of that sexual rivalry which Huxley had pointed out as operative in biological survival. Though all is here resolved with apparent ease there is some ambiguity about 'the knot there's no untying'. The non-human pulsation of sexuality, which is to culminate so powerfully in Tess and Jude, is hinted at when Dick wishes to utter his proposal to Geoffrey Day: 'Dick said nothing; and the stillness was disturbed only by some small bird that was being killed by an owl in the adjoining wood, whose cry passed into the silence without mingling with it' (UGT, iv, II, 166). So Maybold's feelings for Fancy are 'killed' by the unwitting Dick on the walk into Casterbridge, and Fancy's almost predatory role is pointed up by the scene of her netting birds with Shiner, and by her caged canary. A similar ruthlessness is apparent socially: the choir cannot adapt and is doomed to the obsolescence pronounced in the masterly comic scene in the vicar's study. This scene, and the whole book, bears witness to the pagan nature of country life: the deepest religion is a natural one which expresses itself in ancient rituals such as the marriage feast, and the dance at the tranter's — an atavistic religion for which the alleged 'witch', Mrs Endorfield, caters.

Although *A Pair of Blue Eyes*[27] is a less impressive achievement it is of great significance in assessing Hardy's darkening concept of Nature. The central episode is Knight's ordeal on the cliff-face. As Knight clings to the Cliff with No Name Hardy remarks that the 'inveterate antagonism of these black precipices to all strugglers for life is in no way more forcibly suggested than by the paucity of tufts of grass, lichens, or confervae on their outermost ledges' (PBE, XXII, 239). As Knight slips down the 'hostility' of Nature becomes 'a cosmic agency, active, lashing, eager for conquest' (PBE, XXII, 242). This scene dramatizes to chilling effect the Arnoldian withdrawal of faith in a beneficent universal order. It marks a watershed in Hardy's imaginative work. Clinging bravely to the cliff, Knight perceives a trilobite embedded in the rock layers; this leads him to a reflection about successive orders of being, and he is finally rescued by Elfride's ingeniously tearing off her underclothing and making a rope to pull him to safety. The key to this action is to be found in Darwin and Huxley, both of whom several times referred to the trilobite as an example of what Darwin called 'sudden extermination' of whole orders. Knight is thus confronted by an image of primal origin and extinction through failure to adapt. It is Elfride's human ingenuity that gets him off the cliff; but he is finally too highly developed mentally and too inert to win her. The novel closes with Elfride's two ineffectual lovers mourning impotently over the coffin of their beloved — the moral is only too clear. In one of his lectures Huxley told the story of the retreat from Moscow, when a mass of troops were struggling to cross a narrow bridge across a river. One soldier, to extricate himself from the mêlée, clings on to the cloak of a strong French

Cuirassier. This is not simply a source for Hardy: it illuminates what Huxley designates 'selective saving', a concept vital to the novelist — he reverts to it, for instance, when Grace Fitzpiers strips off her skirt to save herself from the man-trap: '[each species] has to fight its way through and struggle with other species; and when well nigh overpowered, it may be that the smallest chance, something in its colour, perhaps — the minutest circumstance — will turn the scale one way or the other'.[28] Knight is one of those who become, through evolution of the mental and spiritual, incapable of fully engaging in the struggle of life — this is to be one of the tragic possibilities and ironies which Hardy is to explore in the later fiction.

The persistence which Knight lacks, allied to an intimate creative relation with Nature, is to be found in Oak. The immense age and stolidity of the earth is suggested at the outset of *Far From the Madding Crowd* in the depiction of Norcombe Hill, 'a shape approaching the indestructible as nearly as any to be found on earth' (FMC, 11, 46), whilst the variety and movement of Nature are conveyed by the interpretation of the differing wind sounds, and by Oak's flute, which is an extension of Nature. Oak embodies the central, subdued optimism of the novel, whose real theme is the care of the land and the tending of flocks. Oak's intuitive rapport with Nature is enacted in the great storm scene, when seeing the toad, he 'knew what this direct message from the Great Mother' meant, and covers the stacks neglected by Troy and the carousing peasants (FMC, XXXVI, 272). This shows how the skills of man evolve fruitfully within the agrarian community — a continuity and tradition of effort made even more explicit in the sheep-shearing scene. But the element of evolutionary struggle is also present, not only in the patient adaptability of Oak but also in the sexual plot. The scene of Troy's swordplay in the hollow is palpably Darwinian in its depiction of sexual attraction. In sexual attraction, Darwin wrote, the 'war is, perhaps, severest between the males of polygamous animals, and these seem oftenest provided with special weapons'. He added, 'the shield may be as important for

victory, as the sword or spear'.[29] The tragedy of Fanny Robin
(the name echoing both Darwinian and folklore elements in
the conception) underlines Troy's essential polygamy. In bird
courtship Darwin recorded that the males 'display their
gorgeous plumage and perform strange antics before the fema-
les'; Bathsheba thus witnesses, and succumbs to such a display. There is a balance in *Far From the Madding Crowd*
between optimistic and pessimistic readings of Nature, but the
novel is profoundly Darwinian. The final stress, upon the
low-toned optimism of the marriage to Oak, emphasises the
theme of continuity and survival matters which become more
pressing as Hardy goes on writing.

In *The Return of the Native* Hardy orchestrates these
themes with a rich new power. In the vision of Egdon, 'a place
perfectly accordant with man's nature', 'slighted and
enduring' and 'suggesting tragical possibilities', Hardy pre-
figures a time when the 'chastened sublimity of a moor' will be
'in keeping with the moods of the more thinking among mankind' (RN, i, I, 34–5). Whilst the heath embodies certain
ancient ways of life, it also acts as a barrier to new thought; its
life and ways are primeval, its rituals derive their sanction
from Nature — Hardy tersely remarks that churchgoing is
'exceptional at Egdon' (RN, i, X, 113). The peasants' taproot
to Nature emblemised in the mummers' play, the bonfires,
Susan Nonsuch's accusations of witchcraft, and the general
culture of the rustics whose impulses Hardy describes as
'pagan still' (RN, vi, 1, 401) — all this suggests the blind
impulsions of an indifferent, all-encompassing Nature which
is unsatisfactorily embodied in the person of Diggory Venn,
one of a class 'rapidly becoming extinct in Wessex' (RN, i, II,
37–8), who saves himself from obsolescence by adaptation
into a dairy-farmer — an unreal transformation which owes
more to Lamarck than to Darwin. For Eustacia, her 'Pagan
eyes, full of nocturnal mysteries' (RN, i, VII, 93), no such
adaptation is possible. Her Bovaryesque longing for Paris, and
her hatred of Nature and the heath, are part of her 'Prom-
ethean rebelliousness'. Clym, by contrast, undergoes a type of

immolation of self to the heath: he is shown willing a return to Nature which he can never attain naturally — a problem Lawrence confronts with Annable. His plans and visions are progressively obliterated — intelligence beyond a certain level cannot accommodate itself to the blind world of process. When he becomes a furze cutter Hardy writes that he 'appeared as a mere parasite of the heath', 'having no knowledge of anything in the world but fern, furze, heath, lichens, and moss' (RN, iv, V, 297). His return from a futile world of money-making is counterpointed by the heroic futility of Eustacia's rebellion against natural law and by Wildeve's descent from socially useful engineer to publican and sinner. *The Return of the Native* is Hardy's most sombre novel so far, with its sense of the dwarfing of man's aspirations by vast evolutionary forces — a sense of which Lawrence has given the best account: 'Close to the body of things, there can be heard the stir that makes us and destroys us. . . . The Heath persists. Its body is strong and fecund, it will bear many more crops beside [these characters]'. 'Man has a purpose', Lawrence concludes, 'which he has divorced from the passionate purpose that issued him out of the earth into being' (STH, 27). The insistence on the fecundity of the earth, where Hardy stresses the barren intransigence of the heath, betrays the author of the opening of *The Rainbow*. But in his account of the lost connexion Lawrence is essentially right; it is in the blind fumblings of Clym that Hardy examines the implications of that 'missing link'. The return to Nature pre-supposes abandonment of self, allowing the 'higher' powers of man, his reason and intellectual and spiritual life, to atrophy. Hardy never fully recognises the implications of this, even with Angel Clare. Clym's preaching is thus no more than an authorial sop; the real pulse of life is left to the peasants, who, as Lawrence says, 'kept this strong, deep root in the primal soil', whilst 'all the exceptional people' are 'reduced' (STH, 29, 27). The inimical processes of Nature, the blind operations of random chance, and the consequent divorce of developed man from the soil, these themes dominate *The Return of the Native*, and impart a new bleak uniformity to the tone.

The Trumpet Major[30] is imbued with a more beneficent sense of country life, its men and women, as Hardy writes elsewhere, born 'with only an open door between them and the four seasons',[31] and the implications of *The Return of the Native* are shelved in favour of a tale of a period when, as Hardy amusingly remarks, 'Nature was hardly invented' (WT, XVI, 154). The main preference for country over town, here and in *A Laodicean*,[32] lies in the abundance of 'such girls' as attract the heroes.[33] Somerset is conventionally said to possess 'a heart susceptible to beauty of all kinds, — in woman, in art, and in inanimate nature' (AL, i, I, 38), but in the Rhineland scenes it is de Stancy who exclaims revealingly, 'I have almost forgotten there's such a thing as Nature, and I care for nothing but a comfortable life, and a certain woman who does not care for me' (AL, v, VII, 350).

Although he later dismissed it as a 'slightly-built romance', *Two on a Tower*[34] shows Hardy's mind more firmly engaged with his central theme. In place of Egdon he introduces nothing less than the universe as background to the human action, speaking in his preface of 'a wish to set the emotional history of two infinitesimal lives against the stupendous background of the stellar universe'.[35] It is often alleged that Hardy fails with this theme, the slightly novelettish love story becoming paramount. Nonetheless, Hardy does convey in several places the contrast the lovers feel 'between their own tiny magnitudes and those among which they had recklessly plunged', those stellar reaches which 'they could not cope with even as an idea, and which hung about them like a nightmare' (TT, VIII, 86–7). St Cleeve, in his fanatical devotion to astronomy, cogitates in his last fatal visit to the column with the 'inexorably simple logic of such men', a reflection of 'the cruelty of the natural laws that are their study' (TT, XLI, 291). Yet Hardy also shows here that the cruel natural law of sexual attraction, which is so to torment Tess and Jude, may be broken down: witness Viviette's abnegation of her emotional claims upon what Bishop Helmsdale designates 'the votary of science' (TT, XXVI, 187). Within a determinist and frightening universe the human being may communicate personal values which, though as ephemeral as human life, bring some meaning to sublunary existence.

Such values are reasserted, to be more profoundly defeated, in *The Mayor of Casterbridge*.[36] The town itself is imbued with many natural qualities. It is, Hardy insists, 'the complement of the rural life around; not its urban opposite' (MC, IX, 88). Casterbridge was the 'pole, focus, or nerve-knot of the surrounding country life; differing from the many manufacturing towns which are as foreign bodies set down, like boulders on a plain, in a green world with which they have nothing in common' (MC, IX, 92). This interdependence, indeed interpenetration, is symbolised by the butterflies which flutter up the High Street, an image which recalls Huxley's exposition of the way humble-bees build nests near towns to procure for themselves the unwitting protection of the local cats against the field-mice which eat their honey.[37] This sense of organic connexion between the town and its surroundings also means that it is vulnerable to fluctuations of weather and crops. This vulnerability opens the way for a critique of the struggle for existence which seems to affect the lives of the characters perhaps more directly than in earlier novels. Although beneficence is apprehended in Nature, for example in the horses, who, in 'contrast with the harshness of the act' of wife-selling, are seen 'crossing their necks and rubbing each other lovingly' (MC, I, 44–5), and notably in Elizabeth-Jane, the 'flower of Nature', the overall picture is bleak, with the powerful but clumsy Henchard overcome by the adaptive Farfrae, whose display of Scottish dancing first attracts Elizabeth-Jane. The mayor's hopeless struggle against subjection to the 'new' man is reminiscent of some obsolescent pre-historic beast. When this central theme is related to the human corruption in Mixen Lane, Hardy's meaning is made plain.

Whilst Henchard largely brings tragedy upon himself, the characters in *The Woodlanders*[38] are viewed far more as pawns in a cosmic tragedy. The resilient art and custom of Oak and Venn is here recreated in the tending of the trees by Giles and Marty; but this resilience no longer guarantees success, or even survival. Giles wields almost magical powers in relation to Nature: 'He had a marvellous power of making trees grow ... there was a sort of sympathy between himself and the fir, oak, or beech that he was operating on; so that the roots took hold of the soil in a few days' (TW, VIII, 93–4). This intercourse with Nature is acquired with a study and skill equalling Fitzpiers' own more barren studies. At the cider press Giles resembles 'the fruit-god and the wood-god in alternation' (TW, XXXVIII, 305). Yet this god-like sense of fruitfulness and regeneration, though genuine, is dramatically undercut by the pervasive sense of waste and blight in Nature. Whilst Fitzpiers spuriously studies physiology and transcendental philosophy, 'so as to discover if possible a point of contact between them' (TW, XVIII, 162), Grace scans the bountiful autumn landscape and recognises that 'some kernels were unsound as her own situation, and she wondered if there were one world in the universe where the fruit had no worm, and marriage no sorrow' (TW, XXVIII, 234). This perception is central to Hardy's later novels: whilst the value of the characters who remain 'in touch' with Nature is endorsed, the reality of that Nature is seen as tragically flawed and at odds with human aspiration. So the superficial society woman, Felise, 'disliked the woods' as Eustacia disliked Egdon (TW, XXXII, 263), and the woodlands present 'features of a world not familiar to Fitzpiers' (TW, XVII, 155). Yet this Nature, which here places the falsity of social and intellectual pretension, is also rotten, Hardy perceiving in the woodlands 'the Unfulfilled Intention, which makes life what it is', ensuring that the 'leaf was deformed, the curve was crippled, the taper was interrupted; the lichen ate the vigour of the stalk, and the ivy slowly strangled to death the promising sapling' (TW, VII, 83). This seminal passage reveals the gulf between Hardy and the sacramental apprehension of Nature discernible in Ruskin or Hopkins with their doctrine of generic plentitude, the beauty and inscape of trees, and of the tree as symbol of the divine plan. The woodlands around the Hintocks compose rather an anti-pastoral, a symbol of the universal Darwinian process. No human villain is now required in the fiction; in both man and his environment the possibility of happiness is ruled out by the pattern of struggle.

This darkened vision is submerged in *The Well-Beloved*,[39] a fantasy in which, as Pierston reflects, 'the immaterial dream dwarfed the grandest of substantial things, when here, between those three sublimities — the sky, the rock, and the ocean — the minute personality of this washer-girl filled his consciousness' (WB, ii, VIII, 113). The darkness, however, overwhelms *Jude the Obscure*.[40] The striking image of Jude bird scaring in the desolate field is glossed by the subsequent events, so that Sue's outcry against 'Nature's Law' as 'mutual butchery' (JO, v, VI, 327), and Phillotson's argument, that 'Cruelty is the law pervading all nature and society; and we can't get out of it if we would' (JO, v, VIII, 338), are both ratified by the substance of the novel. The meliorist potential within evolution is abandoned, 'the wilfulness of Nature' (JO, iii, VIII, 197) being mirrored by the implacability of human law. The final rejection of the Romantic response to Nature is reached here, as the characters achieve their doom with almost nihilistic determinacy. Nature is no longer held up as ideal, since there is no longer any contrast between the predatory in man and Nature. Indeed the palpable presence of Nature recedes, dwindling to a background against which the deracinated individuals wander hopelessly from one urban centre to another. In no other novel is the birth of modern consciousness so painful, or bought at so terrifying a cost.

Discussion of *Tess of the d'Urbervilles* must begin with Mrs Durbeyfield's exclamation after the seduction: ' " 'Tis nater, after all, and what do please God" ' (TD, XII, 117). The novel is an extended gloss on this claim, and consists in essence of definitions and redefinitions of the term 'Nature'. In 1890, whilst working on the text, Hardy complained that contemporary fiction was devoid of 'treatment which seeks to show

Nature's unconsciousness not of essential laws, but of those laws framed merely as social expedients by humanity' (PW, 127). Never before had Hardy shown his characters so connected, in the Romantic tradition, with Nature — landscape, birds, animals — and yet subject to the agency of sexual selection and struggle, that 'stubborn and resistless tendency' (TD, XXIV, 192), he calls it, through which 'the great passionate pulse of existence, unwarped, uncontorted, untrammelled' (TD, XXV, 199) is made manifest with a force which is 'not to be controlled by vague lucubrations over the social rubric' (TD, XXX, 232). This pervasive motif of 'flux and reflux' (TD, L, 399) embraces natural and human worlds alike: the aristocratic Durbeyfields go down to extinction, to be replaced by the industrial *nouveaux riches* Stoke d'Urbervilles. One strand of the book typifies the life close to Nature as a good, not only at the pantheist climax of the novel at Talbothays, but also in the comparison between the primeval life of Cranborne Chase and the 'Slopes', the bogus house of the Stoke d'Urbervilles, and between Sandbourne, a 'glittering novelty' of a pleasure-city set down in that 'tawny piece of antiquity', Egdon Heath (TD, LV, 426). Even the sluttish field-women experience a species of pantheism in their drunken revels, 'themselves and surrounding nature forming an organism of which all the parts harmoniously and joyously interpenetrated each other' (TD, X, 98) — the oblique sexual reference wholly appropriate, since Car Darch was 'till lately a favourite of d'Urberville's', and repeated at Talbothays, where the 'ready bosoms existing there were impregnated by their surroundings' (TD, XXIV, 189). But it is Tess who is centrally 'Pantheistic as to essence' (TD, XXVII, 213): she is created by Hardy in terms of a proliferation of bird and animal imagery. Her baby is described as a 'bastard gift of shameless Nature who respects not the social law' (TD, XIV, 131), and after his death it becomes clear that the 'recuperative power which pervaded organic nature was surely not denied to maidenhood alone' (TD, XV, 135). What are termed her 'essentially naturalistic' beliefs (TD, XXVI, 205), enable her, in administering the *coup de grâce* to the injured pheasants, to embrace 'Nature's teeming family' (TD, XLI, 324) — a family whose multiplicity is a tenet of evolution theory.

Against the free life of Nature, at Talbothays and elsewhere in Wessex, Hardy counters the claustrophobic life-denying moral law of human society which traps Tess 'like a bird in a springe' (TD, XXXI, 238). The subtly coercive power of opinion — a vital topic for Hardy as for George Eliot — is epitomised in the paradoxically harmless figures of Mercy Chant and the Clare brothers, or by the anonymous landlord who expels the Durbeyfields. Hardy characteristically expands this sense of social conformity as inimical to human potential by introducing repeated blows of fate or chance. Tess is raised in a sequestered spot where 'fatalism is a strong sentiment' (TD, XXIII, 186), and her sufferings lead her to a partial acceptance of the fatalistic convictions 'common to field folk' (TD, XXXII, 244) — for example, Mrs Durbeyfield's reliance on the *Compleat Fortune Teller*, or Dairyman Crick's faith in the son of Conjuror Trendle. The d'Urberville traditions heighten this sense of fatality right up to the seemingly inevitable murder of Alec. After the seduction Tess feels 'she could have hidden herself in a tomb' (TD, XIII, 119), and this image of simultaneous surrender to and flight from the judgement of soceity reverberates into the sleepwalking scene, Alec's concealment in the d'Urberville tombs, and Tess's sleep on the sacrificial stone. Tess is dogged by a long 'family of waiters on Providence' (TD, V, 66), and by the sense that she is 'one of a long row only' (TD, XIX, 165). The movement of the novel vacillates creatively between freedom and naturalness, and repression and subjection: the image of the herons which fly from the Froom Valley finally traduced into the 'Herons' boarding-house, presided over by Mrs Brooks, with her 'enforced bondage to that arithmetical demon profit-and-loss' (TD, LVI, 431).[41]

This double vision is centred in Tess herself; the feeling about her is not so much that she represents the ruin of agrarian England as that her human potential is thrown away through ll choice and circumstance. It is thus vital to read the central act as seduction rather than rape. Early in the novel Mrs Durbeyfield sings 'I saw her lie down in yonder green grove; Come, love! and I'll tell you where' (TD, III, 46); Durbeyfield tells his wife that her ancestors disgraced themselves 'more than any o' us' (TD, IV, 57); Tess shares 'the slight incautiousness' of her race (TD, XIV, 126), and in the Chase is 'stirred to confused surrender awhile' (TD, XII, 117). But this is a surrender intimately bound up with what 'Tis Nater' to do, and related to the survival of the race.

Both of Tess's lovers are cut off from the natural world which she embodies. Tess is startled on first meeting Alec; she had dreamed of 'an aged and dignified face, the sublimation of all the d'Urberville lineaments' (TD, V, 69), but instead she discovers the young man lurking 'behind the blue narcotic haze' (TD, V, 71), as he is later to lurk in the weird allotment scene (TD, L). Like the murderer discussed at Talbothays who has 'brimstone flames around him' (TD, XVII, 147), Alec likes to dramatize himself as a 'lost soul' who was 'born bad' (TD, XII, 112). His role is foreshadowed in the flowers and fruit, the wild ride, and the rose-prick which is to be echoed by Tess's blow with the glove at Flintcomb-Ash. The roses and strawberries at the Slopes are forced, products of the world Alec represents — money, as against Nature or tradition. Alec's transmogrification into a ranting preacher possesses a grim rightness, and he remains a threatening figure to the end.

Angel, though sympathetically conceived, is also denatured. He is at the outset little more than a mouthpiece for *Westminster Review* formulae against the church. When he comes to work for Dairyman Crick he attains a new awareness of life in Nature, just as Mill was rescued from barren rationalism by reading *Lyrical Ballads*. Yet both Angel and Tess are blind at Talbothays. Although Angel adapts to become an active farmer and an adept of Nature, making 'acquaintance with phenomena which he had before known but darkly' (TD, XVIII, 157), his courtship of Tess is still flawed by his idealist cast of mind — Hardy's analysis of this type is careful, precise

and sympathetic. Angel is compulsively led to etherealise Tess
into 'a visionary essence of woman' (TD, XX, 170) whose life
seems to him 'actualised poetry' (TD, XXVI, 205). In the
miasmal atmosphere of Talbothays Tess is also blinded, the
force of passion and natural selection rendering Angel 'god-
like' (TD, XXIX, 222), one with the 'soul of a saint' and the
intellect of a seer (TD, XXXI, 234). In exposing Angel's
vulnerability to convention Hardy shows great art. Thinking
he has found a 'new-sprung child of nature', Angel later con-
demns her as 'the belated seedling of an effete aristocracy'
(TD, XXXV, 275). He had, Hardy notes, 'persistently elevated
Hellenic Paganism at the expense of Christianity; yet in that
civilisation an illegal surrender was not certain disesteem'
(TD, XLIX, 389). He might, 'with more animalism' have been
'the nobler man' (TD, XXXVI, 287), but he is sent away to
Brazil under 'the shade of his own limitations' (TD, XXXIX,
309) to learn through suffering what he cannot through
ratiocination. In a Wordsworthian transformation Clare loses
his 'angelic' nature and gains humanity through suffering.
Intellectual freedom is bound fast to emotional and moral
orthodoxy; the education of suffering, by which Brazil
replaces Cambridge, finally allows Angel Clare to share the
second, doomed honeymoon with Tess.

Thus both men fail Tess and each perverts Nature in his own
way, agents of a dehumanisation which is going on progressively in humanity, through industrialisation and education
and all the weapons of the modern state.

Nonetheless, Nature is not conceived as a simple positive to
be set against this: as he contemplates the mess of the Durbeyfield home Hardy berates Wordsworth and demands to know
where the poet gets his 'authority for speaking of "Nature's
holy plan" ' (TD, III, 51). This outburst lays bare the polar
opposites of the novel, the tensions between views of Nature,
the beneficent Romantic view and the Darwinian perspective
of struggle, intensified by random chance. So Tess, though
seen as a child of Nature in a recognisable Wordsworthian
sense, is told by her young brother that she is an inhabitant of a

blighted star (TD, IV, 61), and falls victim to 'the vulpine slyness of Dame Nature' (TD, XXXVI, 287). Lesser characters, such as the maids, are shown to writhe 'feverishly under the oppressiveness of an emotion thrust on them by cruel Nature's law' (TD, XXIII, 187). The cornered animals in the hayfield, the rats in the cornrick, the dying pheasants — all enforce this interpretation, a patterning which runs counter to the poetic concept of Nature elsewhere; but there is no confusion in Hardy's art: his art is fundamentally evolutionary. Tess's tragedy is the myth of struggle for existence allied to the overpowering weight of the burden of heredity.

The crux in Hardy's imaginative grasp of the theory is defined in the contrast between Talbothays and Flintcomb-Ash, the one offering a Romantic, the other a Darwinian conception of man and the universe. The abundant creativity, fertility and potency of Nature are magnificently captured in the Talbothays scenes. Nevertheless at the centre of the section entitled 'The Rally' stands the mysterious garden scene in which Tess walks almost hypnotically through the weeds towards the sound of Angel's harp:

The outskirt of the garden in which Tess found herself had been left uncultivated for some years, and was now damp and rank with juicy grass which sent up mists of pollen at a touch; and with tall blooming weeds emitting offensive smells — weeds whose red and yellow and purple hues formed a polychrome as dazzling as that of cultivated flowers. She went stealthily as a cat through this profusion of growth, gathering cuckoo-spittle on her skirts, cracking snails that were underfoot, staining her hands with thistle-milk and slug-slime, and rubbing off upon her naked arms sticky blights which, though snow-white on the apple-tree trunks, made madder stains on her skin; thus she drew quite near to Clare, still unobserved of him.

Tess was conscious of neither time nor space. The exaltation which she had described as being producible at will by gazing at a star, came now without any determination of hers; she undulated upon the thin notes of the second-hand harp, and their harmonies passed like breezes through her, bringing tears into her eyes.

(TD, XIX, 161–2)

This passage, subject of so much critical discussion, is double-dyed in Darwinism: the harp merely replaces Troy's sword. As Huxley had explained 'Every plant grows up, flourishes, occupies its square foot of ground, and gives off its fifty seeds; but notice this, that out of this number only one can come to anything; there is thus, as it were, forty-nine chances to one against its growing up; it depends upon the most fortuitous circumstances'.[42] So does the love of Clare and Tess depend upon circumstance, chance and struggle — the meeting again, the missing letter, and so on. Huxley wrote elsewhere how the 'very plants are at war': 'The ground is full of seeds that cannot rise into seedlings; the seedlings rob one another of air and light and water, the strongest robber winning the day, and extinguishing his competitors'.[43] Just so does Tess extinguish Izz Huett and the other 'competitors' for Angel at Talbothays. Within the paradisal setting the immutable law of survival and sexual selection works ineluctably, and with tragic misfiring.[44]

The naked struggle in Nature is masked in the rampant bloom and luxuriance of Talbothays; at Flintcomb-Ash it is unflinchingly exposed. Here the beneficent potential of life is withdrawn in a bleak barren upland setting marked only by white flints in 'bulbous, cusped, and phallic shapes' — the landscape, both outer and inner, of *Jude the Obscure*. The girls are here reduced to wage slaves by undeviating harshness in work and environment, surviving only by sheer will-power and heroic stoicism. The suffering reaches its apotheosis in the threshing scene. The threshing machine which keeps up 'a despotic demand upon the endurance' of the workers is motivated by a steam engine whose operator has 'the appearance of a creature from Tophet'. Whilst 'denizens of the fields served vegetation', he served 'fire and smoke', speaking 'in a strange northern accent' (thus linked with the industrial *nouveaux riches* d'Urbervilles, whose scion, Alec, is shortly to appear), and labouring 'in the service of his Plutonic master'. In this great scene Hardy subsumes many contemporary images of agricultural distress. Under this machine dominance the labourers are subjected to incessant toil, thrown into a 'stupefied reverie' by the humming of the machine, their 'tired and sticky faces' lit up by the 'wrathful' sun, and reminiscing nostalgically about hand-threshing methods (TD, XLVII, XLVIII) — a contrast made sharply in the texture of the novel by the more leisurely and graceful account of the reaping at Marlott in which Tess participates as a nursing mother (TD, XIV).

This is a complex scene. A dehumanising mechanism, which reorders the natural rhythms of the countryside, is clearly implied. Yet there is also a sense of mystery and power in the new farm machinery, as Jefferies had acknowledged when he wrote of 'the wonderful effect' the steam plough made 'with its sweep of smoke, sometimes drifting low over the fallow, sometimes rising into the air in regular shape'. This alien invasion was imbued with a strange poetry for the Victorian sensibility:

> . . . ever-rising on its mystic stair
> In the dim light, from secret chambers borne,
> The straw of harvest, sever'd from the corn,
> Climb'd, and fell over, in the murky air.[45]

The scene combines mystery with suffering, a combination which the total experience of Flintcomb-Ash endorses:

> How it rained
> When we worked at Flintcomb-Ash,
> And could not stand upon the hill,
> Trimming swedes for the slicing-mill. . .
>
> How it snowed
> When we crossed from Flintcomb-Ash
> To the Great Barn for drawing reed,
> Since we could nowise chop a swede.
> ('We Field-Women')

The threat posed by the machine is paralleled by Alec's threat to Tess, the violation of agricultural England by the blow on the mouth. Through a dramatic reversal of meaning the tyranny of the machine becomes a metaphor for the iron law of the universe disclosed by evolution theory. The machine, implying fixed determinism, is thus contrasted with the romantic concept of organic growth; Tess's growth is crushed in the struggle for existence — Spencer's philosophy had never been more direly fulfilled. The final scenes of the novel, at Stonehenge and Wintoncester, merely body out the pessimism of Flintcomb-Ash. The raising of the black flag is Hardy's ironic comment upon the doctrine of the survival of the fittest. Yet simultaneously the drawing together of Angel Clare and Liza-Lu bears witness to the nonhuman creative power of a Nature whose purposes remain unknown to the human community.

Notes

1 C.L. Cline (ed.), *The Collected Letters of George Meredith*, p. 1529.

2 T. Hardy, *Desperate Remedies* (1871), (London, Macmillan, 1971, hereafter cited as DR).

3 T. Hardy, *The Hand of Ethelberta* (1876) (London, Macmillan, 1958, hereafter cited as HE).

4 E. Hardy and F.B. Pinion (eds.), *One Rair Fair Woman* (London, Macmillan, 1972, hereafter cited as RFW), p. 139.

5 T. Hardy, *Under the Greenwood Tree* (1872) (London, Macmillan, 1971, hereafter cited as UGT).

6 F.E. Hardy, *The Life of Thomas Hardy, 1840–1928* (London, Macmillan, 1973, hereafter cited as *Life*), p. 185.

7 H. Orel (ed.), *Thomas Hardy's Personal Writings* (London, Macmillan, 1967, hereafter cited as PW), p. 48.

8 J. Holloway, *The Victorian Sage* (London, Archon Books, 1962), p. 265.

9 R. Morrell, *Thomas Hardy, The Will and the Way* (Kuala Lumpur, University of Malaya Press, 1965), passim.

10 J.V. Davies (ed.), *Study of Thomas Hardy and Introduction to These Paintings* (London, Heinemann Educational, 1973, hereafter cited as STH), p. 31.

11 The major source of this idea, powerfully dramatized in *The Dynasts*, was H. Spencer's *First Principles* (London, Williams & Norgate, 1910).

12 Hardy attended Darwin's funeral; described himself as 'among the earliest acclaimers' of *The Origin of Species*; recommended the *Life and Letters* of Darwin to an intellectually troubled clergyman; and conversed upon evolutionary doctrine (*Life*, 153, 205, 259).

13 C. Darwin, *The Origin of Species*, ed. J.W. Burrow (Harmondsworth, Penguin Books, 1970).

14 *Ibid.*, p. 124.

15 *Ibid.*, pp. 150–1.

16 T.H. Huxley, *Man's Place in Nature and Other Essays* (London, Dent Everyman edn., n.d.), p. 236.

17 *Ibid.*, p. 265.

18 *Ibid.*, p. 292.

19 T. Hardy, *The Return of the Native* (1878) (London, Macmillan, 1958, hereafter cited as RN).

20 Huxley, *op. cit.*, pp. 158–9.

21 T. Hardy, *Tess of the d'Urbervilles* (1891) (London, Macmillan, 1974, hereafter cited as TD), Chapter XX, p. 168.

22 Huxley, *op. cit.*, p. 280.

23 *Ibid.*, p. 323.

24 T. Hardy, *Far From the Madding Crowd* (1874) (London, Macmillan, 1973, hereafter cited as FMC).

25 See R. Jefferies 'The Wiltshire Labourer', in E. Thomas (ed.), *The Hills and the Vale* (1909) (London, Duckworth, 1909), pp. 247–69.

26 Preface to the 1895 edition of FMC.

27 T. Hardy, *A Pair of Blue Eyes* (1873) (London, Macmillan, 1920, hereafter cited as PBE).

28 Huxley, *op. cit.*, p. 242.

29 Darwin, *op. cit.*, pp. 136–7.

30 T. Hardy, *The Trumpet Major* (1880) (London, Macmillan, 1972, hereafter cited as TM).

31 T. Hardy, *Wessex Tales* (1888) (London, Macmillan, 1930, hereafter cited as WT), p. 181.

32 T. Hardy *A Laodicean* (1881) (London, Macmillan, 1968, hereafter cited as AL).

33 T. Hardy, *Life's Little Ironies* (1894) (London, Macmillan, 1964, hereafter cited as LL I), p. 113.

34 T. Hardy, *Two on a Tower* (1882) (London, Macmillan, 1912, hereafter cited as TT).

35 Preface to the 1895 edition of TT.

36 T. Hardy, *The Mayor of Casterbridge* (1886) (London, Macmillan, 1964, hereafter cited as MC).

37 Huxley, *op. cit.*, p. 243.

38 T. Hardy, *The Woodlanders* (1887) (London, Macmillan, 1973, hereafter cited as TW).

39 T. Hardy, *The Well-Beloved* (1897) (London, Macmillan, 1910, hereafter cited as WB).

40 T. Hardy, *Jude the Obscure* (1896) (London, Macmillan, 1973, hereafter cited as JO).

41 Hardy had already utilised this symbol, when Mrs Yeobright, exhausted by her fruitless visit to Clym's cottage, sights a heron flying towards the sunlight: 'Up in the zenith where he was seemed a free and happy place, away from all contact with the earthly ball to which she was pinioned;

and she wished that she could arise uncrushed from its surface and fly as he flew then' (RN, iv, VI, 296).

42 Huxley, *op. cit.*, p. 239.

43 *Ibid.*, pp. 348–9.

44 The moral confusion of Tess's descent into the richness of the vale compares interestingly with Newman's reaction to similar landscapes: 'Who has not felt the irritation of mind and impatience created by a deep, rich country, visited for the first time, with winding lanes, and high hedges, and green steps, and tangled woods, and everything smiling, but in a maze?' ('Discourses on University Education'). Hardy's conception of the garden scene may owe something to George Eliot's analysis of a mind 'made up of moods, where a fruitful impulse springs here and there conspicuously rank amid the general weediness' (*Daniel Deronda*, Ch. XXV).

45 C. Tennyson Turner, *The Steam Threshing-Machine* (1868).

5   Richard Jefferies

I

'I am nothing unless I am a metaphysician', Jefferies once asserted.[1] Whilst in one sense this is true, it is certain that in his work, perhaps supremely within the Victorian period, the central theme is the influence of natural objects upon the human mind. Virtually the whole of his work is concerned with man in Nature; the treatment ranges from agricultural journalism to Nature mysticism, but it is always Nature which provides the key to his *oeuvre*. Despite a degree of esteem and popularity with the reading public, for whom he mediated the ways of the natural world, Jefferies remained a solitary. 'Who loves Nature', he once confessed, 'can make no friends, every one repulses, all seem different' (NB, 217). Thus his books are in essence a record of Jefferies's relations with the forces of Nature. This is his theme in both essay and novel. That it was a theme of profound significance for his contemporaries helps to account for the reputation of Ruskin. But Jefferies remained outside the main currents of Victorian thought, and made no attempt to gain an *entrée* to the literary coteries of the day. He professed at the end of his life that he had 'no desire to make money or excel in anything or fame — All I cared for and desired was the fields, the hills, the sea' (NB, 279). He was viewed by his contemporaries chiefly as a sporting writer on the strength of his most popular works, *The Gamekeeper at Home*[2] and *The Amateur Poacher*;[3] secondly as a farming commentator, through many articles and *Hodge and his Masters*;[4] and thirdly as a boys' writer, for *Wood Magic*[5] and *Bevis*.[6] While these are all important strands of his genius, the purity of his finest work remains largely unrecognised. Especially, the originality of his later novels, and their value both in themselves and for the future of the novel, has generally gone unremarked. Jefferies brought the fiction of Nature to its most lyrical fruition. Properly read, they provide a missing link in the English fictional tradition at a crucial growing point.

II

In *Faust* Nature is called 'the living visible garment of God'. If the deity is understood as a life-force, Jefferies would have concurred. The Nature mysticism of Jefferies's Nature writing is one of the most striking Victorian manifestations of T.E. Hulme's 'spilt religion'. While Jefferies's views of Nature were of some complexity and in any case altered radically during his career, his central position may be summed up as Wordsworthian. Jefferies was enabled through Nature to 'see into the life of things'. In Jefferies, as in Wordsworth, moments of passional communion with the natural world recreate fallen man:

> So build we up the Being that we are;
> Thus deeply drinking-in the soul of things,
> We shall be wise perforce.
> (*The Excursion*, iv, 1264–6)

This sense of man's emotional response to the external world, and the way in which it, as it were, creates individual perceptions, is felt across the century — from the journals of Dorothy Wordsworth to those of Hopkins — but nowhere is it accorded more sustained treatment than in Jefferies. Standing apart from the age, Jefferies crystallised the Wordsworthian tradition and expressed it within new prose forms, whether in essay or novel. This is not to claim him as a conscious Wordsworthian like Hale White. On the contrary Jefferies arrived at his insights largely by that habit of meditation and exalted contemplation of Nature which he described in *The Story of My Heart*[7] as beginning in his teens.

Despite controversy after his death there seems no doubt that Jefferies had rejected Christianity at an early stage of his career. The family background was Low Church, and at one time services were held in the barn at Coate Farm, but Jefferies's own attendance seems to have been spasmodic. The first phase of his writings, dealing as it does with local history or agricultural practice, rarely ventures any comment on religion. When it does, Jefferies is content to frame conventional pieties, as in his piece on 'Village Churches' (1875);[8] here the budding leaves and grass in the churchyard 'may naturally be taken as symbolical of a still more beautiful spring-time yet in store for the soul' (HV, 42). Jefferies was soon to repudiate this stock response, and even came to regard churches as a physical blot on the landscape, 'repellent structures', 'out of proportion and jarring to the eye' compared with the 'curious felicity' and 'good proportion' of oast-houses.[9] On a more serious plane the later essay 'Nature and Eternity' places Christianity in terms of Jefferies's litany of Nature, his own private theology. Man 'must no longer stultify the mind by compelling it to receive as infallible what in the very nature of things must have been fallible to the highest degree'. Rather should man root out 'these primeval, narrow, and contracted ideas; fix the mind upon the sun of the present, and prepare for the sun that must rise tomorrow' (HV, 301). *The Story of My Heart* makes it clear that Jefferies dismisses the notion of a presiding deity, either malefic or beneficent:

There is not the least trace of directing intelligence in human affairs. This is a foundation of hope, because, if the present condition of things were ordered by a superior power, there would be no possibility of improving it for the better in the spite of that power. Acknowledging that no such direction exists, all things become at once plastic to our will.

(SH, 97)

This is crucial to an understanding of Jefferies's philosophy, since his worship of Nature is no atavistic rejection of progress in favour of primitivism. The note sounded in his preface to *Round About a Great Estate*[10] is characteristic in its modulated version of perfectibility. 'In this book some notes have been made of the former state of things before it passes away entirely. But I would not have it therefore thought that I wish it to continue or return. My sympathies and hopes are with the light of the future, only I should like it to come from nature' (RGE, xvi). Indeed, demolition of Christianity was to him a necessary adjunct to human progress. 'Sun Life, Sun and Sea are better than any modern gods', he wrote in 1883, though he added pregnantly, 'they cannot help me' (NB, 129). Early in 1887, in the throes of his last illness, Jefferies rejected the notion that his sufferings were 'inflicted by any God'. 'In misfortune you are not to trace it to a deity. Deity and the whole range of superstition invented because of misery.' Another note added, 'If you must pray or think of prayer, pray for knowledge — for the mind to be opened — that we may get outside our circle of ideas'. At the end of February Jefferies wrote that he was 'giving up' Christianity, the 'vice of self-sanctification', and he appended the cryptic interrogative, 'who wants to live in *their* Heaven?' (NB, 222, 236).[11]

Yet Jefferies was profoundly religious. The form his religious impulses took, in *The Story of My Heart* and elsewhere, is widely known; but some rehearsal of the salient features is essential. Nature was to Jefferies primarily an incomprehensible religion in itself, and not a medium for revealing particular religious doctrine. The rhapsodies of *The Story of My Heart* are concerned primarily with celebration:

Lying down on the grass, I spoke in my soul to the earth, the sun, the air, and the distant sea far beyond sight. I thought of the earth's firmness — I felt it bear me up; through the grassy couch there came an influence as if I could feel the great earth speaking to me. . . . I felt an emotion of the soul beyond all definition; prayer is a puny thing to it, and the word is a rude sign to the feeling, but I know no other.

(SH, 20–1)

The chief problem in any reading of *The Story of My Heart* lies in its terminology: Jefferies is compelled to describe one sphere of being in terms of another. In Kantian terminology the phenomenal is connected, by Jefferies, with the noumenal in a causal relation. The stylistic afflatus which commonly attends this sort of transformation is a pitfall which Jefferies does not avoid. But the effort of linking mind and Nature is of the highest value: through the joyful intercourse with Nature Jefferies foresees an expansion of humanitarian sentiment.

A degree of caution must be exercised in isolating this

increasingly dominant Nature worship from the body of Jefferies's work. Looker's words may act as a salutary reminder
of other aspects of Jefferies:

Jefferies loved the beauty of the English scene but knew too the grim realities
of life on the land: awkward weather, poor crops and poor prices, unfair
foreign competition, and the additional handicaps to the small farmer of
lack of capital, partial equipment, and the increasing difficulty of obtaining
skilled agricultural labour in a changing age. He knew, indeed, only too well,
that while 'the wheat is beautiful, human life is labour'.[12]

The transcendental optimism of the confessorial work *The
Story of My Heart* and some of the essays is founded upon a
clear-sighted appraisal of the hardships of rural life in the
nineteenth century. In *Hodge and his Masters* and elsewhere
Jefferies presents the stark reality of peasant life. He is often
thought of as a 'conservative' who turned 'radical'; but beside
his unadorned portraits even Hardy's peasants exude an aura
of romantic nostalgia. Whilst he allows himself to envy the
open air life of the field-women,[13] there is nowhere in Jefferies
the traditional piety of the Wordsworthian peasants. Indeed,
the indifference of the farm-labourer to his surroundings com-
prises a damning indictment of the life he is compelled to lead:
'The solitude of the hills over whose tops the summer sun
seems to linger so long has not filled the shepherd's heart with
a wistful yearning that must be expressed in verse or music.
Neither he nor the ploughman in the vale has heard or seen
aught that stirs them in Nature' (HM, 81). To the ancient
Wiltshire labourer, as to Michael, the trees and meadows may
become 'part of his life' (HM, 365), but Jefferies presents an
unromantic view most cogently in 'The Labourer's Daily Life'.
Through continual hardship the man 'grows insensible to the
weather, so cold and damp; his bodily frame becomes crusted
over, case-hardened; and with this indifference there rises up
at the same time a corresponding dullness as regards all moral
and social matters'.[14] The *fons et origo* of Jefferies's mysticism
is therefore a bleak asseveration that in 'the life of the English
agricultural labourers there is absolutely no poetry, no colour'
(TF, 97).

Neither is it a valid assumption that Jefferies's ideas on Nature were formulated in an idyllic vacuum away from the denaturing effects of mass industrialism. Living as he did in the environs of Swindon Jefferies witnessed the phenomenon of a railway boom-town at first hand. Indeed, for his early 'Story of Swindon' he mastered many of the technicalities of carriage and engine manufacture, and spoke of the metamorphosis from farmland to commerce with enthusiasm (HV, 104–33). He also greeted the mechanisation of agriculture as a presage of advancement, commenting that the steam plough 'makes the violet yet more lovely' by contrast (FH, 142).

This is not to say that Jefferies was blind to the effects of industrialism. His later work shows a deepening awareness of the clash between the city and Nature. In *Nature Near London*,[15] for example, Jefferies notes how the 'dust of London fills the eyes and blurs the vision'. But, he goes on, 'it penetrates deeper than that. There is a dust that chokes the spirit, and it is this that makes the streets so long, the stones so stony, the desk so wooden' (NNL, 209). Jefferies loved London, finding 'a fascination in it' which could not be gainsaid (NNL, 26), and devoting to it many of his finest essays. But as type of the cash nexus he rejected it utterly, commenting sadly, 'the man of merchandise does not see what the man of the field sees' (NNL, 102).

Alongside the rejection of urban culture Jefferies cast aside academic learning and books. His own reading was highly eclectic, and he concluded that he would never find what he sought in the British Museum reading room.[16] In 'Nature and Books' he amplifies upon this; finding 'from the dandelion that there were no books' he underwent a course of having to 'unlearn the first ideas of history, of science, of social institutions, . . . to unlearn the old mode of thought and way of arriving at things; to take off peel after peel . . . almost remaking the soul' (FH, 32–3). This is no simple anti-intellectualism. It is rather a metaphysical pre-condition of a return to Nature, which again finds affinities with Wordsworth:

Nor less I deem that there are powers
Which of themselves our minds impress;
That we can feed this mind of ours
In a wise passiveness.
('Expostulation and Reply')

Through his iconoclastic and heterodox critique of political economy, mass industrialism, Christianity and literary culture Jefferies freed himself from ideological pressures. His analysis of cultural concepts helped towards this assertion; but primarily his intuitive grasp of the natural world, nurtured since childhood, informs all his writings. He found that where 'men and nature have dwelt side by side time out of mind there is a sense of a presence, a genius of the spot, a haunting sweetness and loveliness'.[17] Man may be unconscious of this harmony; indeed as a child he is closest to natural phenomena, like Bevis and Mark who bathed 'in air and sunbeam, and gathered years of health like flowers from the field' (B, 91). At times Jefferies suggests a total unity between man and the sensible world, explaining 'I have never felt so much myself, an individual, as a part of this whole'.[18] The sportsman of *The Gamekeeper at Home* and *Amateur Poacher* graduated towards mysticism with an inexorable logic of the emotions. He explained in a letter how he used 'to take a gun for nominal occupation, and sit in the hedge for hours'. In a revealing passage he goes on to note that the downs are 'literally teeming with matter for thought. I own that the result has been a profound optimism — if one looks at nature metaphysically'. Metaphysics gains the upper hand by the time of the composition of *The Story of My Heart*, where Jefferies prays that he 'might have the inner meaning of the sun, the light, the earth, the trees and grass, translated into some growth of excellence in myself, both of body and of mind'. Later he longs in a Shelleyan mode to penetrate beyond phenomena, with 'inexpressible desire of physical life, of soul-life' (SH, 60, 77). The beauty of the world is intimately related to bodily human beauty; the one reminds the onlooker of the other, as Jefferies recognised in studying the Venus Accroupie in the Louvre. Returning a third time to this sculpture Jefferies identifies its potent attraction: 'it recalled to my memory the loveliness of nature. Old days which I had spent wandering among deep meadows and by green woods came back to me' (FH, 263).

The first stage of Jefferies's belief in the efficacy of Nature is epitomised in the reaction of Felix Aquila in *After London*;[19] awakening in a bountiful landscape Aquila 'did not question or analyse his feelings', content to let his mind go out 'to the beauty of it' (AL, 242). A wise passiveness pervades such moments, when to be 'beautiful and to be calm, without mental fear, is the ideal of nature', and the 'memory of the green corn, fresh beneath the sun and wind, will lift up the heart from the clods' (LF, 21; OA, 209). A childlike relaxation, a faith in the restorative power of the natural universe, characterise this strand of Jefferies's thought, which is simply codified in the wind's catechism to little 'Sir Bevis': 'How can they know anything about the sun who are never out in the sunshine, and never come up on the hills, or go into the wood? How can they know anything about the stars who never stopped on the hills, or on the sea all night?' (WM, 316).

Contact with physical beauty develops a heightened awareness which results, in Jefferies, in a concept not unlike Wordsworth's 'spots of time' or Eliot's 'still point'. The ardour of Jefferies's empathy with the natural universe obliterates the inexorability of time and causal determinism. For Jefferies 'existence is continuous and knows no break. Neither is there any difference between the days: or, indeed, the years, or the centuries; it is all alike (I mean, to me); and what is meant by dates I could never grasp' (OHC, 40–1). There is recognition of this doctrine as early as *Wood Magic*, when the brook explains to Bevis that 'there is no real division betwixt you and the past', and the wind adds, 'It is all one long today' (WM, 141, 319). But the timeless moment, and the resultant delivery of man from history, is expounded most forcefully in *The Story of My Heart*:

It is eternity now. I am in the midst of it. It is about me in the sunshine; I am in it, as the butterfly floats in the light-laden air. Nothing has to come; it is now. Now is eternity; now is the immortal life. Here this moment, by this tumulus, on earth, now; I exist in it. The years, the centuries, the cycles are absolutely nothing; it is only a moment since this tumulus was raised; in a thousand years more it will still be only a moment. To the soul there is no past and no future; all is and will be ever, in now.

(SH, 41)

Later, Jefferies reiterates, 'Now is eternity, now I am in the midst of immortality' (SH, 50).

The final stage of Jefferies's development is the least suscep-tible of analysis. Jefferies indicates that he has tapped a source of knowledge to which the natural world is the key. Nature therefore finally becomes a means, and ceases to be an end in itself. If *Bevis* may be judged biographically, Jefferies became aware of this teleological interpretation of Nature in boyhood; the famous passage where Bevis lies on the grass and contemp-lates the Zodiac traces the mysterious and resonant origins of this experience (B, 288–9). Once again, the sustained record of Jefferies's mysticism is to be found in *The Story of My Heart*; but elsewhere his essays bear witness to the contemplation of this 'worshipper of earth' (FH, 6). 'Mystery is forever about us' (OA, 44), and even the severe practicality of *The Amateur Poacher* concedes that in Nature 'something that the ancients called divine can be found and felt there still' (AP, 352). Through recognition of the 'vast prodigality' of the phen-omenal world (OHC, 68), Jefferies aspires towards what he terms 'the Beyond'. It is 'as if the great earth sent a mystic perfume — an immaterial influence — through the frame' (OHC, 191). A late essay, 'On the Downs', expresses some of the insights of *The Story of My Heart* in a less rhapsodic style. Space is finite because the mind can conceive of it in a moment of time, and yet the mind itself, Jefferies holds, remains largely unemployed within the confines of modern civilisation (HV, 270–9). Another late piece, 'Nature and Eternity', returns to this need to expand the mind 'till it grasps the idea of the unseen forces which hold the globe suspended and draw the vast suns and stars through space' (HV, 296). Man's relation with these 'unseen forces' receives treatment on an exhaustive scale in *The Story of My Heart*, which is in some respects a less satisfactory vehicle for Jefferies's thought, with its strangely erotic insistence on violent action and the quest for a leader. This nonetheless remains the *locus classicus* for the student of Jefferies's ideas on Nature, showing as it does how Jefferies longed for his soul to be 'enlarged' by going 'straight to the sun, the immense forces of the universe, to the Entity unknown'. At the conclusion of his spiritual autobiography Jefferies reveals how 'an inner and esoteric meaning began to come to me from all the visible universe, and indefinable aspirations filled me' (SH, 74, 125). *The Story of My Heart* left Jefferies finally dissatisfied, both in expression and content. To the end of his life he continued his endeavour to formulate his mysticism more clearly, and specifically to express what he called 'Sun Life' or his 'Lyra Prayer' for a communion which transcended physical bounds. The notebooks are full of references to this endeavour, which never reached fruition, being perhaps an attempt to express the inexpressible. One of the last notes shows Jefferies still grappling with this problem: 'I see the sands and the stars, and the subtle cosmical material far up, and feel through, and the more I touch these the greater grows my soul life and soul touch' (NB, 283).

However, it must be stressed that Jefferies's apprehension of Nature was not soft-centred. Indeed he often seems to imply with Coleridge that 'we receive but what we give And in our life alone does Nature live'. In 'Hours of Spring' the point is made that 'The earth is all in all to me, but I am nothing to the earth' (FH, 5). This 'cruel way of nature' (FH, 217), and all its indifference, is exemplified in manifold contexts, as when Jefferies comments, in Hardyesque vein on Exmoor, that the 'vast moors have simply swallowed up the efforts of man to conquer them'.[20] 'Walks in the Wheatfields' contains a passage on the cruelty of the tropical forests which in some ways pre-empts Aldous Huxley's strictures on Nature mysticism. Jefferies delineates the 'fearful bloodthirstiness that makes a tropical forest so terrible in fact, under its outward show of glowing colour. There, with cruel hawks and owls, and serpents, and beasts of prey, a bird's life is one long terror' (FH, 138).

Notwithstanding the romantic pretensions of *The Story of My Heart*, it is here that Jefferies firmly contradicts any animistic version of the Universe and asserts its non-human otherness. 'All nature', he holds, 'is anti- or ultra-human, outside, and has no concern with man'. Later he iterates that there is 'nothing human in nature or the universe', which he characterises as 'force without a mind' (SH, 54–5). The furthest limits of Jefferies's vision are reached in the late notebooks; it is here, in painful communion with himself, that his final idea of Nature may be discerned. Already in April 1883 he was writing, 'No soul in Nature — no law deducible from it — soul quite separate — could make it much better'. During the four years that remained Jefferies amplified this position, but he is found repeatedly toying with the notion that in Nature 'there are many things, facts — but no reasons'. If 'there is no heart in Nature' then 'Man must supply it'. Jefferies is no philosopher in the strict sense, but he writes here in the Romantic tradition, regarding mind and imagination as the creative sources of life. By entering into sympathy with the physical creation man might be uplifted, but as in Coleridge and the German Idealists the ultimate stress falls upon the creativity of man. It is this capacity which Jefferies sees as 'too large for present knowledge — capacity so great — hence the constant desire for something more, hence perhaps the thought of Something Beyond, the mind that *is* full'. Towards the end, Jefferies sounds an unfamiliar note of despair; as when he protests, 'I have been through nature, I am weary of nature, nothing there'. Two days later he writes with tragic intensity, 'I hate nature. I turn my back on it. Works of man greater than nature — nature works without a mind as the sea sculpturing the cliffs'. Yet the next entry gives a loving description of a whitethroat in the garden; but Jefferies soon reverts to his theme, lamenting his 'absurd veneration of works of nature as if they were divine — no mind in it at all'. These anguished notes go beyond the scope of the novels, which neither explore the implications for man of an indifferent creation nor express coherently the doctrine of the Beyond. The notebooks break off with a profoundly characteristic affirmation: 'I dream of Ideality' (NB, 135, 207, 227, 251, 259, 260, 290). When these entries are perused it becomes clear why a contemporary held that for Jefferies, 'Nature was a beautiful, but destroying angel'.

III

In his fiction Jefferies extricated himself from the formulae of the three-decker with its ramifying sub-plots and host of minor characters, and worked towards a new poetic naturalism. Produced in isolation from the cultural centres, and devoid of that direct relation with an audience which Hardy both enjoyed and deplored, the Jefferies novels constitute a remarkable artistic achievement. They embody a radical response to the problems of writing fiction, and sustained imaginative effort to create a new genre. Writing at a time of debate about the possibilities of the novel Jefferies opted for neither French naturalism nor Jamesian impersonality, but struck out on his own. The extent of this emancipation can be measured by an examination of the early novels, which reveal the young Jefferies travailing within a tradition wholly foreign to his talents.

The first essays in fiction date from 1866, when Jefferies was working as a journalist in Swindon, and take the form of long short stories or novellas. The editor of these juvenile pieces rightly detected in them an 'indication of Jefferies's want of acquaintance with the social life which he attempts to describe'.[21] These callow sketches exhibit little talent and much plagiarism. The most substantial, 'Henrique Beaumont', contains some natural touches, and there are foretastes of *Greene Ferne Farm*[22] in a striking scene in a Druid circle, and in the character of Bob Austin, the miller. Regrettably the plot, involving a mysterious Hindu servant in an English village behaving according Wilkie Collins, reduces the characters to the merest types. Another story, 'Who Will Win?', is a ludi-crously breathless variant of the American tall tale, with a shipwreck scene which both recalls Cooper and looks forward to the artistry of *Bevis*. There is a pause in the narrative when the protagonists, alone on the prairie, express something rec-ognisable as consonant with Jefferies's later ideas, 'an inde-scribable feeling of immensity and a sensation of incapability of corresponding expansion; an idea, an impression of little-ness' (EF, 152). Otherwise these tales are notable only for their vapidity.

The same may be said on a large scale of the first three novels. These are the apprentice work of a writer unfamiliar with the upper reaches of the society which he depicts. Yet they still repay close study for reasons well urged by W.J. Keith: they contain themes 'which are to develop and mature in the later fiction — the contrast between the natural (or "Nature") and the artificial, the tentative presentation of Jefferies' ideal of womanhood, and his general concern for spiritual aspira-tion'.[23] These, and other characteristic concerns of Jefferies, are here enmeshed within the paraphernalia of the Victorian society novel.

Jefferies's first novel, *The Scarlet Shawl*,[24] was noticed in the *Athenaeum*, the *Graphic*, and the *Globe*, though none of the reviewers could praise it, and it made no money either for Jefferies or for Tinsley, the publisher. The plot concerns the amours of Percival Gifford; he is in love with Nora, but becomes enslaved by the seductive Pauline Vietri, while Nora gets involved with other suitors. The development of the story is conventional, though the loss of two letters at crucial points in the drama may be a shadowing forth of that more famous lost epistle from Tess to Angel (SS, 263, 278). The main interest lies in those few moments of heightened awareness experienced by the characters in which forces beyond them take possession, as when Nora plays the organ, 'playing, not from the mind, but from unconscious cerebration', an emotion Jefferies later reverts to as she walks by the sea, 'utterly uncon-scious of everything but the sounds of the waves — listening to the great organ of nature'. This again suggests Hardy — the organ-scene of *Desperate Remedies*,[25] published three years earlier. The power of the sea, and its deployment as a metaphor for human passion, is reinvoked in the *dénouement* when wind and sea mirror 'a crisis of nature — the throes of a great being' (SS, 93–5, 273). Percival, though he is woodenly conceived, is possessed of qualities which will be fully articulated in later protagonists. The grandeur of London eclipses the 'littleness' of his soul for a moment of revelatory disclosure, and the sky, clouds and water 'filled him with a sense of a higher life. If he could only drink in this beauty always he should be immortal' (SS, 159). He is differentiated from the vapid parliamentarian, Sir Theodore Stanley, precisely by his excitement at 'the glories and beauties of nature — of the stars, the sea, the powers of art' (SS, 255). The praise of the multitude, he recognises, is nothing compared with 'the fresh breeze of the downs, or the salt bracing air of ocean' (SS, 208). *The Scarlet Shawl* does not aspire to the grandeur of the three-decker, and the narrative consequently has a degree of economy. But the inspirational passages are grafted awkwardly on to the foreign body of a society plot, with predictable results.

In *Restless Human Hearts*[26] Jefferies grapples with a scale and amplitude proper to the three-decker. Whilst it remains true that here again he was dealing with topics of which he knew next to nothing, the real Jefferies begins to announce himself in the depiction of man in relation to Nature. At the outset he remarks that so many 'now dwell in an atmosphere of smoke and a scenery composed of brick walls, that the existence of persons whose whole being vibrates to the subtle and invisible touch of Nature seems almost incredible' (RHH, I, 2–3). Such a person is the heroine, Heloise Lestrange, who lives in the downs with her aged father, a modest man who 'lived in accord with nature' (RHH, I, 22). Like the young Jefferies, it is her wont to climb up 'the steep-sided downs, and choosing a hollow sheltered from the wind, lay down upon the soft thymy turf' (RHH, I, 33; see RHH, I, 229). This prelapsarian idyll is blighted when Heloise marries Louis, a young *roué* who soon tires of his innocent young wife and takes up with her half-sister, the passionate Carlotta. Once again Jefferies involves himself in the sensation plot, suitably garnished with violence and *nostalgie de la boue*. On the model of Scott and Thackeray, Jefferies introduces a second pair of lovers, Georgiana Knoyle and Neville Brandon, and the characterisation, though perfunctory, is of some interest. Neville is a dreamy introvert, 'ever seeking to discover the true relation of man to nature' (RHH, I, 182), in contrast to his battle-scarred brother Noel; and Georgiana, a powerful and statuesque figure, is the archetypal modern woman entering upon a three-year 'trial' marriage with Neville.[27] This relationship is fraught with difficulties, since Georgiana is a headstrong extrovert, whilst Neville knows 'the mysterious awe which falls upon the mind in the near presence of its Creator', and merges pantheistically into 'the life of the tree, of the grass . . . finally of the broad earth underneath' (RHH, II, 290, 227). Once more the theme of the intuitive recognition of natural forces and their regenerative power in the modern world is submerged beneath a labyrinthine plot, and the characters remain little more than gestures. Heloise, abandoned by Louise, becomes haplessly involved with Noel. There is a finely wrought scene in which they take a boat and sail downstream, the physical and psychological treatment suggesting that Jefferies may have read *The Mill on the Floss* — he knew *Scenes of Clerical Life* well.[28] The third volume, after a violently improbable sequence of somewhat Dickensian incident,[29] contrives the marriages of the two couples and concludes strangely with Neville building a 'temple of Nature' on the downs (RHH, III, 292–5). This is not an adult novel; yet some advances may be traced in Jefferies's handling of his themes.

World's End,[30] the last of the early trilogy, is also the most ambitious; but once again its successes are peripheral to the structure, the author becoming bogged down by the length and complexity of the story. The subject was broached by Jefferies in a letter to Tinsley:

The story centres round the great property at Birmingham, considered to be worth four millions, which is without an owner. A year or two ago there was a family council at that city of a hundred claimants from America, Australia, and other places, but it is still in Chancery. This is the core, or kernel, round which the plot develops itself. I think, upon perusal, you would find it a striking book, full of original ideas.

Tinsley published the book, but the inevitable comparison with the victims of Chancery in *Bleak House* exposes the poverty of Jefferies's imaginative capacity to handle this type of plot.

Nevertheless, this is a richer and more rewarding novel than its predecessors. Book I, entitled 'Facts', is a graphic description of the growth of the city of Stirmingham out of a swamp — an exercise from which Jefferies benefited when he wrote the masterly opening of *After London*. In *World's End* he shows how a great city grows up bringing both progress and crime. Indeed the formation of the community here accords with Freud's theory of the primal crime, and the mark of Cain is placed upon the warring families at the outset, finally resulting in a plan to murder all the claimants at one blow. In Book II, 'Persons', the focus shifts to World's End in the downs, and to Aymer Malet, his fiancée Violet Waldron, and her aged father Jason. Malet is the Jefferies figure, reading voraciously and full of curiosity 'to understand the stars that shone so brilliantly upon those hills — the phenomena of Nature with which he was brought in daily contact', eager to translate that 'mystic language' (WE, II, 11–12). There is stress here upon fate and necessity in a grimly Hardyesque vein, and on their wedding day Violet's father is murdered. Through a journalistic career similar to Jefferies's own, Aymer Malet is drawn into the maw of the Baskette claims and finally proves the legitimacy of the Waldrons' entitlement to the fortune. The events leading up to the mining of the theatre holding all the claimants from America, and the clumsy engagement of the two plots, make the last third of the novel unwieldy; but there are some scenes of real imaginative power — Esther Herring's visit to the deserted Waldron house in a snowstorm, for instance, and the decay in Nature after the loss of the estate, are presented with a stark directness which Hardy might have admired (WE, II, 140–1, 148). The tormented personality of Lady Lechester, a figure familiar enough to the adept in Victorian fiction, is vividly dramatized in terms of her environment, notably in her moody haunting of the pool at Kickwell Pot which is finally to claim her: 'In winter a weird and sinister spot, when the trees were bare and dark, the fir trees gloomy and black, when the snow lodged in great drifts upon the Downs, and the murmur of the river rose to a dull, sullen roar, resounding up the strange, natural funnel' (WE, III, 156).[31] The characterisation of Aymer, Violet and Lady Lechester, and the descriptive writing, bear witness to a deepening of Jefferies's talent. The problem for him was to invent a suitable form for his real subject — the interrelation of man and Nature.

Before examining the mature novels in which he found this form, it will be valuable briefly to consider Jefferies's short rural tales. Whilst these are little more than sketches, even in the early attempts Jefferies displays a mastery which is absent from the first novels and which has to do with consonance of style and content. The mode of presentation sometimes makes it difficult to differentiate between fiction and heightened journalism exemplified in such pieces as 'John Smith's Shanty' (TF), 'One of the New Voters' (OA), and many chapters of *Hodge and his Masters*. Two tales of 1876, 'Gaudy as a Garden' and 'The Midsummer Hum',[32] rehearse a single situation, the involvement of a humble village girl with a young man of higher class. This type of *imbroglio* was staple fare of current melodrama, yet Jefferies contrives a freshly individuated version, and in both stories permits a happy ending. In 'Gaudy as a Garden' the rough but genuine love of John Young, a labourer, for Molly Green, is threatened by the intervention of the local farmer's son who is attracted by the gay apparel affected by Molly, 'a bad'un' according to the village women. After a lively sketch of the village 'Feast' with its attendant gypsies and country musicians, the *éclaircisse-ment* reveals that Molly's clothes are bought from the relat-ively innocent profits of poaching, to which 'Master William' has amorously turned a blind eye. The situation is comfortably resolved by William's father, who arranges for John and Molly to marry and work in his employ. Despite the received wisdom of the format there are fine individual touches, such as the old man who eats all day to spite his wife. ' "cos she becrutches I" '. In 'The Midsummer Hum' the same *donnée* is explored, this time the intervention coming from the landed gentry. The midsummer haymakers are amused to see a young gentleman from the squire's, 'in light trousers, a velveteen jacket, and straw hat', coming to join their labours. Mr Martin is drawn to the field by his admiration of Lucy Luckett, a 'thoughtless, impulsive creature, full of life, joyous as the sunshine', and once again there is an affronted suitor of her own class. Whilst dallying in an assignation with Mr Martin, Lucy is shocked to her senses by the sight of her true lover, drunk and heartbroken, falling into the undergrowth. Martin, recognising the true nature of the relationship, arranges that the couple shall marry. Jefferies illuminates this tiny drama with many authentic touches, such as the story of the fiddler who fiddles to his wife on her death-bed. He also lightly brushes upon social reform, as when the garrulous mason tells of his days as a ploughboy, or when Martin talks to the local farmer 'on the agricultural labourer question', or the vicar speaks loftily of the 'labouring class'. At a deeper level the title, which refers to the indeterminate sound of Nature at mid-summer, provides a *leitmotif* which pervades the story, placing the human within a natural context. The tale ends suggestively: whilst Lucy and her lover prepare to settle down together in the village, 'Mr Martin went back to London, riding on his wheel [i.e. bicycle]'. Many of Jefferies's over-riding themes are here subsumed in miniature: the organic village community set against the mechanical and urban. They had appeared earlier in the grimmer sketch called 'A True Tale of the Wiltshire Labourer' (TF, 259—85).

Jefferies's later rural tales, grouped under the titles 'The Field Play' and 'Bits of Oak Bark' (LF, 22–52), all date from 1883. They show marked development, for where Jefferies has earlier endorsed the prevailing structure of country life, he now exposes it to a radical critique. Stylistically, also, these later pieces often display a new fluidity and originality. The first part of 'The Field Play', 'Uptill-a-thorn', is founded on a plot which replicates 'The Midsummer Hum'; indeed, the seduction theme echoes some of the most potent social undercurrents of the age, as works ranging from *The Red Barn* to *Adam Bede* and *Tess* amply illustrate. A lissome peasant girl dallies with the men, to the annoyance of the other field-women, and attracts the attentions of the roughest labourer and of the farmer's son. But in this instance the idyll is flawed and the girl ruined. An easy simplicity is the keynote, but the felt life of the lower agricultural orders is finely rendered. The girl, Dolly, is at once characterised as she carelessly tears her dress on a thorn hedge on the way to hay-making. Her 'mingled poverty and carelessness — perhaps rather dreaminess — disappeared when once you had met the full untroubled gaze of those beautiful eyes'. Dolly possesses the 'most seductive' of female characters, 'yielding, sweet, and gentle'; this quality proves her downfall, for, despite her charm for 'Mr Andrew', it is Big Mat with whom she becomes entangled. They disappear from the harvest field, and when Dolly reappears she is permanently subdued. She lives with Mat and bears his child, whilst he alternates between alcohol and violence, finally hitting Dolly and putting out one of her eyes. When Mr Andrew returns to the village after an absence he does not recognise his former sweetheart, 'this ugly, repellent creature' whom he fends off with a half-crown. There is no dramatic conclusion: life drifts on, 'but Dolly was like a violet over which a waggon-wheel had rolled'. With a delicate symbolism Jefferies concludes, 'The thorn had gone deep into her bosom'. The sombre desolation here in the picture of Dolly's altered state presents a truth such as is to be found fully worked out in Cresseid's final meeting with Troilus in Henryson's poem;

Jefferies's vision, though rustic and unheroic, is scarcely less moving in its anguish at the ruins of time.

The second story, 'Rural Dynamite', is less successful. Here Jefferies sacrifices a taut narrative for passionate propaganda on behalf of the rural poor. The plot concerns an outbreak of rick burning, which, being finally laid at the door of Big Mat, leads Dolly's brother to drink himself to death whilst Dolly ends her days in the workhouse. Jefferies's digression is humane and outspoken, and marks a shift in his social thought. But a comparison with Faulkner's 'Barn Burning' shows what can be achieved on this theme without authorial intrusion.

A masterful lucidity is envinced in 'The Acorn Gatherer', the first part of 'Bits of Oak Bark'. The gatherer is a boy who is discovered asleep in the fields by his grandmother and soundly beaten for his pains. Some days later he is sent on an errand and disappears, his body finally being fished out of the canal. This rural drama is encapsulated in the opening emblems: 'Black rooks, yellow oak leaves, and a boy asleep at the foot of the tree'. The rooks at the acorns, Jefferies remarks, are the 'happiest creatures in the world', and this is transferred to the boy united with Nature, his forehead fixed in a frown 'like the grooves in the oak bark'. When the boy is found in the canal Jefferies asks, 'Does anyone sorrow for the rook, shot, and hung up as a scare crow?' After the old woman had forcibly awakened him with her stick Jefferies reveals his history: he is the illegitimate son of the old woman's daughter, now dead; as his drunken father neglects him he is at the mercy of this severe harridan. In death, as in life, he is neglected; a dealer thinks there is an object in the water, but 'did not want any trouble', so passes by; a barge-woman who sees the little corpse sails placidly on to the public house; when a labourer ultimately recovers the body the old lady feels 'no twinge: she had done her duty'.

The fluid poetics of *Greene Ferne Farm* are without parallel in earlier English fiction. In a letter to Tinsley Jefferies had explained of an earlier unpublished novel, that the 'scenery is a description of that found in this county, with every portion of which I have been familiar for many years. The characters are drawn from life, though so far disguised as to render easy identification impossible. I have worked in many of the traditions of Wiltshire, endeavouring, in fact, in a humble manner to do for that county what Whyte Melville has done for Northampton and Miss Braddon for Yorkshire.' This might apply equally to *Greene Ferne Farm*, except that Jefferies has here penetrated far beyond his exemplars, even the Hardy of *Under the Greenwood Tree.* The novel constituted a growing-point both for his own later work and for that of others.

The subject-matter is conventional enough: Valentine Browne and Geoffrey Newton are friendly rivals for Margaret Estcourt, the daughter of the widowed owner of Greene Ferne Farm; and her friend May Fisher is wooed by the Reverend Felix St Bees. The rivalry of the young men culminates in a gun battle, and the upshot is a double wedding, with Valentine renouncing his claim to Margaret. The protagonists are supported by a range of ballad figures, from the bluff Squire Thorpe, through the grasping miller Fisher, and the knowing farmers Ruck and Hedges, down to Jabez the shepherd. Such a gallery, with variants, was stock fictional material. It is Jefferies's power, through his comment on this society and his inwardness of tone, and through his new poetic narrative procedure, to transmute this worn-out matter into a striking work of fiction.

The narrative consists of a discontinuous set of dramatic scenes of an almost symbolist quality. Each chapter thus leads the story forward, whilst enabling Jefferies to jettison the three-decker conventions. The first chapter, 'Up to Church', is a superb example of his art. The action is introduced by means of the choric figures of Hedges and Ruck. They have met every Sunday for the last thirty years, wearing away the moss on the churchyard wall. Ruck, 'shaped something like one of his own mangolds turned upside down', wears costume which makes

manifest his rise in society: smock (peasant), breeches (yeoman), beaver hat (landowner). The scene is pastoral,
dominated by the rounded ridge of the Downs, with the larks
singing, and water glistening; but this atmosphere is soon
modified by the pigs grunting and gobbling at the base of the
wall. The congregation arrives whilst the choirboys play
among the tombstones. The plot is casually inserted into the
conversation, and Jefferies parades his characters before us,
from Shepherd Jabez, who sucks a thrush's egg to clear his
throat, to the young ladies and Mrs Estcourt, the widowed
owner of the farm. Inside the cold church, 'a rather superior
tomb', Jefferies delineates a subtle class structure, noting that
'it was possible to tell the rank of the congregation as they
entered, by the length of time each kept his hat on after getting
through the door'. The deathly church, though hallowed by
ancient usage, stands in stark contrast to the 'soft warm air,
the green leaf and bud without'. In the ruminations of Squire
Thorpe during the sermon Jefferies accurately mirrors a dis-
integrating agricultural society, the squire regretfully noting a
'general divorce, as it were, of the people from authority'.
Finally the focus shifts to the heroine, Margaret Estcourt, a
natural and attractively simple girl. As the congregation
emerge into the sun they are amused to see Jabez, chased by the
choir boys, collapse among the pigs, the chapter closing with a
subtle compound of sacred and profane. Jefferies, in announ-
cing his theme, depicts his society with a pointed wit that may
be fairly called Chaucerian.

   The second, slighter chapter, 'The Sweet New Grass', serves
to develop the love theme, and introduce the remaining chapters. After an inconclusive encounter between Geoffrey and
Margaret in the woods, Jefferies introduces the idealistic Felix
St Bees. Although possessed of private means St Bees acts as
curate in the nearby conurbation of Kingsbury; in the course
of his duties 'the little black figure in black penetrated everywhere without risk'. In the image of Kingsbury Jefferies incor-
porates into his fictional world the pressures which will destroy the rural economy. He does not fall into the trap of

imbuing the country with too great a weight of paradisal tonings: man's fallibility is exemplified at a harmless comic level by the drunken old soldier, Augustus Basset, and as malignant evil by Fisher the miller.

Chapter III, 'The Nether Millstone', introduces Fisher at the mill house. At ninety he sits passively in his beehive chair, and it is part of the man that natural beauty 'touched him not'. His heart is likened to his own millstone crushing the seed, and Jefferies mentions in passing 'the carter whom he had partly blinded by a blow from his whip-handle . . . the ploughboy he rode over and lamed; the fogger whose leg he broke with a kick', and Peggy, seduced then married off at Fisher's expense, and his own family, all dead except for May. When Felix St Bees arrives to ask for May's hand he is beaten out of the house. The second episode, in which Geoffrey Newton and St Bees visit the poor of Kingsbury, in its vision of an urban hell, is germane to Jefferies's purpose. The men thread their way through children who 'with naked feet, played in the gutter among the refuse of the dust heap, decayed cabbage, many curs, and filth'. 'At the end of a new street hastily "run up cheap" and "scamped", they found a large black pool, once a pond in the meadows, now a slough of all imaginable filth'. The unemphatic tone, with its fleeting echo of Bunyan, serves to focus attention upon the alienation between man and his environment implicit in an uncontrolled and indiscriminate surrender to industrialism. In one of the jerry-built houses they visit a young man who has been injured in a factory accident. The man, suffocating in a room whose windows are made not to open, had earlier been a shepherd on the downs, and ruminates sadly about his present fate. The effects of mass labour and the factory system are touched in with a fine compressed humanity.

Chapter IV, 'The Wooden Bottle', reverts to the rural scene. In his recreation of a hay-making scene Jefferies shows considerable psychological power. As the labourers have struck Mrs Estcourt enlists the help of the gentry to bring in the hay, under the bibulous direction of the old soldier Augustus Basset. The ensuing debate gives rise to some telling comedy:

'. . . they have only struck work on my place, thinking, no doubt, that, being a woman, I must give way — will be obliged to do so, and some of them are not able. Many have called and begged me not; and Mr Thorpe says the same. Yet I don't like it. We have always been on good terms with the men.'

'O yes, you pets 'em up,' said Augustus, 'just like so many children; and, of course, they ain't going to work for you.'

'The struggle of capital and labour,' began Felix learnedly, then a sudden jolt of the springless wagon threw him off balance, and he had to cling to the sides.

'O, mind the gatepost!' cried Mrs Estcourt, in some alarm.

(GFF, 74)

The hay-lifting acts as a catalyst to the rival lovers, each of whom tries to out-pitch the other, virtually burying the luck-less Augustus on the cart. As the heat of the amorous contest subsides the party reclines under the hedge and listens to Felix reciting poetry. A debate on metre is cut short by the return of the recalcitrant labourers. On the way back to the farm the party falls in with a group of mowers, and both Geoffrey and Valentine try their hand with the scythe — playing at what is to others a whole way of life. The mower explains that the design of the sythe has deteriorated in his lifetime: ' "I minds when [the handles] wur made of dree sart of wood, a main bit more crooked than this yer stick, and sart o' carved a bit; doan't 'ee see? It took a chap a week zumtimes to find a bit a 'wood as ud do. But, bless 'ee, a' moast anything does now." ' As they walk away, Felix reflects upon the decline of ancient crafts in an elegiac vein which links Jefferies here with Hardy, Morris and George Bourne.

The emotional centre of the novel lies in the sequence of chapters, 'Evening', 'Night', and 'Dawn', in which Geoffrey and Margaret get lost and spend the night together on the downs. Jefferies treats this material with a new poetic inten-sity: the image of the man traversing the empty downs in 'Evening', for instance, creates memorably an impression of the vastness of the hills and the littleness of man. It is an instance of that bird's-eye-view point which Hardy often adopts also, the mind attuned with Nature microscopically

suddenly lifting itself out and beyond, creating a subtle interplay of feeling between characters, setting and narrator. On
the return journey Margaret and Geoffrey are surrounded by
mist and their antagonism melts away. They take refuge in a
dolmen whose environs recall 'the spirits haunting such magic
circles of the Past'. Margaret feels a 'sense of loneliness', as the
silence of the vast expanse around weighed upon her'. Jefferies adumbrates the mystery hanging over this primeval
edifice, whose elemental stones suggest both a connexion with
ancient Britain and the life and youth of the lovers. There is no
forced melodrama, but a sensitive poetic realism which goes
beyond what can be spoken:

'I must rest,' she said, and went back to the trees and sat on a boulder.
Opposite, the pale glow in the east shot up into the sky; as it rose it became
thinner and diffused. Slowly the waning moon came up over the ridge of the
distant hill, whose top was brought out by the light behind it, as a well-
defined black line against the sky. Vast shadows swept along and filled the
narrow vales — dark as the abyss of space; the slopes that faced eastwards
shone with a faint grey. The distorted gibbous disk lifted itself above the edge
— red as ruddle and enlarged by the refraction: a giant coppery moon, weird
and magical. The forked branches of a tree on the hill stretched upwards
across it, like the black arms of some gibbering demon.
'Look round once more,' he said, as the disk cleared the ridge. 'Perhaps
you may recognise some landmark, and I will run and bring assistance.'
'And leave me here alone!' reproachfully.
'No, I will never leave you.'

(GFF, 118–9)

Jefferies looks with almost scientific particularity at Nature
here, with the distortion and refraction that the mist produces;
the unusually appropriate 'gibbous' and 'ruddle', the echoing
of 'gibbous' in 'gibbering', and the clinging to human contact
— all this is executed with tact and immediacy. When Margaret finally agrees to sleep inside the dolmen, with Geoffrey
on guard outside, Jefferies notes 'her heart was turning
towards him'. The dawn scene confirms this, in its vivid
dramatization of man alone with Nature:

The mist drove rapidly along; after a while gaps appeared over-head, and
through these he saw broad spaces of blue sky, the colour growing and

deepening. The gaps widened, the mist became thinner; then this, the firs
wave of vapour, was gone, creeping up the hillside behind him like the
rearguard of an army.

Out from the last fringe of mist shone a great white globe. Like molter
silver, glowing with a lusciousness of light, soft and yet brilliant, so large and
bright and seemingly so near — but just above the ridges yonder — shining
with heavenly splendour in the very dayspring.

(GFF, 130

Geoffrey's consciousness is here adapted to, and yet somehow creating what he sees: he now possesses the girl, and the
ensuing narrative is only concerned to reproduce the union in a
socially acceptable form. Here the loose structure which Jefferies uses pays off, the novel naturally opening out into this
lyrical climax. Yet this is balanced by dramatic irony, the
soaring joy of the lovers being pierced by the voice of earth, ir
the person of Jabez the shepherd, who claims to have been
misled by ' "The Ould Un hisself" ' who ' "abides in thuck
place wur them gurt stwoanes be" '. The primal energies, both
Christian and pagan, of the places are suitably caught, though
not insisted upon in the way that Hardy presses home the
significance of Stonehenge.

As the novel follows the cycle of the seasons, so the rivalry
displayed in the hay-making is balanced by a similar outburst
in Chapter VIII, 'A-Nutting'. The party goes on a nutting
expedition in the autumnal sun, and Margaret shows to great
advantage with the 'excitement, the *abandon* of the moment'
Geoffrey, wrought to a pitch of anger by jealousy, wrenches at
a stubborn bough and breaks it, leaving the nuts scattered on
the grass. He is at odds with himself, and at this juncture, out
of sympathy with Nature. Once again the slightness of inci
dent reveals the more tellingly the psychological currents, the
feelings exposed by the rustic minutiae. But in Andrew Fisher
the miller, all feeling is dead; and in the ensuing chapter
'Gleaning', Jefferies depicts the scene around his corpse. He is
shown seated as always in his beehive chair in the beams of the
setting sun. The 'wearyful women' tramping home from the
gleaning catch a glimpse of the old rogue in his accustomed
position, and his meanness is mirrored in theirs. But in their

case the life of toil has produced its ill effects: 'Their forms had lost all semblance to the graceful curve of women; their faces were hard, wrinkled, and angular, drawn with pain and labour.' They are blind to the beauty of Nature, 'for their hearts were pinched with poverty'. They drop a curtsey to the old man, cursing him beneath their breath. Only later is it revealed that he is long dead, his home stripped bare by two ancient harridans. The reflection of a bloody sunset enters his chamber and evokes the image of the Day of Judgement. Jefferies reverts here to St Bees who is riding over the downs to make peace with Fisher. En route he comes upon a crowd of workmen excavating an ancient skeleton, the *disjecta membra* being unceremoniously dumped into a bucket to be snuffled by a donkey while the men retire to a hostelry. Unearthed with the skeleton is a piece of brass with the motto *Gaudeamus*. When the curate discovers the corpse of the miser and the locals hail the news with delight, the tag is imbued with a new meaning. The miser's death is metamorphosed from literary cliché into a scene of delicacy and realism. Even in the looted house, the shepherd who accompanies St Bees is pleased to pocket a guinea dropped by the crones who have stripped the place bare: Fisher's qualities have not died with him.

The repressed animosity of the rivals erupts in Chapter X, 'A Fray', in which they engage in a shooting match through a double mound hedge. The issue is never really in doubt, and the final 'Feast' chapter sees the respective couples, Geoffrey and Margaret and Felix and May, married off and the whole rural community celebrating in Mrs Estcourt's barn. This bucolic finale bows to the traditions of the rustic tale, but it also orchestrates those themes of fertility and fruition which are as vital here as in *The Winter's Tale*. As if to reinforce its cyclic form the novel ends as it began with the choric persons of Hedges and Ruck arguing their property rights, and Jabez alcoholically poised astride a stile, giving voice to an ancient ballad.

The infusion of a poetic sensibility into the matter of the rural tradition, which characterises *Greene Ferne Farm*, is

Jefferies's major contribution to the art of the novel. In its successors he was more daringly experimental in abandoning traditional requirements of story-telling and characterisation, but *Greene Ferne Farm* exists in its own right as an impressive artistic achievement.

Jefferies worked on *The Dewy Morn*[33] over a period of five or six years. It existed first under the title *Wild Thyme* (FF, 178), though it was prematurely offered to the publishers in 1878 under the later title. Bearing in mind Jefferies's copious output a lengthy gestation argues deep personal involvement in the novel. Some hints of the earlier version are obtained from Jefferies's note of May 1879: 'Excise evil characters, make all "sweet" and pleasant'. Melodramatic events were to be expunged. A little earlier he had announced his central intention: 'Atalanta. Take a classic name: heroine so interesting as to be far more interesting than the plot'. One Swinburnian name was dropped in favour of another, but the conception of the heroine remained crucial. In his creation of Felise Goring Jefferies unequivocally justifies his abandonment of the social novel of his predecessors. As he reminds himself in a note eighteen months later, 'there must be no Realism round her'. The tangle of old and new plots is uncovered in a long note at the end of 1881, but the heart of the matter, a 'girl out of doors and the romance of the meadows', is now divined by Jefferies. This was the period of *The Story of My Heart*, and much of the intensity of vision spilled over from autobiography to novel. This intensity suffuses the great bathing scene, which Jefferies was planning in the summer of 1883. It is to be a 'Poem of Love' centring upon Felise as a 'Goddess of Nature'. Jefferies insists upon the pagan nature of his character: 'Felice and the classics because of the sun, and stream, love of the Greeks'. The discontinuity of narrative begun with *Greene Ferne Farm* is to be further cultivated: 'To go on by central incidents and explain any as progress'. In the completed novel Jefferies requires his readers to 'let me write my scenes one after another, and supply the connecting links for me out of your own imagination'. The density of plot notation which ensues in the notebooks is mainly concerned with detail of action, though once again Jefferies's key ideas — on female beauty, chance and circumstance, and rural poverty — are adumbrated. The vision and revision which a perusal of the notebooks reveals destroys the myth of Jefferies as artless rural journalist (NB, 41, 32, 103, 125, 145, 147–53). In the groundwork for *The Dewy Morn* there lies a challenge to the hegemony of the Dickensian novel; the rural tradition of the Howitts and even of *Adam Bede*, is transfigured by a new intensity and compelled to yield an imaginatively realised truth to inner life.

The opening chapters attain a rare hieratic quality. Felise, a young girl living in the depths of the country with her uncle, Mr Goring, climbs to the top of the downs, attuning herself, like Jefferies, to the benediction of Nature. She is climbing, like the women of ancient Greece, to worship the dawn: 'She was gathering from sunlight, azure sky and grassy fields, from dewy hills and all the morning, an immense strength to love' (DM, I, 6). Jefferies tempers these raptures with touches of living colour. Felise is easily diverted: 'An ash-branch stood out to bar her path. She stopped and touched it, and counted the leaves on the sprays; they were all uneven' (DM, I, 2). The delicate actuality of her shifts of mood is thus a modifying factor in the 'mysticism' of her Nature worship, just as her spiritual ascent is rooted in earthly reality: 'Up — from thyme-bunch to thyme-bunch, past gray flat flints; past rusty ironstone fragments . . . up, straight for the summit' (DM, II, 8). She climbs, in true Romantic style, to gain contact with the Universal: 'to have more of herself — to have the fullness of her own existence'. In this way she attains bodily perfection: 'The wind, the sun, the fields, the hills — freedom, and the spirit which dwells among these, had made her a natural woman' (DM, II, 10–11). Despite these heightened emotions it is typical of Felise that she fails to see the sunrise. Like Eustacia Vye she is restlessly impulsive, and so full of emotional currents that, as Jefferies puts it, 'she loved before she had seen the object of her love' (DM, III, 17). The object she

fixes upon is a local tenant farmer, Martial Barnard, and as
Felise descends the hills the two meet accidentally. Barnard,
who is on horseback, does not yet reciprocate Felise's love; a
broken engagement to an heiress in the nearby town of Maasbury has left him cynical and uninvolved. Through gesture,
such as Felise's gently stroking the horse, Ruy, Jefferies conveys subtle undercurrents of emotion. The nervous vitalism of
the horse acts as a totem of the flow of desire in a scene which
centrally anticipates Lawrence:

At a touch Ruy halted. She looked up at him; he carefully avoided her glance.
The horse, growing restless, began to move again; again, for courtesy's sake,
he was compelled to check him. Not a word had been spoken while this show
was proceeding.

Barnard's face grew hot with impatience, or embarrassment, or a sense
that he was doing wrong in some manner not at the moment apparent.
Sideways, she saw his glowing cheek. It only inflamed her heart the more,
the bright colour, like the scarlet tints in a picture, lit up his face. Next he
controlled himself, and forced his features and attitude to an impassive
indifference. He would sit like a statue till it pleased her to let him go. Ruy
pulled hard to get his neck free that he might feed again.

She stopped and gathered him some grass and gave it to him. Twice she fed
him. Barnard remained silent and impassive. Still not a word between them.
The third time she gathered a handful of grass; as she rose her shoulder
brushed his knee. She stood there, and did not move. Her warm shoulder just
touched him, no more; her golden hair was very near. She drew over a tuft of
Ruy's mane, and began to deftly plait it. Barnard's face, in defiance of
himself, flushed scarlet; his very ears burned. He stole half a glance
sideways; how lovely her reseate cheek, the threads of her golden hair
against the bay's neck! Ruy was turning his nostrils round to touch her, and
ask for more grass. She swiftly plaited his mane.

At that moment another horse neighed over the hill; they both looked
round — no one was in sight. But Ruy answered with a neigh, and in the
same instant stepped forward. Barnard pressed his knee; Ruy began to move
faster. Barnard bowed; his voice was temporarily inarticulate, and he was
gone.

(DM, VI, 35–6)

Felise longs to announce herself to Barnard; she is a girl for
whom the 'forms of society were nothing', as Jefferies writes,
'she had already broken them' (DM, IX, 50). The contained
eroticism of the scene on the downs is balanced by the more

explicit sequence of images that make up the bathing scene
(DM, XI). It is a scene which recalls Manet's *Déjeuner sur
l'herbe* in its joyful physicality, and its slightly voyeuristic
delight in the flesh. Through Dionysian physical movement
Felise reaches full self-hood:

In the moment when her rounded right arm was sweeping backwards,
clearly visible in the limpid water — just as the stroke was nearly completed
— the sculptor might again have obtained an inspiration. . . . There was
something almost sacred to her in the limpid water, in the sweet air, and the
light of day . . . she knew her own fullness of existence.

(DM, XI, 64–6)

The unity of action, human erotic beauty and Nature is
finely realised by Jefferies. The overt presentation of physical
passion is one of the great achievements, one of the openings
made, by the Nature novelists, and nowhere more notably
than here:

That shoulder — the left — raised a little higher than the other, on account of
her position, was partly bare, the tunic having slipped somewhat. Unconsciously she pressed her cheek against it, feeling and caressing it. Her
shoulder lifted itself a little to meet the embrace of her cheek, and the tunic
slipped still more, giving it and that side of her bust freedom to the air.

(DM, XI, 69)

In a bold stroke Jefferies goes on to retrace the first two scenes,
this time from the point of view of Martial Barnard, thus
giving each sequence a double perspective of relevance and
interpretation.

Gazing out of the shrubbery at Felise in the pool, Barnard
feels stirrings of an emotion he has tried to stifle, and Jefferies
does not disguise its physicality: 'The dew upon her knees, wet
from the limpid water, glistened in the sunshine. Till this
instant he had never met anything that answered to the poetry
— the romance — in his heart' (DM, XIV, 91). This love idyll,
whilst it remains the core of the book, is now placed within the
wider, and harsher social context. Jefferies's quasi-symbolist
mode permits him to transfer from one social group to another
with artistic assurance.

In Old Brown and his wife, who have worked all their lives

upon the Cornleigh estate, and their eviction from the tied cottage, Jefferies introduces peasant realism. The eviction is to be effected by the squire's hard-fisted agent, Robert Godwin. The portrait of Brown is unfailingly verific, Jefferies slipping neither into grotesque caricature nor rural docility and whimsy. Whilst the authorial denunciations of the evils of the tied-cottage system are weighty (DM, XVII, XXX, XLV), there is no compensatory idealisation of the suffering peasantry. On the contrary, the brutality of their lives is categorically stated; but Jefferies adds, 'These morals are born of generations of cruel poverty, and they are perpetuated by the brutal modern system which leaves for the worn-out labourer or labourer's wife no refuge but the workhouse or the grave' (DM, XXIX, 210). The point is borne out in Brown's rank ingratitude at Felise's attempt to gain him a sympathetic hearing (DM, XXXV). Nonetheless Jefferies is unequivocal in apportioning the blame for this state of affairs upon the land-owning class: as in Lawrence, the erotic and the social revolutionary go hand-in-hand. The subtle moral balance of the novel might here have been upset by a familiar gallery of ferocious aristocrats and conniving agents. Jefferies avoids this, embodying the negative forces of the book in the agent Robert Godwin, 'no set villain of a piece, no unscrupulous tyrant for the sake of evil' (DM, XX, 136). The old *schema* of humours which is a strong residual element in many Victorian novels gives way to a psychological study of some complexity.

Like his philosophical namesake, Godwin is a man absolutely without imagination; he is scrupulous and fair in business transactions but devoid of human warmth. This inner nullity is expressed by a failure to respond to Nature, 'the sunrise, the colours of sunset, the stars so clear seen at an altitude — these mere imaginative things were invisible to him altogether' (DM, XIX, 126). He is the polar opposite of Felise, and whilst she is conceived in terms of imagery of vigour and fertility, the imagery connected with Godwin is deathly. In his garden 'nothing had been planted afresh for generations; the boughs fell away with age. . . . The apples had ceased to bear'

(DM, XXXVII, 259). Yet the portrait is never reductive, and Godwin never dwindles into an automaton. He is rather a man possessed by an *idée fixe*. As a child Felise has lived close to Nature, 'led along by unknown impulses, as if voices issued from the woods calling her to enter' (DM, XXII, 153). Godwin had glimpsed her in the fields, and was transfixed by her dancing (DM, XXIII, 165). The agent's life is thus ruled by a furtive and futile passion. When Felise buys Barnard's horse, which Godwin has seized as a settlement of debts, and returns it to her beloved, Godwin is bitterly apprised of the true situation. In a daring exploration of masochism Godwin is shown arranging for the couple to meet on his premises so he can watch their love developing whilst sublimating his desire in paperwork (DM, XXXIX). The dualistic nature of Godwin's behaviour is determined by his thwarted love for Felise, and culminates in his attempt to seduce her surrogate, Mary Shaw, the maid (DM, XXIX), and his harrassment of both the Browns and old Goring, her independent guardian.

Behind the agent stands another 'hollow man', Squire Cornleigh, a nonentity whose silence is taken by the locals for inscrutability. During a quarter of a century in parliament he has never uttered a word, and is thus to be rewarded by a baronetcy. When presented with a simple human problem, such as Felise brings to his notice in the plight of Brown, he ceases to exist, and hides behind his agent. Again Jefferies is at pains not to present a villain; the squire is youthful and pleasing in appearance, and is kind to his dogs. Yet in his way he is as psychologically incapacitated as Sir Leicester Dedlock, and like that bastion against 'levelling tendencies', is a mouthpiece of reaction and repression. He is ruled by his wife Letitia, who has destroyed the ancient park and church and robbed Maasbury of many amenities, in obedience to what Jefferies, in a rare reference to the Oxford Movement, calls 'the swarm of shaven clericalism around her' (DM, XXXI, 221). It is Letitia Cornleigh who sternly enforces the estate law that where illegitimacy occurs the whole family is turned out of doors — a law also affecting Tess. Felise's maid, Mary Shaw, becomes pregnant by Abner, the son of old Brown, and in an hypnotic scene, throws herself into the mill pool (DM, XLII' which 'Black and still, unruffled while the wind blew above' was always 'waiting like fate' (DM, XV, 96). She is rescued by Barnard, gives birth to a daughter, and dies (DM, XLIV). The suicide is motivated by the estate law on illegitimacy, so the principles of the Cornleighs are reaping their reward, and Jefferies has dramatized a social problem central to the agricultural depression.

In the meantime the Felise–Barnard relationship is deepening, and in a rich pastoral chapter it ripens with the wheat. In the heat of summer with the sky blue and 'in the distance some large clouds ... motionless', Felise's 'exalted passion strung her naturally fine and sensitive nature; she seemed to feel the sun's majestic onward sweep in the deep azure — her love made earth divine' (DM, XLI, 286–90). Barnard, inflamed by her beauty, recalls the bathing scene: her dress is 'transparent to his eyes — the image of the beautiful knees dewy from the bath could never fade. No dress could hide her' (DM, XLI, 295). Even now Jefferies makes it clear that Barnard does not love Felise for herself. Before the personal clarification, however, the wider implications of the novel are exposed in the social *dénouement*.

The great public meeting in Maasbury to honour Squire Cornleigh is addressed in tones of stringent radicalism by Barnard, who exposes the rottenness of the land-owning system to its unwitting victims (DM, XLVII, XLVIII, XLIX). The scale and acuteness of the attack leave little doubt that here Barnard is the authorial mouthpiece.

In the final stages of the novel, a maddened Robert Godwin waylays Felise and ties her up, dragging Ruy towards her in an attempt to mutilate the beauty which can never be his. Barnard intervenes, and is compelled to shoot the horse; this moment of crisis finally unites the lovers, and Godwin shoots himself (DM, L, LIII). This type of Nemesis, baldly recited, sounds melodramatic, but the essence of the three personalities has been subtly delineated by Jefferies and the events merely lay bare the deep underlying psychological clash. The technique here stands half-way between Victorian convention, the sensation novel and the new psychological poetry of Lawrence. At the notebook stage Jefferies had observed that 'Artistically R.G. ought not to die — it gives a cold deathly sense — but he really could not help it, for it was his nature' (NB, 158). This 'nature' of deathliness, extending to a whole culture, is precisely Lawrence's method in characters like Annable, Gerald Crich and Chatterley.

The novel ends with Felise and Martial married, and in a cyclic pattern Felise once again looks towards the downs and the summer sunrise: 'The stars were gone, and the deep azure of the morning filled the sky. By the ridge of the hill the white light shone brightly; above it a purple mingled luminously with the blue; towards the zenith the loveliness of the colour is not to be written' (DM, LV, 394). In its portrayal of Felise as hierophant of Nature *The Dewy Morn* is most original; in its account of the incipient land problems of the period it is valid and truthful documentary; in its distillation of the transient beauty of the earth it is poetic; and in its plastic conception of the formation and deformation of character it is adventurous. The work throughout is imbued with a lyricism and structural control, a unifying sense of image and theme, which looks forward to the achievements of the modern novel. Although Jefferies did not have the time or energy, through his fatal illness, to extend the achievement, *The Dewy Morn* forms a significant link with future novelists on the Nature theme.

Amaryllis at the Fair,[34] the least characteristic of Jefferies's mature novels, is the only one to have gained any measure of critical acceptance. Its fragmentary structure, doubtless rooted in Jefferies's final illness, may be accepted as a valuable rendition of real life. It is a novel of great strengths in its presentation of urban and rural society. The characters are drawn with the loving precision of autobiography, and throughout, the grave tone qualified even those characters whom Jefferies would appear to be endorsing. The sombre voice of the last notebooks may be discerned in the subordination of rustic incident to the central theme of Amaryllis and her development. The Nature worship which is Jefferies's pabulum, and which is the touchstone of the earlier novels, is here present only in muted and elegiac form. Yet it is hard to escape the conclusion that the static ambience, the exiguous plot, and the substantial digressions mirror a debilitated creativity and a response to country society felt to be *in articulo mortis*.

It is no coincidence that the most vital pages are those which relate the heroine to her natural surroundings. In the contrast between Iden, prosaically putting in his potatoes, and his daughter excitedly responding to the daffodils, for instance, Jefferies juxtaposes two attitudes to life which are to clash throughout the novel (AF, I). When Mrs Iden, in an excess of that marital tension which is a constant undercurrent, tramples on the daffodils, Amaryllis's education is taken a step further (AF, V). The texture of a rural homestead is a felt presence in the novel, and in the portraits of Farmer Iden, hubristic Grandfather Iden, Alere Flamma the indigent artist, and the sensitive Amaryllis herself, Jefferies creates a valuable microcosm of English rural society at a time of change. In the virtual transformation of Iden from a lifelike picture of Jefferies's father into an avatar of Pan (AF, XXVI), the potent imagination of the earlier work is once more evident. 'It was his genius to make things grow — like sunshine and shower', Jefferies records of Iden. He is 'a sort of Pan, a half-god of leaves and boughs, and reeds and streams, a sort of Nature in human shape'. In his garden of plenty, and most fruitfully in his summerhouse, the maimed spirits of Amadis and Alere Flamma are revived and reintegrated by 'magic power of healing'. After the harrowing interlude in Fleet Street and the city of dreadful night, the culmination of the novel in the meadows, with Amadis and Amaryllis 'as full of love as the meadow was of sunshine', imparts a gleam to this least optimistic of Jefferies's novels.

A remark of Leavis's that 'no great novelist can be a Benthamite' furnishes a clue to the novels of Richard Jefferies. They are based upon the primacy of Nature and of the natural in man. His insights into character and environment follow from his doctrine. It was not a new thought, but it was felt upon the pulses, and with a living immediacy which renders Jefferies's essays in fiction bold and original. In tracing the bases of behaviour, and relating man to the circumambient universe, Jefferies upheld and extended the Nature tradition in vital new ways.

Notes

1 S.J. Looker (ed.), *The Nature Diaries and Notebooks of Richard Jefferies* (London, Grey Walls Press, 1948, hereafter cited as NB), p. 282.

2 R. Jefferies, *The Gamekeeper at Home* (1878) (London, Oxford University Press, World's Classics edn., 1960, hereafter cited as GAH).

3 R. Jefferies, *The Amateur Poacher* (1879) (London, Oxford University Press, World's Classics edn., 1960, hereafter cited as AP).

4 R. Jefferies, *Hodge and His Masters* (1880) (London, Methuen, 1937, hereafter cited as HM).

5 R. Jefferies, *Wood Magic* (1881) (London, Collins, n.d., hereafter cited as WM).

6 R. Jefferies, *Bevis* (1882) (London, Dent, Everyman's Library edn., 1966, hereafter cited as B).

7 R. Jefferies, *The Story of My Heart* (1883) (London, Constable, 1947, hereafter cited as SH).

8 R. Jefferies, *The Hills and the Vale* (1909) (London, Duckworth, 1909, hereafter cited as HV).

9 R. Jefferies, *Field and Hedgerow* (1889) (London, Longman, 1910, hereafter cited as FH), p. 125.

10 R. Jefferies, *Round About a Great Estate* (1880) (London, Eyre & Spottiswoode, 1948, hereafter cited as RGE).

11 See 'No benevolence therefore no intelligence. Nothing to expect but the action of forces. I find nothing. Nothing but the feeling by the sea' (NB, 224).

12 S.J. Looker and C. Porteous, *Richard Jefferies, Man of the Fields* (London, Country Book Club, 1966, hereafter cited as RJ), pp. 223–4.

13 R. Jefferies, *The Open Air* (1885) (London, Dent, Wayfarer's Library edn., n.d., hereafter cited as OA), p. 31.

14 R. Jefferies, *The Toilers of the Field* (1892) (London, Longman, 1892, hereafter cited as TF), pp. 95–6.

15 R. Jefferies, *Nature Near London* (1883) (London, Chatto & Windus,

1904, hereafter cited as NNL).

16 R. Jefferies, *The Life of the Fields* (1884) (London, Chatto & Windus, 1908, hereafter cited as LF), p. 217.

17 R. Jefferies, *Wild Life in a Southern County* (1879) (London, Nelson, n.d., hereafter cited as WL), p. 207.

18 S.J. Looker (ed.), *The Old House at Coate* (London, Lutterworth Press, 1948, hereafter cited as OHC).

19 R. Jefferies, *After London* (1885) (London, Duckworth, 1929, hereafter cited as AL).

20 R. Jefferies, *Red Deer* (1884) (London, Eyre & Spottiswoode, 1948, hereafter cited as RD), p. 17.

21 G. Toplis (ed.), *The Early Fiction of Richard Jefferies* (London, Simpkin, Marshall, 1896, hereafter cited as EF), p. xv.

22 R. Jefferies, *Greene Ferne Farm* (1880) (Hounslow, Foster, 1940, hereafter cited as GFF).

23 W.J. Keith, *Richard Jefferies* (London, Oxford University Press, 1965), p. 123.

24 R. Jefferies, *The Scarlet Shawl* (1874) (London, Tinsley, 1874, hereafter cited as SS).

25 T. Hardy, *Desperate Remedies* (1871) (London, Macmillan, 1970).

26 R. Jefferies, *Restless Human Hearts* (1875) (London, Tinsley, 1875, hereafter cited as RHH).

27 The conception of Georgiana reflects the 'Girl of the Period' controversy sparked off in 1866 by Mrs Linton's articles in the *Saturday Review*.

28 S.J. Looker (ed.), *Field and Farm* (London, Phoenix House, 1957, hereafter cited as FF), p. 42.

29 Francis's attempted suicide on the rails and Carlotta's train journey (RHH, III, 197, 201) resemble episodes in *Dombey and Son*.

30 R. Jefferies, *World's End* (1977) (London, Tinsley, 1877, hereafter cited as WE).

31 The scene of the dragging of the Pot on the eve of the wedding is another effective nodal point for the narrative. Lady Lechester's weird cousin Odo is visualised as a Pan figure, and contributes something to the atmosphere.

32 S.J. Looker (ed.), *The Chronicles of the Hedges* (1948) (London, Phoenix House, 1948, hereafter cited as CH), pp. 191–202.

33 R. Jefferies, *The Dewy Morn* (1884) (London, Bentley, 1891, hereafter cited as DM).

34 R. Jefferies, *Amaryllis at the Fair* (1887) (London, Nelson, n.d., hereafter cited as AF).

6   W. Hale White

I

Hale White, a profound admirer of Dr Johnson, once remarked that the doctor was 'not the only man who finds it easier to confess himself in a book, which can be had in any bookseller's shop for money, than in talking'.[1] Each of White's pseudonymous novels may be read as a confession of unbelief, an exploration of spiritual isolation. These feelings were shared by many of the leading intellects of the age — a point ably made by White's son; the great Victorian moralists, he observed, 'were characterised by no nobler quality than their profound sense of the troubles of the time, and the courage with which they faced the current orthodoxies and insisted on the need of fundamental solutions'. With his father in mind he added, 'Their melancholy may have been the measure of their sense of failure, but their courage and intellectual integrity remained unaffected'. Whilst this melancholia intermittently assumed almost pathological proportions in White's case, it is a mark of his purposive sense of character that it never overwhelmed him or his fiction. His novels are in some sense victories won against this sense of oppression or futility. Although they convey a modern sense of alienation, they increasingly embody a transfiguration of that sense into a new, wider awareness of fellowship through communion with Nature. Hale White, with his passionate nature, could never rest content simply to abandon the puritanism of his youth. In the task of recouping his loss of faith he had only inner experience to guide him. To approach Hale White simply as a representative of the Puritan tradition fails to do justice to his achievement as a novelist of Nature. The man who exclaimed, 'How rare, how precious are the pages which clouds and fields might have indited!' (LP, 280), frequently exhibits a sensibility scarcely less attuned to Nature than Jefferies's own. Whereas

Jefferies intuitively felt a deep rapport with Nature, Hale White underwent a long spiritual journey. In reaching this affirmation, in the struggle which it entailed, he jettisoned traditional novel form in favour of a new, flexible structure which has the plasticity of a diary, as of the mind turned inwards upon its own contemplation. The detritus of the Victorian novel, like the outworn formalism of the chapel, is replaced by an art which stresses authenticity, fidelity to experience, spontaneity and the autonomy of the individual.

II

Hale White's immersion in Midlands nonconformity and his subsequent revulsion is a too familiar behaviour pattern to require rehearsal here. It is a curious coincidence that the young man who attended Bunyan's chapel in Bedford should undertake so long and arduous a pilgrimage. Whatever the theology which he abandoned, White never lost that characteristic Puritan sense of life as a spiritual drama. The fundamental separation between himself and a communal body of belief seemed to White to demand a resolution both in terms of his own personality and in the lives of his characters. He was constitutionally incapable of remaining an unbeliever, yet he could find in no system of belief a worthy resting-place. White's novels evince very clear Bunyanesque qualities in the spiritual-journey theme and in the plain style. Each work goes beyond a statement of unsettled agnosticism. Whilst the early novels emphasise the collision between sensitive humanity and rootless modern existence, the later novels reveal powers and agencies of a new order.

In *The Autobiography of Mark Rutherford*[2] and *Mark Rutherford's Deliverance*[3] it is possible to trace, beneath the fictional disguises, the course of Hale White's rebellion. His explusion from dissenting college in 1852, and the attendant *odium theologicum*, dramatized his rejection of a dead creed. It was followed by a species of dark night of the soul in London. This, and the pictures of clerical drudgery, have led to the critical view of Hale White as a delineator of urban misery and anguish. This view is valid of only one phase of his development and thought, as a record of the nadir of his spiritual existence. Hale White was incapable of lapsing into the Laodicean somnolence which characterised the latitudinarians of all churches. The quest for God, or for belief, is the theme of all the novels. Like many documents of romanticism, the postulates which they embody may not be susceptible of logical categorisation. Nevertheless, they aptly reproduce that exploratory spirit so typical of White; not the least valuable part of his Puritan inheritance was his hostility to mere aestheticism. That is not to suggest that Hale White, after an intense Puritan upbringing, rejected his cultural heritage and began consciously to construct an alternative. Indeed, most of the matter of his new faith lay at hand during his adolescence. Under the pressure of the collapse of the old order new ideas were forged. The sources of these ideas cast illumination upon Hale White's art and thought.

The passage from orthodoxy into heterodoxy was not accomplished in isolation. In his self-imposed task of reassembling the heap of broken images bequeathed to him by the atrophy of his puritan heritage White turned instinctively to his intellectual mentors. Hale White was, as Middleton Murry observed, a man with many questions and no answers; but the act of questioning itself constituted a new type of faith. 'Hale White when he was expelled from New College was certainly very unorthodox', a fellow student recalled; 'His favourite authors were Carlyle, Emerson, Goethe, and some other German authors'. Two significant names must be added: Wordsworth and Spinoza.

Hale White's reminiscences of boyhood exhibit an unconscious love of Nature strikingly similar to passages in *The Prelude*. Recalling his swimming, boating, fishing and skating activities he wrote: 'There woke in me an aptness for the love of natural beauty, a possibility of being excited to enthusiasm by it, and of deriving a secret joy from it sufficiently strong, to make me careless of the world and its pleasures'.[4] Thus in the unemphatic Bedfordshire landscape he gained his first experience of bliss. These days were etched in his memory, and in old age he remembered passing 'whole days in the fields about Bedford, dipping in and out of the Ouse'.[5] A brief return to the town brought back with Proustian force the 'slow river, rushes, willows, meadows, and villages to which no visitor ever goes, and where nothing is heard save the drowsy sound of the scattered farms'. He confided to a friend, 'I have left Bedford for a great many years. It is closer to me now however than ever it was'. The 'glad animal passion' of boyhood soon gave way to a deepening awareness of the higher powers of Nature, and a recognition that Nature worship would form the basis of his worship had mingled with his religious experiences. This was crystallised by the reading of 'Tintern Abbey'. Wordsworth gave definition to White's thoughts in a way wholly attuned to his own being. This reading brought him secret joy, and effected a revolution in his relation to the world about him. The best documentation of Wordsworth's role is to be found in *The Autobiography of Mark Rutherford*, where the boy first reads *Lyrical Ballads*. All the systems of thought of his youth 'decayed' and 'fell away into nothing', and allied to this sloughing-off process came 'the birth of a habit of inner reference'. In a passage of great importance Rutherford goes on to observe that Wordsworth's 'real God is not the God of the Church, but the God of the hills, the abstraction Nature, and to this my reverence was transferred'. The God of this new dispensation 'dwelt on the downs in the far-away distances, and in every cloud-shadow which wandered across the valley'. Thus Wordsworth recreated Rutherford's divinity, 'substituting a new and living spirit for the old deity' (AMR, II, 18–19). The Judaeo-Christian God is replaced by romantic pantheism; indeed Hale White came to feel that 'a man who devotes himself to Wordsworth and is religious and a lover of beauty will find himself looking at the world in a certain way; it will no longer be what it was without Wordsworth; hills, clouds, sea, and human beings will not be the same' (LP, 93). In the same essay, 'Revolution', he adds,

'When I first read Wordsworth I saw God in Nature. As I grew older I felt a difficulty in saying so much. Nevertheless, the "something added" has always remained and will remain as long as I live' (LP, 94).

Wordsworth's poetry did not enable Hale White to erect a traditional system of belief, but educated him in new modes of feeling. During his pilgrimage to the Quantocks White made this point. In quoting from 'The Ruined Cottage' he remarked that 'the religion by which Wordsworth lives is very indefinite', but added that because it was indefinite 'it is not therefore the less supporting'.[6] His Quantocks dairy also contains an entry relevant to the novels, making the vital connexion between natural objects and man: 'If Wordsworth's love of clouds and mountains ended there it would be no better than the luxury of a refined taste. But it does not end there. It affects the whole of his relationships with men and women, and is therefore most practical' (MP, 200). The ecstatic communicant with Nature is thus fitted for social action by this worship; this proves to be a fruitful theme in the novels, where Nature becomes an ethical influence or presence. The protagonists of the novels, however oppressed by their social condition, discover in Nature an analogue for their aspiration; the later heroines move towards that communion which Hale White discerned in Dorothy Wordsworth: 'She is one with earth, sky, and humanity, and our relationship to them is our relationship to her' (LP, 242). Where the characters are at odds with natural piety, and wrestle mentally against wise passiveness, they fall into error, like the heroine of the story 'Esther', who reflects bitterly upon the exchange she has made of Blackdeep Fen for the urban wilderness of Homerton: 'I little understood that such things and the ease which is felt when our surroundings grow to us make a good part of the joy of life' (MP, 41).

Few Victorians were more deeply immersed in Wordsworth than Hale White; but another tutelary spirit was Carlyle, whose *Latter Day Pamphlets* were 'devoured' by the adolescent (GD, 190). His sketch of 'A Visit to Carlyle' in 1868 recalls the reviewers' attacks on the *Pamphlets*, and his own 'eager journey to the bookseller for each successive number'. During his adolescence, White recalls, the books were 'read with excitement, with tears of joy, on lonely hills, by the seashore and in London streets, and the readers were thankful that it was their privilege to live when he also was alive'.[7] This sounds a note of excited release from the life of the chapel and prayer-meeting into the larger sphere. White seems to have read the bulk of Carlyle, but it was *Heroes and Hero-Worship* and *Sartor Resartus* which 'drew him away from the meeting house': 'They laid hold on him as no books had ever held, and the expansion they wrought in him could not possibly tolerate the limitations of orthodoxy' (EL, 28). Although White came to disagree with Carlyle on negro slavery, Arnold's attack upon the master as a 'moral desperado' would have been unthinkable for him; he remained a staunch disciple to the end, and his final verdict was consonant with that first flush of enthusiasm over half a century before: 'Carlyle remains to me — this is now my irreversible verdict on him — the voice which in our century came from the deepest depths. In nobody do I find the immovable rock as I find it in him'.[8]

In addition to the general impact of Carlylean doctrine in terms of high strenuousness in morals, an unbending concept of duty, and a critique of industrialism, it may well be that Hale White's ideas on Nature were expanded by reading Carlyle.

The doctrine, which Carlyle inherited from Goethe, of the world as the 'living visible garment of God', provides him with the basis for a new religion designated 'Natural Supernatural- ism'. The section devoted to this concept in *Sartor Resartus* is vital to an understanding of White's position. Each phenome- non of the Universe is miraculous, according to Carlyle, but as the wonder ebbs we lose our sense of its religious quality. If we could unseal our eyes then the primal wonder returns:

this fair Universe, were it in the meanest province thereof, is in very deed the star-domed City of God; . . . through every star, through every grass-blade, and most through every Living Soul, the glory of a present God still beams.

But Nature, which is the Time-vesture of God, and reveals Him to the wise, hides Him from the foolish.

(*Sartor Resartus*,iii, VIII)

This dogma restores to Carlyle and his disciples something like the Calvinist idea of 'election', and under an acceptably romantic guise. Elsewhere, Carlyle accounted for Nature in accord with transcendental idealism: 'There is, in fact, says Fichte, no tree there; but only a manifestation of Power from something which is *not I*. The same is true of material Nature at large, and of the whole visible Universe, with all its movements, figures, accidents and qualities; all are impressions produced on *me* by something *different from me*'. Here the German Idealist position merges with Spinozism. Carlyle suggests that both Nature and the perceiving mind are manifestations of a divine presence; 'this so solid-looking material is, at bottom, in very deed, Nothing; is a visual and tactual Manifestation of God's power and presence, — a shadow hung out by Him on the bosom of the void Infinite' (*Heroes and Hero-Worship*, Lect. II). This is more rhapsodically expressed in 'The Everlasting Yea':

How the fermentest and elaboratest in thy great fermenting vat and laboratory of an Atmosphere, of a World, O Nature! — Or what is Nature? Ha! why do I not name thee GOD? Art not thou the 'Living Garment of God'? O Heavens, is it, in very deed, HE, then, that ever speaks through thee; that lives and loves in thee, and lives and loves in me?

(*Sartor Resartus*, ii, IX)

Whilst it would be wrong to claim that Hale White swallowed Natural Supernaturalism whole, the placing of this Nature philosophy within a context of religious unorthodoxy must have exerted a powerful attraction over him. Carlyle helped him to locate God increasingly within Nature.

The links between Carlylean idealism and Emersonian transcendentalism may have led White from one to the other. White seems to have read Emerson whilst at college, and his admiration for the New England philosopher was doubtless increased during his sojourn at John Chapman's, since Chapman published a good deal of Emerson, and Transcendental ideas were current in that circle. By the time of his visit to Emerson in 1873, therefore, there can be little doubt that White was a disciple.

The Carlylean idea of election through devotion to Nature is amplified in Emerson's 'Woodnotes': 'These echoes are laden with tones Which only the pure can hear'; and some of the later lines must have appealed to White:

> Behind thee leave thy merchandise,
> Thy churches and thy charities;
> And leave thy peacock wit behind;
> Enough for thee the primal mind
> That flows in streams, that breathes in wind;

Emerson's *ideé fixe*, the identity of all being, is expounded throughout his work: unity of man with Nature, unity of Nature with God are recurrent notes. 'Who shall define me as an Individual', he asks in the *Journals*. 'I behold with awe and delight many illustrations of the One Universal Mind. I see my being imbedded in it; as a plant in the earth so I grow in God. I am only a form of him. He is in the soul of me'. This was heady reading for the initiate of the Bunyan Meeting, and may have laid the foundation for White's study of Spinoza. It seems certain, at any rate, that the idealist strain found a ready response in White's consciousness, and became part of his way of apprehending the world.

White began reading Goethe whilst still at college, and his son said that he had studied Goethe 'profoundly'. He made a pilgrimage to Weimar, and refers to the German poet with a frequency which denotes the deepest intimacy with Goethe's ideas. When his second wife asked for his opinion of Goethe he replied, 'You might just as well ask me, "What do I think of the sea or the sky?" ' (GD, 318). In Goethe each reader finds reflection of his own self. There is in the poems an acceptance of Nature, and a recognition of man's role within it, combined with a quasi-mystical union with the cosmos. Nature is eternally active, and the detection in botany of morphological processes gives the poet a feeling of joy most notably rendered in the song of the Erdgeist in *Faust*, and in the association there between spiritual rebirth and the reviving life of Nature. Goethe, with his sense of wholeness, does not make a distinction between the indifference of Nature and the sensibility of man. He characteristically takes Nature as a source of inspiration which may enable the artist to transcend time and place, an enlargement of his faculties. Indeed, man may be the interpreter of Nature. As a scientist Goethe retained a realist awareness of Nature, and his evolutionary naturalism must have encouraged White in his quest for an acceptable creed.

Goethe was quick to correct Jacobi, under whom he studied philosophy, when Jacobi argued that 'Nature hides God'. 'Spinoza does not prove the existence of God; existence *is* God', replied the young poet. What Spinoza did teach, according to Goethe, was 'to see God in Nature, and Nature in God'. Whether Hale White came to Spinoza through Goethe is not clear; that Spinoza's influence was crucial is undeniable. Work on Spinoza was the major scholarly effort of White's life; his translation of the *Ethics* first appeared in 1883, and it was revised for later editions. White also edited the *Tractatus* in 1895, and wrote a number of articles on the Jewish philosopher.

In considering Hale White's relation with Spinoza it is valuable to ponder the view he held that the 'contact of a *system* of philosophy or religion with reality is that of a tangent with a circle. It touches the circle at one point, but instantly the circle edges away' (MP, 240). White's testimony on the potency of Spinoza is irrefutable. In 'Evolution' he recalled a saying of Spinoza's which had remained with him for fifty years: 'The mind and the body are one and the same individual, which at one time is considered under the attribute of thought, and at another under that of extension' (LP, 89; recalling *Ethics*, Prop. XXI, Pt.2, Scol.). The efficacy of this assertion in banishing Cartesian dualism is a major tenet of Spinozism. White's essay on Spinoza is eloquent in its assertion that the philosopher's works were 'productive beyond those of almost any man I know of that *acquiescentia mentis* which enables us to live' (P, 58). On this evidence Spinoza was a moral and ideological power in White's life.

White derived from Spinoza a sense of the immanence of God in the material world; a habit of reference to the inner authority of conscience; and a vitalistic view of matter. The novels are infused with these ideas, but most importantly, with Spinoza's pantheism. The Romantic furore over *Pantheismus-streit* may be read as a confrontation between Spinoza and Kant. It is a conflict between God as transcendent and imma-nent presence. At the heart of the question stands Spinoza's assertion that 'God is the indwelling, and not the transient cause of all things' (*Ethics*, Pt. 1, Prop. XVIII). That is, God is not the creator of things, but the things themselves. The school of philosophy which treats the self or subject as primary can never be logically reconciled with the school which treats the object as primary. Since, according to Spinoza, 'Whatever is, is in God, and nothing can exist or be conceived without God' (Pt. 1, Prop. XV), it follows that it is 'only God, to whose nature alone existence appertains' (Pt. 1, Prop. XIV, Cor. i). Therefore, 'particular things are nothing else than a modifi-cation of attributes of God' (Pt. 1, Prop. XXV, Cor.). Since there is no substance but God, all substance is God. By placing all existence within the context of '*Deus, sive Natura*', the perceiving mind as separate entity is done away with; the philosopher holds that 'in the nature of things nothing is given save substances and their modifications' (Pt. 1, Prop. VI, Cor.). Thus what is normally termed the understanding is contained within the monistic doctrine of substance. The pantheist equation of One and Many is arrived at in this manner. It remained for German Idealism to develop its implications. It follows axiomatically from Spinoza's position that man can make only a fleeting appearance in the world of Nature, and that humanised Christian dogma, such as free-dom of the will and personal immortality, is set aside. There is some evidence that White was attracted to this hypothesis, and certainly the necessitarianism of Spinoza's thought is rigor-ously applied, all notion of final causes being dismissed as figments of the imagination. In Spinoza, as Novalis found, 'lives this divine spark of the understanding of Nature'. 'All Nature is in Him', White wrote of the Spinozan God, arguing for a type of immortality from the pages of the *Ethics* (P, 39). It was through Spinoza that White renewed himself intellectually, just as through Wordsworth he had renewed himself spiritually. The man who comprehends Spinoza, he held, understands 'that he is not a mere transient, outside interpreter of the universe, but himself the soul or law which is the universe' — a crucial insight to an 'outsider' of White's fastidious temperament. Armed with this revelation, man will 'feel a relationship with infinity which will emancipate him' (P, 38–9). It was this 'relationship with infinity,' through the mediation of Nature, which became the commanding theme of the later novels.

To sum up: Wordsworth, Goethe, Carlyle, Emerson and Spinoza expanded Hale White's consciousness beyond the stifling confines of dissent. In transporting him *extra muros*, and laying bare the decadence of Puritanism, they showed the way to a new religion founded in Nature.

On the matter of White's relation with his literary contemporaries there is less to say. 'He tells me most emphatically that he was never in the literary world', his second wife noted, 'not educated for literature; not trained for literature; has known hardly any literary people' (GD, 33). This is an excusable exaggeration. Upon his expulsion from New College White was briefly befriended by Kingsley and F.D. Maurice; during his years at John Chapman's he was close to Marian Evans, and mixed freely with her radical circle, meeting Lewes, Spencer, Froude and others, and making himself *au courant* with their ideas, however distasteful; during his years at the Admiralty, and during his retirement, he had contact with Ruskin, Morris, Coventry Patmore, Dykes-Campbell, Swinburne and others, and struck up a close friendship with Philip Webb. He was isolated, but did take part in the ideological debate and its social implications. It was naturally George Eliot whom he valued most highly. She shared White's cultural milieu, and he admired her as the type of those 'insurgents' who appear in his own fiction. Speaking of her Midlands connexions he wrote, 'She owed to them the foundation of what she was, but they, through her, became vocal. She was exactly the right person, and came at exactly the right moment' (LP, 137). He came to regret having lost contact with her, and it may be this lost opportunity he refers to in the strange 'Confessions of a Self-Tormentor', when the narrator explains that his curse 'has not been plucking forbidden fruit, but the refusal of divine fruit offered me by heavenly angels' (MP, 120). His final verdict on George Eliot was an expression of awe at her powers: 'There are submarine caves which she has sounded, into which no plummet but hers has been dropped'; he added that 'she ranks as a first explorer' (LTF, 180).

White had particular interest in novels of Nature. He urged a friend to read *Lavengro*, and enthused over *Lorna Doone*, 'as good a story in my judgement as we have had, at any rate, in this last half-century, full of all the light, scent and colour of Exmoor, a land I love, and the work of a genuine artist' (LTF, 47, 367). In the context, the most significant literary contemporary was Jefferies. White was a profound admirer of Jefferies: in the autumn of 1887, when he heard of Jefferies's death, he commented to his friend Mrs Colenutt, *à propos* of 'My Old Village', 'Every scrap of his is precious. Just look for example at his last article, the last he ever wrote, the one in *Longman's Magazine* for this month, or rather October. Never was there such a naturalist and lover of the country. His two or three novels, poor fellow, were written, they say, for a living. I have not read them as yet' (LTF, 36–7). Some weeks later White reverted to this: 'I told you to read the article in Longman. Read also *Wild Life in a Southern County.* To me chapter four has few rivals in beauty of pure English prose and in suggestiveness' (LTF, 38). A little later he wrote again to Mrs Colenutt: 'Ask your husband, if he wants to refresh his memory with the most vivid description of Dissenting life in country places which has been written for a long time, to turn to the collected fragments of Richard Jefferies just published, called *Field and Hedgerow*, and read 'The Country Sunday'

(LTF, 43). It was Jefferies to whom White felt closest, in his reading of Nature, and the articulation of the Nature theme is seen in its purest form in their novels.

III

In tracing Hale White's involvement with Nature, and in recalling the influence of Wordsworth, Carlyle and Spinoza, it should not be supposed that he wholly jettisoned the tenets of Christianity. On the contrary, when faced with the 'cold negativism' of the Chapman circle, most of whom derived their animus against religion from Strauss and Feuerbach, Hale White confessed to his father that he was driven back again 'to all my old friends who appear more than ever perfect, and Jesus above them all'. His biblical essays show Hale White examining man's suffering and reconciliation with God. If the 'origin and reason of religions' is to 'bring Heaven and earth together' (LP, 116), there can be no question of White's discarding the Christian belief *in toto*. Rather, ancient truths yield a fresh insight, and new formulations are made. In a virtuoso sketch, 'F–E–D', White adopted an unusually prophetic stance:

The sea was the same light greenish-blue with the cloud shadows sailing over it. I began to ask myself whether I was sure that modern tendencies are irreversible; whether the road has no turning which leads to anarchy and defacement of beauty, to millionaires . . . to modern gunnery and bomb-dropping aeroplanes, to wars engineered by finance-mongers, in which millions of people are slaughtered who never had the least grudge against one another.

White goes on to speculate that 'what we call the intellect may one day be deposed, and a claimant with a better title to the imperial throne may be discovered' (LP, 69). Here, and elsewhere in his *oeuvre*, White strains towards an optimistic reading of the future of mankind, averring that there is 'a great Power in existence', that it is feasible to 'hear afar off, a triumphal note'.

The foundation of this triumph will be Nature. For a man

afflicted with melancholia White bears a few scars of the post-Darwinian *angst*, which settled upon his generation. Indeed, on reading Darwin he recorded in letters that *The Origin of Species*[9] showed that both gods, 'the God after the Pentateuch and the God of the development are good, very good in their ways'. Evolution thus becomes 'the God of the development' capable of delivering man from the commercialised determinist present. Within Nature good and evil coexist: 'Everywhere in nature we see exaction of penalties down to the uttermost farthing, but following after this we discern forgiveness, obliterating and restorative! Both tendencies exist'. This forms the dialectic for many of the novels. Man has failed to interpret Nature rightly: thus a storm prompts the thought that 'this great drama had been enacted again and again through all these thousands of years, and yet man was no nearer a knowledge of what all that energy *meant* or what it *did*'. Wind and weather are reminders of the 'Titanic forces in the world which we shall never tame and which care not a rush for us'. An existential cosmos was an impossibility to Hale White: 'What is the ultimate design of the Universe we do not know, but that there is no ultimate design is incredible' (LP, 281).

Hale White's writings on Nature are not generally so abstract. As with Wordsworth and Jefferies, White seems to have progressed from intuitive delight in Nature towards quasi-mystical experience. His second wife was struck by his saying that the 'only thing he had ever been *sure about* was *beauty*' (GD, 107). This originates in a fluid response to sensory experience. On the Rhine he observed that the sunset 'was a new order of beauty not to be preconceived . . . adding to one's estimate of Nature's capacity' (LTF, 16). The emotional effulgence associated with sunsets seemed to him 'akin somehow to passion' (GD, 113), and in the novels the passional characters are those attuned to the 'simple unit of transcendent loveliness' in Nature (MP, 154). Thus the heroine of 'Kate Radcliffe', watching natural forces at work in the Lake District, feels the emotion of her author; 'her heart lay bare: she wondered, she was bowed down with awe, and she also longed unspeakably' (MP, 73). Nature, so conceived offers a continuous critique of human pretensions, whilst simultaneously imbuing man with higher aspirations. In an interesting sketch a familiar Calvinist vision of eternal damnation, of nugatory value to the listening holidaymakers, is serenely placed by the sea where the preacher speaks, the hellfire intensity doused by the unemphatic recession into geological time, 'the sound of their soft, musical plash filling up his pauses and commenting on his texts' (MP, 159).[10] The communion with Nature presupposes a humanity raised above the narrow potential laid down by human systems. 'This sunset, which is common to the whole county, is more to me than anything exclusively mine' (MP, 225). Thus man is led to the Wordsworthian concept which informs Hale White's mature work, and which is expounded by the fictional author of 'Judith Crowhurst', that Nature 'is not merely beautiful, but that she can speak words which we can hear if we listen devoutly' (MP, 141). At times this 'listening' leads Hale White towards a sense of human futility: 'How much better to be a breath of that south-west wind than to be a pitiful *personality* like myself, crouching over a fire' (LP, 288). This, despite bouts of melancholia, is untypical. Yet whilst the great events of Nature more often leave him 'quivering with beautiful, awful earnestness' (LTF, 292), flooded with that 'sounder hope and deeper joy' (MP, 153), which the 'silent solemnity' of the 'divine spectacle' (GD, 103) prompts in the witness, that act of witness occasionally raises a doubt in Hale White's mind which is most cogently expressed in a notebook entry:

Lying in the field this July day I take up a tall grass stem in flower. Its delicacy, grace, the poise of its head, are lovely beyond speech. But the whole field, ten acres of it, is covered with tall stems equally delicate, graceful, and with the same perfect poise. For whom does this beauty exist?

(LP, 293)

White is sounding once more the problem of mind and objective reality which is subsumed in Spinozism. Often his reaction is more instinctive, as when he observed that lichen-covered trees 'are not there to be spoken: they are there to be seen' (GD, 11). Nature is 'too much for words, too much for thinking' (GD, 357). Through openness to its promptings man's capacities are enlarged and renewed. White gained his 'deliverance' from the harsh intellectual vacuum of dissent through Nature.

No analysis of White's relation to Nature should seek to impose a spurious unity upon a body of thought which is diverse and shifting, whose essence is immediacy. Whatever White's intellectual proclivities, he was an imaginative rather than a ratiocinative writer. The role of Nature in the early novels is that of moral agent, but there is also in White a strain of mysticism which reveals a more intense awareness of the potency of Nature. This is evinced as a type of symbiosis enacted between man and his environment:

After a lovely day out of doors by myself I saw that a single act of admiration is of little use. We must live with beauty, without any straining effort to admire, quietly attentive, absorbent, until by degrees the beauty becomes one with us and alters our blood.

(LP, 309)

This transmutation of the blood implies a sensibility preter-naturally commingled with Nature. 'When we see a tree mutilated', White demands, 'should we feel the same if it were foreign to us, if there were no relationship whatever between ourselves and it?' (LP, 283). Of this central relationship White was convinced. 'The sea with its shifting shades; the gleam on its horizon — what are they? Water, vibrations, nothing. But the relationship to me is not nothing. That is an adamantine fact. So beauty becomes real as granite' (LP, 289). From Schleiermacher he may have recalled the definition of revel-ation as every 'original and new communication of the Uni-verse to Man'. Nature thus relates man to the infinite, as Christianity had claimed to do. 'What a man is conscious of, is not himself, but that which is not himself. Without a belief in the existence of an external world, I could not believe in my own existence' (MP, 251). White is here edging towards the annihilation of the self/not-self distinction which is the key feature of Spinozism, and which is the final end of all Nature mysticism, with its insistence upon the union of observer and observed. This process of intent contemplation leading the perceiving mind towards a merger with the sources of sense data was explored by Hale White in relation to a field near his house at Groombridge, a commonplace field which, he noted, 'I am just beginning to understand after having paced it a hundred times' (LP, 303). A true adept of Nature, White came to recognise in this field 'something which I cannot exhaust' (LP, 35). He explained more fully to Philip Webb: 'There is a field just above me bordered with trees so lovely *always* that I feel it would be foolish to go to Switzerland. It is nothing but a common field, but until I have done with it why should I travel?' White added pregnantly, 'I never shall have done with it' (LTF, 311). The final transformation of Baptist into pantheist is celebrated in these notes, the object no longer union with an anthropomorphic god but with all created life. The consummation of this phase of White's thought is recorded in 'An Epoch'. Of this final stage little can be said: like Jefferies in his essays White here attempts expression of the inexpressible:

> One morning when I was in the wood something happened which was nothing less than a transformation of myself and the world, although I 'believed' nothing new. I was looking at a great, spreading, bursting oak. The first tinge from the greenish-yellow buds was just visible. It seemed to be no longer a tree away from me and apart from me. The enclosing barriers of consciousness were removed and the text came into my mind, *Thou in me and I in thee*. The distinction of self and not-self was an illusion. I could feel the rising sap; in me also sprang the fountain of life uprushing from its roots, and the joy of its outbreak at the extremity of each twig right up to the summit was my own: that which kept me apart was nothing. I do not argue; I cannot explain; it will be easy to prove me absurd, but nothing can shake me.
>
> (MP, 182–3)

IV

Nonconformity traditionally discouraged the cultivation of fiction, and the art of dissent is strenuously didactic. Yet the culture of chapel or meeting-house was not barren, as the careers of Hale White or Lawrence amply bear out. Nonetheless, to reduce White to the company of Froude, Mrs Humphry Ward and J.M. Shorthouse, as an examiner of that dissenting background, is a false critical manoeuvre. His theme is relationship, expressed in a variety of modes throughout the novels; but the deliverance and renewal which all his protagonists seek becomes ever more firmly centred in the relation with Nature. This does not imply withdrawal into mystical contemplation; rather, as in Wordsworth, Nature is a reviving and ennobling presence authenticating both social and metaphysical ideals. The search for a fictional instrument which could adequately reproduce not only the confession of a second-rate sensitive mind in the Mark Rutherford novels, but also the pantheist aspiration and quest of his later heroines, removed Hale White from accepted fictional modes. The puritan mind is prone to introspection, and certainly the inwardness of experience related in Hale White's later novels was not susceptible to either the realist or romance genres then in the ascendancy. White was not content with the human typology of Thackeray or Trollope. 'What cardboard puppets are the creations of fiction', he exclaimed, 'compared with a common man or woman intimately known!' In his imagined world the 'common man or woman' could only be intimately known through an interrelated pattern of analysis, exposition and symbolism: 'If emotion be profound, symbolism, as a means of expression, is indispensable' (MP, 224–5). Thus it is that White's method in narrative, whilst resembling that of his friend George Eliot, in terms of analysis of motive and reticulation of causal relations, goes further than her in its poetic conception of man's relation to his environment. Lacking the comprehensive social vision of his great contemporary, Hale White nonetheless extends the frontiers of fiction in terms of a poetic rendition of life. His utterly frank version of the crisis of faith in the era of honest doubt, and its renewal through pantheism, gives him a unique position in the development of the novel.

Discussion of Hale White's fiction should take into account

his obsessive use of pseudonyms. All the novels were published in the name of 'Mark Rutherford', the 'Dissenting Minister' whose autobiography had begun the series. The enigma was further increased by the provision of a further intermediary between writer and audience, in the shape of 'Reuben Shapcott', Rutherford's friend, who was advertised as 'editor' of the novels. Hale White, who rarely discussed his work in the family circle, placed himself at three removes from his work: a sign perhaps of inner conflict. The adoption of distrust at the making of fiction which goes back tbrough Defoe to the seventeenth century. It may also be that the *mélange* of supposed authorship and editorship constitutes one of those rhetorical devices which Wayne Booth has explored, and provides an apt illustration of the authorial 'second self'. Through the personae of Rutherford and Shapcott White projects a distorted mirror image of his real self, scrupulously excising aspects of his own personality and career, so that no simple correlation between fiction and fact can be proposed, however close the parallels may appear. In fact, the later novels rely very little upon this technique: as White's art matured he felt less need for concealment, and though he retains the pseudonyms he speaks out as clearly through them as George Eliot had done through hers.

In a poem which prefaces *The Autobiography of Mark Rutherford* White, or his *alter ego*, writes:

> For I was ever commonplace;
> Of genius never had a trace;
> My thoughts the world have never fed,
> Mere echoes of the book last read.

Yet this deathbed confession closes with a seraphic vision of the sunrise. This spiritual vacillation precisely delineates the character of Mark Rutherford: fully conscious of his poverty, material and mental, yet possessed of deep aspirations. Rutherford is a convinced Darwinian, but not a pessimist. 'The law of the universe everywhere', he writes, 'is rather the perpetual rise from the lower to the higher; an immortality of aspiration after more perfect types; a suppression and happy forgetfulness of its comparative failures' (AMR, VI, 76). In the thwarted career of Rutherford, White dramatises this theme, the 'perpetual rise' of aspiration counterpoised by the fall of his fortunes. Though gloomy, the final impression of the book is far from one of unrelieved gloom. Unlike Hardy, White finds a core of optimism in man's struggle for affirmation.

In many particulars the story of Mark Rutherford is the story of the young Hale White. 'Childhood' shows Rutherford growing up in the dissenting society of a small Midlands town. Memories of school are less vivid than memories of summer holidays 'passed half-naked or altogether naked in the solitary meadows and in the water', or the winter break, with its delights of football and skating across the reaches of fenland ice (AMR, I, 4). The warmth and joy is set against the bankruptcy of dissent in the 1840s. The platitudes and deathly sleep of the chapel service are unfailingly rendered, the boy even envying the candle-snuffer who is permitted to move around during the interminable services (AMR, I, 7). The nadir of the boy's chapel career is reached when at the age of fourteen he is required to undergo 'conversion', professing to a change of heart of which he has no experience (AMR, I, 10–11). These manifestations of nullity and spiritual charade lay the foundations for his tormented character. In 'Preparations' White gives a devastating account of the dissenting college where Rutherford is to train for the ministry. Here the baleful grip of a decadent puritanism is clearly articulated. The biblical scholarship turns out to be a 'sham', the confutations of neology 'a mere sword of lath', and the proofs of God 'the chattering of sparrows' (AMR, II, 13). The inmates of the college, from the president, author of many 'prim little tracts', to the most successful of the students, with his vicious combination of theological rhetoric, acquisitiveness and covert eroticism, are the first of that gallery of dissenters which is to extend through the novels.

Rutherford is delivered by a genuinely Pauline conversion, the *Lyrical Ballads* inculcating in him a type of evolutionary pantheism. Although 'God is nowhere formally deposed' in Wordsworth, the true deity is Nature, 'and to this my reverence was transferred'. God was removed from the conventicle 'and dwelt on the downs in the far-away distances, and in every cloud-shadow which wandered across the valley' (AMR, II, 19). This act of self-renewal has predictable doctrinal repercussions: the atonement became 'an exemplification, rather than a contradiction, of Nature' (AMR, II, 22). Unlike White, the hero completes his studies and goes on probation to a chapel in the East Midlands. White's portrait of Water Lane Chapel, dominated by the oleaginous draper Mr Snale, the Dorcas tea-meetings, and his account of Rutherford's melancholia, rivals the art of George Eliot. The dialectical tug-of-war takes the form of a struggle in Mark Rutherford in which the puritan opposition of good and evil is transposed to the agnostic opposition of faith and despair. After a sermon to the uncomprehending congregation in which he recreates Christ in his own lonely image,[11] Rutherford falls prey to hypochondria and imagines his sanity is threatened. The stifled grief which fills this section recalls Tennyson:

> O weary life! O weary death!
> O spirit and heart made desolate!
> A damned vacillating state!
> ('Supposed Confessions of a Second-rate Sensitive Mind')

Temporary relief through Nature comes one morning in Devon, when the hero becomes 'aware of a kind of flush in the brain and a momentary relief' (AMR, III, 37). Gradual recuperation is stimulated by acquaintance with a freethinking compositor, Mardon, and his daughter Mary. Rutherford, his faith crumbling beneath the weight of Snale's chicanery and Mardon's stern rationalism, abandons the chapel and becomes a unitarian. This episode, based on White's preaching at Ditchling, begins inauspiciously enough with a dismal dinner party and damp walk home. But again Nature hints at a transcendence of this meagre reality: he walks along 'miserable and desponding', but suddenly 'the clouds rolled off with the south-west wind into detached, fleecy masses, separated by liquid blue gulfs, in which were sowed the stars'; the effect is 'a sense of the infinite, extinguishing all mean cares' (AMR, VII, 95). Immured in the rigmarole of village unitarianism, and bereft of the companionship of Mardon, Rutherford finds solace in a new acquaintance whose lepidoptery is the compensating activity for a tragic personal life: in his eager, yet quiet manner this man epitomises a sense of Nature's unity which Rutherford despairs of finding. His ideal of service seems doomed to failure: 'I had not then learned to correct this natural instinct to be of some service to mankind by the thought of the boundlessness of infinity and of nature's profuseness' (AMR, VIII, 111). The Carlylean sense of duty pulls Rutherford back to London, and at a school in Stoke Newington Rutherford enacts that dark night of the soul which White had undergone, 'the great light of London, like some unnatural dawn' overwhelming him with 'the most dreadful sense of loneliness', a 'nameless dread' and consequent 'efflux of all vitality' (AMR, VIII, 113). Again Tennyson, like White a master of nameless dread and the frisson of nervous disorder, is suggested:

> Be near me when my light is low,
> When the blood creeps, and the nerves prick
> And tingle; and the heart is sick,
> And all the wheels of Being slow.
> (*In Memoriam*, L)

From the treadmill of schoolmastering Rutherford escapes to the treadmill of publishing, acting as agent for Wollaston (John Chapman), and meeting his niece Theresa (Marian Evans). In this drudgery the apostle of Wordsworth can find little outlet for his pantheist enthusiasm: 'London lay round me like a mausoleum'. Yet the urban prison acts to heighten his sense of beauty: 'the very pressure of London produced a sensibility to whatever loveliness could be apprehended there' (AMR, IX, 122). With the death of Mardon the book drifts to an indeterminate close.

Mark Rutherford's Deliverance, as is proper to a sequel, continues the narrative but also suggests new growing —

points and thematic transmutations. The isolation of the first volume is tempered by a new warmth and human contact. In reading the unrelenting sketches of lower-class urban life, and of Rutherford's spiritual martyrdom, a remark of Hale White's is apposite: 'a truer sympathy is that which may require some effort, pity for common, dull, and deadly trouble that does not break out in shrieks' (MP, 147). White admires stoicism, that ability to hold fast which is one of the lessons of Spinoza. Writing of an Arctic explorer he regretted 'that so little is made as an education or as a religion of the lives of such men, for it is upon resolution such as theirs that almost all virtue depends' (LP, 66). This emphasis reveals the meaning of *Mark Rutherford's Deliverance*: his rejection of orthodox faith does not entail a rejection of morality; like George Eliot, White places the accent firmly on duty and social commitment. In his work with M'Kay in the poverty of Drury Lane, in his marriage, and especially in his relationship with his stepdaughter Marie, Rutherford is faced with the task of forging connexions.

This final stage of 'deliverance' is all the more remarkable because of the implacability of social organisations enshrined in the novels. The clerical slavery, the degradation of the lowest social strata, the gross and bitter hopelessness of the metropolis is experienced to the full by Rutherford. In a key passage he reveals how his pantheist faith is challenged by London. In the country, he writes, 'the pure sky and the landscape formed a large portion of my existence'. This led him to wonder 'how men could be worth anything if they could never see the face of nature'. The 'smoke of the streets' exposes traces of self-deception in his Wordsworthian faith, and he attacks 'literary' treatment of Nature: 'It might be imagined from much of this literature that true humanity and a belief in God are the offspring of the hills or the ocean; and by implication, if not expressly, the vast multitudes who hardly ever see the hills or the ocean must be without a religion.' These works of literature, inculcating love of scenery, 'are most depressing' since they hold out a vision of the unattainable (MRD, I, 5–6). Engaged in the drudgery of parliamentary reporting with his friend M'Kay, Rutherford is now schooled in the realities of urban economy. The streets around his lodgings in Goodge Street resemble hell:

The inhabitants drag themselves hither and thither in languor and uncertainty. Small mobs loiter at the doors of the gin palaces. Costermongers wander aimlessly, calling 'walnuts' with a cry so melancholy that it sounds as the wail of the hopelessly lost may be imagined to sound when their anguish has been deadened by the monotony of a million years.

(MRD, II, 17)

The *ennui* which these Gissingesque scenes produces in Rutherford is checked by M'Kay, who has 'a passionate desire to reform the world'. His arguments go to the heart of the Victorian social debate: 'What a farce, he would cry, is this poetry, philosophy, art and culture, when millions of wretched mortals are doomed to the eternal darkness and crime of the city'. The educated classes occupy themselves with 'speculations upon the Infinite', 'addresses to flowers', 'worship of waterfalls and flying clouds', 'while their neighbours lie grovelling in the mire' (MRD, II, 22). In response to this crisis M'Kay and Rutherford form their community in the Drury Lane slums, with its strange and pathetic gallery of disciples. They soon learn that they 'could not make the slightest impression on Drury Lane proper'. The realisation of this social impotence is described by Hale White with a biblical grandeur:

Our civilisation seemed nothing but a thin film or crust lying over a volcanic pit, and I often wondered whether some day the pit would not break up through it and destroy us all. Great towns are answerable for the creation and maintenance of the masses of dark, impenetrable, subterranean blackguardism, with which we became acquainted. The filthy gloom of the sky, the dirt of the street, the absence of fresh air, the herding of the poor into huge districts which cannot be opened up by those who would do good, are tremendous agencies of corruption which are active at such a rate that it is appalling to reflect what our future will be if the accumulation of population be not checked. To stand face to face with the insoluble is not pleasant.

(MRD, V, 65)

From this vision of universal damnation it is possible to

salvage some hope for humanity. 'No theory of the world is possible', Rutherford concedes; but whilst acknowledging the misery and horror he also points to 'an evening in June, the delight of men and women in one another, in music, and in the exercise of thought' (MRD, VI, 85). That is the 'Drury Lane Theology', far removed from the blank intransigence of the Water Lane Chapel variety.

With Rutherford's marriage to his former sweetheart, Ellen, and his entry into deadening clerical work, the final movement of the novel begins. At Somerset House Hale White suffered a kind of living death owing to the combined effect of the tedium of the work and the coarseness of his fellow-clerks: 'It is very terrible to think that the labour by which men are to live should be of this order. . . . Immense masses of [labour] in London are the merest slavery, and it is as mechanical as the daily journey of the omnibus horse' (MRD, VIII, 106). Rutherford's sufferings are lightened by his marriage, and by the growing awareness of the human value of his step-daughter, Marie.

This expansion of sympathy is subsumed in the Nature theme which, with its hints of a psychic resurrection, dominates the close of the novel. This effect is the more telling because of the harrowing quality of the preceding scenes. Thus the brief family visits to the country are no mere escape: they enact a return to the wellsprings of creative energy which Rutherford felt unconsciously as a boy playing in the river, or as a student discovering Wordsworth. There is nothing at the end of a conventional *coup de théâtre*. Rather do we feel that Rutherford, a sadder and a wiser man, still affirms the unity in love of all created life. The day-trip to Hastings evokes a new serenity, and a quiet sense of beauty. Free of the 'litter and filth' of London, 'its broken hedges, its brickbats, its torn advertisements', the family 'tread the immaculate shore' and watch a long row of porpoises, an appropriate symbol of natural delight, intelligence and movement. It was, says Rutherford, 'perfect in its beauty' because 'Everything breathed one spirit' (MRD, IX, 118–9). The novel closes with a picnic in the Surrey hills. Ellen has suffered a long illness, but there is also a sense here of Rutherford's own recuperation through Nature's healing powers. Although, as Shapcott abruptly informs the reader, Rutherford was 'dead and buried' a month after this, the closing pages record a true and credible deliverance:

We sat down on the floor made of the leaves of last year. At mid-day the stillness was profound, broken only by the softest of whispers descending from the great trees which spread over us their protecting arms. Every now and then it died down almost to nothing, and then slowly swelled and died again, as if the gods of the place were engaged in divine and harmonious talk. By moving a little towards the external edge of our canopy we beheld the plain all spread out before us, bounded by the heights of Sussex and Hampshire. It was veiled with the most tender blue, and above it was spread a sky which was white on the horizon and deepened by degrees into azure over our heads. . . . Everything in the future, even the winter in London, was painted by Hope, and the death of the summer brought no sadness. Rather did summer dying in such fashion fill our hearts with repose, and even more than repose — with actual joy.

(MRD, IX, 127–8)

Hale White's third novel, *The Revolution in Tanner's Lane*,[12] takes a more controversial form. The attempt to render the dissenting tradition at both zenith and nadir imposes a strain, which is felt in the architecture of the book. The fissure in the narrative is perhaps a result of the novelist's fidelity to his material, and a mark of his indifference to novelistic technique. Significantly, *The Revolution in Tanner's Lane* is the only Hale White novel in which the transfer from urban to rural implies a dilution of emotion and sensibility. Its dialectic thus places it outside the Nature tradition; the first section deals with the exploits of a radical printer, Zachariah Coleman, in revolutionary circles in London during the closing years of the Napoleonic Wars, and the second section moves to Cowfold, a sleepy Midlands town during the mid-century. The revolution of the title refers ironically not to the ferment surrounding the insurgent cabal centred on the Caillauds and Major Cartwright, but to the ejection of the Reverend Broad from the Tanner's Lane Chapel in Cowfold, a kind of dissenting Barchester. Of revolution in the true sense there is no conception in Cowfold. Rather, the fervour of the Caillauds dribbles away into the liberal decency of the Allens, honourable but parochial, out of touch with the new urban centres of thought.

In none of the novels is Nature simply an escape from pressure, and in the first section of *The Revolution in Tanner's Lane* White shows how the figures of the cadre, entombed in the city, possess a deep sense of the potency of Nature. Thus the life-enhancing passion of Caillaud and his daughter is imaged in a striking accession of Nature into the metropolis: their work-room is 'on a level with an innumerable multitude of red chimney-pots pouring forth stinking smoke', but occasionally 'Nature resumed her rights, and it was possible to feel that sky, stars, sun, and moon still existed'. On wild autumn nights 'the Great Bear hung over the dismal waste of smutty tiles', and in summer 'the heights of Highgate were visible, proclaiming the gospel of a beyond'.[13] White adds that the Caillauds liked 'the excitement of the city, and the feeling that they were so near to everything that was stirring in men's minds' (RTL, V, 65–6). Pauline Caillaud is presented much as a force of Nature. In the dancing scene, so puzzling to the puritan mind of Zachariah, her intuitive and passional forces are dramatized with Lawrencean power (RTL, V, 74). Such an episode exposes the inadequacy of puritanism as a belief, related to Zachariah's tormented marriage, and is indeed a paradigm of Hale White's art. Unlike Pauline, Zachariah finds no solace in the *crise de conscience* brought to a head by his loveless marriage. Questioning God for a reason for his suffering he gazes out at the stars: 'There was nothing to help him there. They mocked him rather with their imperturbable, obstinate stillness' (RTL, VII, 106). Yet in a later crisis, walking from Liverpool to Lancaster to see Caillaud in his death cell, Coleman feels the sanative power of Nature:

Over in the east the intense deep blue of the sky softened a little. Then the trees in that quarter began to contrast themselves against the background and reveal their distinguishing shapes. Swiftly . . . the darkness was thinned, and resolved itself overhead into pure sapphire, shaded into yellow below and in front of him, while in the west it was still almost black. The grassy floor of the meadows now showed its colour, grey green, with the dew lying on it, and in the glimmer under the hedge might be discerned a hare or two stirring. Star by star disappeared, until none were left, save Venus, shining like a lamp till the very moment almost when the sun's disc touched the horizon. Half a dozen larks mounted and poured forth that ecstasy which no bird but the lark can translate. More amazing than the loveliness of scene, sound, and scent around him was the sense of irresistible movement. He stopped to watch it, for it grew so rapid that he could almost detect definite pulsations. Throb followed throb every second with increasing force, and in a moment more a burning speck of gold was visible. . . . He slowly turned his eyes away and walked onwards.

(RTL, XV, 223–4)

The juxtaposition of this with the death-cell scene reveals that Nature can redeem and transcend the human imbroglio. Such metaphysical communing is wholly foreign to the provincials of Cowfold, in whose lineaments White depicts a pietism which epitomises the final surrender of nonconformity to utter conformity. In his masterly evocation of Calvinism in decay, in the hidebound social and religious mores which are the vestiges of the dynamic of puritanism, White sums up the meaning of his novel. The renewal of society promised in the first part dwindles to the insignificant manoeuvrings of clergy and laity in the second, crystallised by the personality of the Reverend Broad, as his name suggests the epitome of *acedia*. Like Wordsworth's Immortality Ode, *The Revolution in Tanner's Lane* essentially deals with loss of vitality and inspiration, and visualises a retreat into a willed, manufactured religion. Nature is ineffectual here, and the characters are held in the iron grip of historical necessity.

Cowfold appears in a slightly different light in White's novella, *Miriam's Schooling*.[14] The heroine, Miriam Tacchi, is one of White's 'insurgents'. Born to the dull round of Cowfold as she perceives it in her father's watchmaking shop, the narrative traces her provincial upbringing, her immersion in the turbulence of London, and her final acceptance of the Cowfold ethos through her love of her craftsman husband. The successive stages of her schooling, and education of the emotions no less thorough than that accorded to Jane Austen's heroines, are bound up with the Nature theme. Indeed, her 'salvation' is wrought through her intuition of the immense rhythms of the universe revealed to her by astronomy, and a resultant expansion of humanity and acceptance of her own personality.

At the outset White explicitly sounds a note of conflict between the heroine and her environment. Miriam is ill-adapted to the conformist pressure of a country town: 'Her room was never in order. Nothing was ever hung up; nothing was put in its place. . . . With her lessons she did not succeed'. Similarly, although she is musical her voice is 'altogether undisciplined'. She has fondness for animals, and a concern for cleanliness, both quirks which mark her off from the towns-people. But what most sets her apart is her refusal to court *aura popularis*: 'a certain originality in her criticisms on Cowfold men, women, and events, a certain rectification which she always gave to the conventional mode of regarding them' (MS, 52–3). This is pathetically dramatized in her defence of Mr Cutts, whom Cowfold gossip has convicted of arson. Her altruistic visit to the county-town solicitor to testify to the good character of Cutts before an uncomprehending audience defines the gap in sensibility and idealism between Miriam and her environment, but it also signals the dangers of a refusal to compromise. This tension can only be resolved by leaving the claustrophobic inanity of Cowfold for London. This takes the schooling much further. The self-deception of Miriam's romantic day dream is tellingly reproduced in the first experience of Miriam and her brother on their arrival in town:

They had fancied an outlook on a gay promenade, and they had in its place a waste expanse of dirty dull roofs and smoking chimneys. If they looked down below, they saw a series of small courtyards used for the purpose of storing refuse which could not be put in the dustbin — bottles, broken crockery, and odd bits of rusty iron.

(MS, 73)

Surrounded by these scraps the boy and girl are drawn into an atmosphere of dissolution as into a whirlpool, Andrew succumbing to alcohol and Miriam becoming entangled with the

Byronic music-hall singer, George Montgomery. The slough of despond is plumbed in a river-side scene where Miriam's anguish expresses itself in a desire for extinction. The urban landscape takes on the quality of a nightmare as Miriam enters this 'dismal, most depressing region' in which the 'spirits were smitten as if with paralysis'. White observes that Miriam 'did not know that her misery was partly a London misery, due to the change from fresh air and wholesome living to foul air and unnatural living'. Once again in Hale White, Nature intervenes, and a thunderstorm, with lightning flaming 'round the golden cross of St Paul's', restores to her some sense of perspective (MS, 112–14).

Miriam suffers a fever, and is moved to 'one of the villages lying by the side of the Avon in Wiltshire, just where that part of Salisbury Plain on which stands Stonehenge slopes down to the river'. Here the leading motif of the story emerges, the Wordsworthian belief in the regenerative powers of Nature. Miriam becomes sensible to the 'exquisite beauty' of the landscape: 'the downs are chalk, and though they are wide-sweeping and treeless, save for clusters of beech here and there on the heights, the dale with its water, meadows, cattle, and dense woods, so different from the uplands above them, is in peculiar and lovely harmony with them'. This paradisal setting is contiguous with a more primitive assertion of natural power and desolation, at Stonehenge. On his own visit to the stones White experienced 'a perfectly worthless depression begotten by the idea of the transitory passage of the generations across the planet', and Miriam shares this emotion. Yet this leads her to the resolve 'that she must do something for her fellow-creatures' (MS, 116–7). The schooling is not over, and Miriam fails in her chosen career as a nurse because of her 'general looseness and want of system'. Her duty lies in the more limited sphere of Cowfold. Careless as to what becomes of her Miriam marries a local man, Didymus Farrow. There is little mutual understanding, but an agent of salvation appears, in the person of a country vicar who, like Hale White, has taken up astronomy. Astonished by the vicar's praise of her husband's skill in making the telescope box, Miriam gazes through the instrument: 'what affected her most was to see Jupiter's solemn, still movement, and she gazed and gazed, utterly absorbed, until at last he had disappeared' (MS, 140). As in *Two on a Tower* or Lawrence's story, 'The Captain's Doll', astronomy here connects the individual with cosmic forces, and compels a *rapprochement* between the man and woman.

When Farrow constructs an orrery, Miriam for the first time recognises and honours his true worth. Her love of the stars becomes inextricably bound up with her feelings towards her husband. As Venus rises after a storm, 'glittering like molten silver', her 'first thought was her husband' (MS, 147). This emotional revaluation is counter-pointed by her interview with Fitchew, 'creature of all work in Cowfold, one of the honestest souls in the place'. Fitchew emerges as a kind of noble savage: despite physical suffering and a difficult marriage he counsels a dignified stoicism, reminding Miriam that ' "we are as we are, and we must make the best of it" ' (MS, 148–51). The tale closes with a moving transfiguration of the commonplace. After a night of rain the south-west wind, 'pure, delicious, scented with all that was sweet from fields and woods', hailed in Meredithian tones as 'the Life-Giver', streams across Cowfold. Miriam rises in the dawn and goes into the fields, her thoughts flowing 'with rapidity and intensity'. As the sun rises Miriam falls sobbing to her knees: her education is complete. The conflict is resolved, and she is able to accept and love her husband:

She was about to get up to cut some bread and butter, and she went behind him and kissed the top of his head. He turned round, his eyes sparkling. . . . He mused a little, and when she sat down he said in a tone which for him was strangely serious — 'Thank you, my dear; that was very, very sweet.'

(MS, 151–3)

In the companion-piece, *Michael Trevanion*, Hale White achieves a similar compression of emotion. The fervent love of the Cornish stonemason for his son, which drives him to interfere in the boy's love-affair, is recreated with tact and understanding. The tug of passions, with the boy in the middle, is an unusual topic for White, and he deals with its complexities in a dramatic manner. The nub of the tale, the girl's rescue from drowning by the boy, is a recollection of a similar incident from White's boyhood (EL, 53). Robert Trevanion is one of those Hale White characters who have a peculiarly close affinity with their natural surroundings, especially the sun and the sea. When the sun burns down in the summer 'the landscape and seascape were all changed for him', they become 'visionary rather than actual'. Robert is conceived as a figure in a landscape:

A boat lay here and there idle, with its shadow its perfect double in unwavering detail and blackness. Just beyond this cerulean lake the river ebb . . . rippled swiftly round Deadman's Nose. . . . Beyond and beyond lay the ocean, unruffled, melting into the white haze which united it with the sky on the horizon.

(MS, 162–3)

Michael does not share his son's dreamily poetic temperament, being 'fervently religious, upright, temperate, but given somewhat to moodiness and passion' (MS, 155). He has made a bad marriage, and focusses all his hopes on his son. Of the girl he feels deeply suspicious, having a nonconformist 'horror of women who could swim' (MS, 159). The rescue brings the lovers together, and the sensuous passion, so foreign to the father, is delicately rendered by White. Michael, brought up 'in a narrow sect, self-centred, moody', misuses a letter to interfere between the lovers, and succeeds in driving away his son. In a mirror image of the first bathing scene he is himself rescued by the girl, to whom he is reconciled at the cost of his sectarian dogmatism. Tracing his son to Plymouth, they too are reconciled in a death scene which subsumes both the themes and landscapes of the tale:

It was a perfectly unsullied night, with no moon, but with brilliant stars. Father and son sat upon a bench facing the sea, and the lighthouse from the rock sent its bright beam across the water. There is consolation and hope in those vivid rays. They speak of something superior to the darkness or storm — something which has been raised by human intelligence and human effort.

In the novels composed during the 1890s Hale White refined his art to a final synthesis. His themes are here articulated with the greatest profundity: the struggle between passion and duty; the conflict between inner conviction and conventional morality; the reverence for the autonomy of the individual conjoined with a desire for social commitment; and the conception of man's place in Nature — a theme which assumes crucial importance for his heroines.

The spiritual drama of *Catharine Furze*[15] is enacted in the fenland town of Eastthorpe, and its nature is symbolised by White's description of the town huddled round the river, but surrounded by the fens, 'the large expanse of sky, the soft clouds distinct in form almost to the far distant horizon and, looking eastwards, the illimitable distance towards the fens and the sea' (CF, I, 9). Catharine is a girl of large, if cloudy, aspiration who finds no fulfilment in the society furnished by the customers of her father's ironmongery, or the chapel respectability of her mother's tea parties. This cramping atmosphere is caught with economic wit in the opening scene between the local worthies in Mr Furze's back parlour. The conversation, full of sly references to horseflesh, cattle, property and widows, properly defines the mentality of masculine Eastthorpe, whilst Mrs Furze's adjurations to her daughter — and her keen avoidance of the earthier topics of the man's world — illumine the feminine view of the proprieties (CF, I, 11–18). Hale White once wrote that 'to one man the world is a collection of material facts. To the other it is incessantly awful and mysterious', and this aptly formulates the clash between Catharine and her environment, a division first made apparent when the shop burns down and her mother proposes a move to the fashionable 'Terrace'. From the muffled etiquette of the new home Catharine escapes to her friends the Bellamys at Chapel Farm. This rural retreat lies 'bare to the winds, breezy, airy, full of light. In summer the front door was always open', and in the garden apricot and plum flourish. The place is ruled over by Mrs Bellamy, who despite her sickliness, embodies the plenitude of Nature: 'She loved plenty. The jug was always full to overflowing with beer, and the dishes were always heaped up with good things, so that nobody was ever afraid of robbing his neighbour'. Catharine is 'never weary' of the farm, 'and the living creatures on it were her especial delight' (CF, IV, 55–7).

Thus the farm becomes an emblem of more than simple rusticity; the resonance here is that of a place in which human and natural are enveloped in a unifying rhythm. On her return to the terrace Catharine finds that Mrs Furze 'was doing everything she could to make herself genteel', decking out her new house with lighter furniture and oleographs which 'professed to represent sunsets, sunrises, and full moons, at Tintern, Como, and other places not named' — the sham cult of Nature, with its glance at Wordsworth, juxtaposed with Catharine's love of the farm, a love aptly declared by her very name (CF, V, 73–4). The ache for respectability which seduces Mrs Furze from chapel to church, is comically acted out in the condescending visit of Mrs Colston, the brewer's wife, at a moment of domestic upheaval compounded by the 'vulgar' intrusion of Mrs Bellamy with her rural ancedotes (CF, V, 76–91).

The removal of Catharine to the educational establishment of the Misses Ponsonby at Abchurch serves to heighten and develop the novel as *Bildungsroman*. The Misses Ponsonby conduct their tutelage by the light of Calvinist Evangelicalism, and espouse the need 'to conceal or suppress all individuality on subjects disputable in their own sect' (CF, VI, 98). Their platitudes are undermined, however, by the tuition of the village clergyman, Theophilus Cardew, whose ardent seriousness stirs an immediate response in Catharine. After hearing his first sermon she experiences an awakening which is likened to a process of Nature: 'It was with her as we can imagine it to be with some bud long folded in darkness which, silently in the dewy May night, loosens its leaves, and, as the sun rises, bares itself to the depths of its cup to the blue sky and the light' (CF, VI, 115). Cardew's almost demonic quest for truth, and his neglect of a sympathetic but inarticulate wife, is examined in some complexity, and his attractiveness for Catharine has been carefully prepared. When Mrs Cardew persuaded her husband to expound Milton to her, in an attempt to ingratiate herself, the result is that he draws closer to the younger girl (CF, VIII, 136–41).[16] Finding in Catharine a soul-mate, Cardew presses his attentions upon her, and 'it seemed as if she was being sucked in by a whirlpool and carried she knew not whither' (CF, VIII, 144). The relationship is cemented in secret by her reading a manuscript of Cardew's, and when she retreats to Chapel Farm she is confronted by him in a scene of great power, rendered through Nature.

At first she is blissfully united with the landscape: 'Clouds, massive, white, sharply outlined, betokening thunder, lay on the horizon in a long line', and Catharine feels it to be 'a day of exultation' when summer 'passed into her blood and created in her simple, uncontaminated bliss'. Cardew appears, and though the conversation is overtly trivial he is 'literally possessed'. 'The more he thought about her, the less did he see and hear of the world outside him, and no motive for action found access to him which was not derived from her'. The relationship is delicately balanced: 'She loved this man; it was a perilous moment: one touch, a hair's breadth of oscillation, and the two would have been one'. In Lawrence the 'perilous moment' would be ratified by Nature; in Hale White Nature supervenes to preserve the proprieties: 'The first note of the thunder was heard, and suddenly the image of Mrs Cardew presented itself before Catharine's eyes'. This is not an easy resolution, the tensions are deftly realised; but the openness to Nature presages an extension of the heroine's human sympathies:

The sky was clearing in the west, and suddenly in a rift Arcturus, about to set, broke through and looked at her. . . . What inexplicable contrasts! Terror and divinest beauty; the calm of the infinite interstellar space and her own anguish; each an undoubted fact, but each to be taken by itself as it stood: the star was there, the dark blue depth was there, but they were no answer to the storm or her sorrow.

(CF, IX, 176–81)

The presentation of the ebb and flow of emotion here, the chilling recession into astronomical time, and the tension between fulfilment of desire and altruistic renunciation, has a rich maturity which belies the judgement that Hale White cannot handle romantic love. The relationship is depicted with a sense of the interrelated tissues of motive, and balance of intellectual, emotional and social claims which George Eliot would have endorsed; it is adult in the fullest sense.

Catharine's fate, like Dorothea's, is to have been born into the wrong epoch. As White explains, 'the world as it is now is no place for people so framed'. Her progress was not to be 'uniform from sixteen to sixty'; rather, she undergoes a 'new birth': 'The sun shone with new light, a new lustre lay on river and meadow, the stars became something more than mere luminous points in the sky, she asked herself strange questions, and she loved more than ever her long wanderings at Chapel Farm' (CF, X, 188–9). The gradual slide of Furze's business towards bankruptcy, and Mrs Furze's matrimonial ambitions for Catharine, with the consequent disgrace of Tom Catch-pole, Fruze's invaluable assistant and Catharine's secret admirer, serve to intensify and prolong the quasi-illicit liaison between the protagonists. Tom, wrongly dismissed from his post at Mrs Furze's instigation, seeks out Catharine at the farm in order to declare both his innocence and his love. But the weather, 'cold and dark', with 'nothing in the heavens or earth which seemed to have any relationship with man', shows this interview to be a wan parody of the earlier scene between the lovers (CF, XVII, 284–7). Not even the Edenic ministrations of Chapel Farm can revive Catharine, possessed as she is by 'vague and misty' terrors, and wrestling with 'shapeless, cling-ing forms' (CF, XVII, 299). From this crisis she is temporarily delivered by the atheist Dr Turnbull, who turns her thoughts to the misfortunes of others, and specifically to her former servant who is dying. This has some effect, and Catharine nurses the girl in her rural hovel; the lineaments of poverty are shown here uncompromisingly. In death the girl, and all her family, return forgotten to the earth, in a sense fulfilling Turn-bull's materialist philosophy: 'in one season the sorrel and dandelions took possession, and Phoebe's grave became like all the others — a scarcely distinguishable undulation in the tall, rank herbage' (CF, XVIII, 325).

A final interview between the clergyman and Catharine opens Cardew's eyes, and he makes restitution to his wife; but the heroine's fate is pre-figured in the narrative: Mr Furze goes bankrupt and his property is sold up, and Eastthorpe is inundated by a flood.[17] The last movement is set at Chapel Farm, where a beautiful May day holds a fleeting promise of renewal for Catharine, as she looks out over the stream at the place of her first interview: 'Never had a day been to her what that day was. She felt as if she lay open to all the life of spring which was pouring up through the earth, and it swept into her as if she were one of those bursting exultant chestnut buds, the sight of which she loved so in April and May'. The nascent moment of resurrection through Nature, framed in an almost sexual mode, fades, and she dies gazing out at the meadows, watched over by a transformed Cardew (CF, XXI, 361–5). This moving *dévoilement* reveals, White remarks, that 'By their love for each other they were both saved', the religious and the natural providing a fitting epitaph for this great novel.

Turnbull's nostrum of social commitment as the antidote to thwarted passion comes to fruition in *Clara Hopgood*.[18] Despite similarities in the theme of provincialism and personal destiny, that *Clara Hopgood* is the more ambitious novel is shown by the contrasts in the personalities of the two sisters. Although the note of foiled idealism again dominates the action Hale White's viewpoint is now more wide-ranging. The Hopgood girls, as much as the Dashwoods, Schlegels or Brangwens, act out a dichotomy in the author's mind between intuition and ratiocination. The danger of schematisation is avoided by the deeply felt rendering of both provincial and urban scenes, and by White's authoritative moral presence. If *Clara Hopgood* lacks the intensity of the Mark Rutherford books there is a gain in terms of a wider social range, a more pluralistic sense of life's possibilities, and a contemplative yet passionately felt philosophical standpoint.

Fenmarket, where the sisters live with their widowed

mother, is another Eastthorpe or Cowfold, and White again draws attention to the sense of freedom in the vistas of space, 'the wide, dome-like expanse of the sky', the 'freedom' and 'the stars on a clear night' (CH, 1, 2). Collisions with the educational establishment have fixed in Madge 'a strong insurgent tendency', and both girls count themselves Goetheans from the time they were in Weimar. The oppression of Fenmarket is intensified by memories of German culture; their visits to *Egmont* or *Fidelio* are now replaced by 'a travelling waxwork show', 'psalm-tunes', and the orthodoxy of Ram Lane chapel substitutes for their debates on Straussian neology (CH, II, 24–5). The isolation of the girls is extreme, their education having removed them entirely from the orbit of Fenmarket. By opening with a game of chess between the sisters White makes visible the differences in personality, and through their discussion of instinct the subsequent action is prepared. Clara enjoys in chess the 'planning and forecasting', and the 'consequences of manoeuvres', whilst Madge is all instinct and intuition. Yet the sisters are given real human dimensions, and never dwindle into types. The analogical role of the chess is revealed when Madge sweeps the pieces away and the girls argue about love, Clara emphasising the risks inherent in a sudden onset of passion and Madge deploring that reason should be employed on such a topic (CH, III, 29–36). This theoretical debate gains practical application with the arrival of Frank Palmer, son of an old family friend. He is attractive and likeable, yet at the centre of his personality is a nullity which emerges when he plays and sings: 'There was a curious lack in him also of correspondence between his music and the rest of himself' (CH, IV, 47). Through involvement with amateur theatricals in which they play Ferdinand and Miranda (an echo perhaps of *Mansfield Park*) Madge and Frank are drawn together. Despite the false notes in Frank's character, exposed by his professed love of Tennyson, a love based upon 'a very good review' which he half remembers, Madge argues that love is a force which is 'independent of views': 'How handsome he was, and then his passion for

her! She had read something of passion, but she never knew till
now what the white intensity of its flame in a man could be'
(CH, VIII, 84–8). Clara, though seeing the situation with
perspicacity, refrains from comment, fearing to inflame her
sister. Walking in the country the lovers disagree, significantly
over Wordsworth, are reconciled and take refuge from a storm
in a nearby barn. Here the seduction scene, imaged by lightning striking an elm, takes place. The thunder which kept
Catharine and Cardew apart has thrown Madge and Frank
together. He is sent abroad on business, but proposes marriage. She feels 'no true love' for him, and though pregnant,
refuses his offer, an act which defines all the attitudes to life
around her. Mrs Hopgood reflects, 'This fine life, then, was a
failure, and a perfect example of literary and artistic training
had gone the way of the common wenches whose affiliation
cases figure in the county newspaper' (CH, X, 103).

The social disgrace of illegitimacy removes the family from
les convenances of Fenmarket, and they take up dismal lodgings in London. The juxtaposition of urban and rural which
informs earlier novels here attains a new poignancy. Clara
recollects the vision of sun and stars in the country, and tries to
carry herself above the 'filthy smother' of fog and dirt, 'a
loathsome composition of everything disgusting which could
be produced by millions of human beings and animals packed
together in soot' (CH, XVIII, 166–7). Yet though the suffering is intense the intercession of Nature, endorsing the
higher aspirations of mankind, and promising a transcendence
of mortality, is more potent than ever before in Hale White. At
Letherhead Madge becomes susceptible to the beneficence of
natural forces: 'Sick at heart and despairing, she could not help
being touched, and she thought to herself how strange the
world is — so transcendent both in glory and horror ... a
world infinite both ways' (CH, XI, 110). This sense of infinity
is crucial for the characters; but the immediate emanation of
Nature and its goodness is the earthy, gossiping figure of Mrs
Caffyn, whose simple hospitality and openness to experience
endear her to Madge. Mrs Caffyn is esteemed 'little better

than a heathen' by the local parson for her practical view of
morality and sin; in fact she takes the form of a natural force
unmediated by convention or compromise, a residual centre of
wisdom.

A more erudite repository of man's knowledge and historical experience appears in the person of Baruch Cohen, an
instrument-maker who befriends Clara and obtains a job for
her. For the first time in Hale White's novels, Spinoza's
philosophy is explicitly expounded, appropriately by a
middle-aged Jew:[19]

In nothing was he more Jewish than in a tendency to dwell upon the One, or
what he called God, clinging still to the expression of his forefathers
although departing so widely from them. In his ethics and system of life . . .
there was the same intolerance of a multiplicity which was not reducible to
unity.

(CH, XIX, 181)

His creed, when he is taxed by Madge, is pure Spinozism, and
the whole-hearted pantheism places the lives of all the characters in a new light: ' "I believe that all thought is a manifestation of the Being, who is One, whom you may call God if you
like, and that, as It never was created, It will never be destroyed" '. Given this postulate of unity, Cohen holds ' "the
difficulties which arise from the perpetual and unconscious
confusion of the qualities of thought and soul with those of
body disappear" ' (CH, XXVIII, 277). Those characters who
are to be 'saved' will to some extent recognise this unity, and
their place within the great cosmic pattern.

Cohen is not, however, simply a mouthpiece for Spinozan
commentary. He is fully drawn by Hale White, who shows
him to be ardently seeking a woman who may respond to his
mixture of passion and intellect, and falling deeply in love with
Clara. Yet at the moment of his unspoken declaration to
Clara, aware of something which 'fell and flashed before her
like lightning' she renounces his love in favour of her sister
(CH, XXVII, 265). This is a seminal moment: it answers Mrs
Furze's strictures about the futility of a 'fine life' devoted to art
and literature and the cultivation of personal feelings. Clara's

compassionate renunciation is one of the many moments which look forward to Forster — the evolution of her inner resources has 'paid off'. A chance meeting with the exiled Mazzini brings the group into contact with 'a saint of the Reason', and raises most acutely the problem of commitment — a commitment which Cohen feels unable to give. Clara, however, is driven to cogitate deeply upon the Italian cause and the possibilities of action.[20] Her giving up personal love and happiness is not puritan but Goethean, as White's translation of a key passage in Goethe shows: 'To be disinterested in everything, but most so in love and friendship, was my highest desire, my maxim, my practice'.

Cohen and Madge are drawn closer, and the novel ends joyously with Mrs Caffyn presiding over an excursion into the Surrey hills. Here the whole party experiences that unity with Nature which Cohen has propounded, and which Hale White has explored in each of his novels. The final movement opens with Clara watching the dawn:

High up on the zenith, the approach of the sun to the horizon was proclaimed by the most delicate tints of rose-colour, but the cloud-bank above him was dark and untouched, although the blue which was over it, was every moment becoming paler. Clara watched; she was moved even to tears by the beauty of the scene, but she was stirred by something more than beauty. . . . In a few moments the highest top of the cloud-rampart was kindled, and the whole wavy outline became a fringe of flame. In a few moments more the fire just at one point became blinding, and in another second the sun emerged, the first arrowy shaft passed into her chamber, the first shadow was cast, and it was day. She put her hands to her face; the tears fell faster, but she wiped them away and her great purpose was fixed.

(CH, XXIX, 284–5)

Her purpose — to fight for Italian unity and independence — is thus directly related to her pantheism, a love of all created life replacing the narrower human love. In this context the 'strange and supernatural peace' which falls on her, as an intimation of death, is felt as fulfilment rather than tragedy. Later in the day, standing with the valley beneath them and the Sussex downs in the distance, Madge and Cohen reach an understanding which involves their own rejection of Mazzini's appeal. As Cohen reflects, ' "I have sometimes thought . . . that the love of any two persons in this world may fulfil an eternal purpose which is as necessary to the Universe as a great revolution" '. So 'the indifference of Nature to the world's turmoil' endorses both views, all is subsumed beneath a Spinozan design for the evolution of man (CH, XXIX, 290). The epilogue, revealing that Clara has died in the republican struggle, does not modify the peace and tranquillity, the unity in brotherhood, which Nature confers in the triumphant closing scene.

Hale White's novels chart in a unique form the passage from puritan to pantheist, and the humanity and wisdom which informs their varied structures is directly related to his concept of Nature. In no case does Nature-worship offer a simple escape; White's experience of the world was too real for that. But Nature comes to offer a new perspective, a mode of transcendence, to a suffering humanity, and in exploration of this theme Hale White has few peers.

Notes

1   W. Hale White, *Last Pages from a Journal* (1915) (London, Oxford University Press, 1915, hereafter cited as LP), p. 76.

2   W. Hale White, *The Autobiography of Mark Rutherford* (1881) (London, Fisher Unwin, 1903, hereafter cited as AMR).

3   W. Hale White, *Mark Rutherford's Deliverance* (1885) (London, Fisher Unwin, 1923, hereafter cited as MRD).

4   W. Hale White, *The Early Life of Mark Rutherford, By Himself* (1913) (London, Oxford University Press, 1913, hereafter cited as EL), p. 61.

5   D. White (ed.), *The Groombridge Diary* (1924) (London, Oxford University Press, 1924, hereafter cited as GD), p. 29.

6   W. Hale White, *More Pages from a Journal* (1910) (London, Oxford University Press, 1910, hereafter cited as MP), pp. 196–7.

7   W. Hale White, *Pages from a Journal* (1900) (London, Oxford University Press, 1930, hereafter cited as P), pp. 2 and 12.

8   W. Hale White, *Letters to Three Friends* (1924) (London, Oxford University Press, 1924, hereafter cited as LTF), p. 107.

9   C. Darwin, *The Origin of Species*, ed. J.W. Burrow (Harmondsworth, Penguin Books, 1970).

10 See *'Under Beachy Head'*, with its marked resemblance to Jefferies: 'On a morning like this there is no death, the sin of the world is swallowed up; theological and metaphysical problems cease to have any meaning' (MP, 170).

11 See Rutherford's later remarks that the 'story of Jesus is the story of the poor and forgotten', and that Christ attracts 'every one who has walked in sadness because his destiny has not fitted his aspirations' (AMR, IV, 47–8).

12 W. Hale White, *The Revolution in Tanner's Lane* (1887) (London, Fisher Unwin, n.d., hereafter cited as RTL).

13 See Edwin Reardon's London eyrie, with its command of the 'green ridge from Hampstead to Highgate, with Primrose Hill and the foliage of Regent's Park in the foreground'. Though Gissing writes that 'Sunset often afforded rich effects, but they were for solitary musing', Nature offers no sense of transcendence to his urban personae (*New Grub Street*, IV).

14 W. Hale White, *Miriam's Schooling and Other Papers* (1890) (London, Fisher Unwin, n.d., hereafter cited as MS).

15 W. Hale White, *Catharine Furze* (1893) (London, Fisher Unwin, 1913, hereafter cited as CF).

16 See the narrator's dismissal of Margaret in 'The Sweetness of a Man's Friend': 'as she had never read 'Paradise Lost', and knew nothing of the laws of blank verse, I did not go on and was disappointed' (LP, 39).

17 The parallels with *The Mill on the Floss* scarcely need stressing. They include striking similarities in character and situation of the two heroines; that sense of interconnexion so prevalent in George Eliot, and often voiced in similar terms by White, for example, 'Tom's appearance even was not an accident, but a thread carefully woven, one may say, in the web that night' (CF, XII, 229); the parallel between the downfalls of Tulliver and Furze; the renunciation by each heroine, in a river scene, of the key temptation, followed in both cases by death; the presence in each novel of a 'guardian' figure (on her visit to Dr Kenn, Maggie meets family friends called Turnbull); and in each novel, a flood scene, the rescue of 'Orkid Jim' by Tom Catchpole, whom he has wronged, echoing George Eliot's finale.

18 W. Hale White, *Clara Hopgood* (1896) (London, Fisher Unwin, 1913, hereafter cited as CH).

19 Linda Hughes has argued that the conception of the sisters is in itself Spinozan, and that the characters develop in the light of White's renewed interest in the philosopher. See L. Hughes, 'Madge and Clara Hopgood: Hale White's Spinozan sisters', *Victorian Studies*, XVIII (1974–5), pp. 57–75. This is plausible; however, the conception of Baruch Cohen probably owes a good deal to *Daniel Deronda*: like White's Jewish seer, Mordecai Cohen is associated with a second-hand bookseller, and his

prophecies are justified by reference to Spinoza; the cause of Italian unity, and Mazzini's role in the struggle, is adverted to by Deronda in the debate at the 'Hand and Banner'.

20 Clara's enlistment in the *risorgimento* may be modelled upon the career of Jesse White Mario. On the growth from personal to impersonal idealism, see White's note: 'The tree does not develop first at this point and then at the other. *All over* it proceeds to perfection. So should the growth of character be, and so it is when it is divinely prompted' (LP, 256).

7 E.M. Forster

Forster once said that Ibsen's characters, 'as they wrangle among the oval tables and stoves are watched by an unseen power which slips between their words';[1] and he went on to identify this power with the Norwegian landscape. Similar powers are at work in his own novels, in which a social comedy harking back to Jane Austen is, as he once remarked of a book by Lowes Dickinson, 'supported by an intense emotion which is never allowed to ruffle the surface'.[2] The union of poise and passion is peculiarly Forsterian, a union of the paternal Thornton sobriety and the maternal Whichelo love. For Forster, standing at the fag-end of Victorian liberalism, the search for the harmonisation of these elements in his being may be seen as a quest for a new theology. He once defined his central theme as 'the importance of personal relationships and the private life',[3] and it is upon this centrality that his claims as a novelist rest. The idea of the heart 'untrained and untutored' is a recurrent one in Forster with his vision of a civilisation resting upon 'undeveloped hearts' (AH, 15). His characters are either blindly unaware of this lack of development, or struggling towards a psychic renewal within a stringent code of moral values which has to be rejected or overturned.

The novel is implicitly concerned with society as a residuum of human values and conduct; but Forster's imagination constantly impels him beyond the merely social. Thus in formal terms there is a clash between the social interaction implied by plot and narrative and the timeless metaphysical values which place that action within a more cosmic framework. There is a dialectic, that is to say, between history and transcendence, between the symbolic or poetic, and the comic or realistic. It is in this friction that the sources of Forster's art are to be discerned. He maintained that the work of art 'is a self-contained entity, with a life of its own' possessing an 'internal order' (TC, 88); as such, it must be made sufficiently plastic to contain these disparate elements. Forster's own career as a novelist is specifically a vindication of this concern with plasticity. Lowes Dickinson's work, he recognised, 'became more tantative as his grasp on reality tightened' (GLD, 94), and a similar movement is to be found in his own work, beginning as it does with the tightly economic social comedy novels and culminating in the pluralistic universe of *A Passage to India*.[4] The stylised antitheses of the early closed novels open out first into the compromise ending of *The Longest Journey*[5] and then into the lyrical indeterminacy of *Maurice*[6] and *A Passage to India*. The sense of an ending is crucial to Forster's concept of the novel: 'Expansion. That is the idea the novelist must cling to. Not completion. Not rounding off but opening out'.[7]

In his concern for humane values, in his stress upon individual response, and in his criticism of conformity both social and religious, Forster stands as heir to Romanticism. To his omnipresent themes of sincerity, freedom and culture should be added one which comes to assume crucial significance: the primacy of Nature, and man's organic connexion with the natural world.

II

'Most of the inhabitants of India do not mind how India is governed. Nor are the lower animals of England concerned about England, but in the tropics the indifference is more prominent, the inarticulate world is closer at hand and readier to resume control' (P I, X, 111). Thus does Forster define the social life of his characters in India; those whom he ratifies show some awareness of the presence and overwhelming power of Nature ready 'to resume control' — a natural order which, in the caves, seems implacably turned in upon itself in a final nullity. Forster often presents the natural universe as one which is beyond human understanding, and one from which man has become disconnected. The ambiguity in Nature is reflected both in the vatic utterances of Professor Godbole, and in the descent into silence of Mrs Moore. But in earlier stories and novels Nature is the archetypal emblem of Words-worthian insight and transcendence. One of Forster's earliest pieces was a school essay on 'The influence of climate and physical conditions upon national character'.[8] In a sense his life work was an exploration of this theme.

The corollary, in Romantic ideology, of any kind of Nature mysticism, was a critique of capitalist industrialism, and it is this which links Forster with his predecessors. Tolstoy's outlook, he wrote, 'was agricultural: he never realised the implications of the machine' (TC, 204). Forster's own work is an attempt to realise the implications of the machine for humanity. In his anti-Wellsian story, 'The Machine Stops', he envisions a time when men have 'harnessed Leviathan' and become victims of their own technology. Predictably, in such a situation, 'the old literature, with its praise of Nature and its fear of Nature, rang false as the prattle of a child'.[9] The denaturing effects of mass production are more subtly treated in the novels, where they manifest themselves in the erosion of human relationships, the dwindling of humane values, the death of passion, and in a suffocating suburbia which is both physical and psychic. Yet the novels, in some ways, set out to reverse the trend: *The Longest Journey, Howards End*[10] and *Maurice* all finally endorse the supremacy of Nature, and the genuine human life as one organically connected with Nature.

The instinctual in man links him with natural processes, and this link is best exposed in human evolution and continuity through the family. Nature therefore is a symbol not only of otherness but the vital channel of continuity. This vital impulse is often impaired in the novels: the death of the baby in *Where Angels Fear to Tread*,[11] or the death of Rickie's daughter, are mere *exempla* of a tendency to inanition which besets the characters. Nature as procreation forces itself upon the novelist, and becomes the key to the wider issue of the survival of the race. Yet Forster is not really comfortable in his hand-

ling of Stephen with his daughter, and Helen's child remains a
cipher. His treatment of the cycle of generation is external by
comparison with Lawrence, and he recognises this by turning
his back upon it in his finest analyses of human relations —
Rickie and Stephen, Alec and Maurice, or Fielding and Aziz.
Yet Forster's homosexuality, and the effect it has upon his
material, does not stifle his recognition of the centrality of
Nature. On the contrary, the teeming multiplicity of the
natural world contains and endorses all forms of passionate
relation.

Forster searches, often in vain, for a society with an organic
connexion with the soil of the kind envisaged by Edward
Carpenter. This is why his guardian figures, sharing with
Lowes Dickinson the 'enhanced sensibility' which comes to
them 'through scenery' (GLD, 150), are rooted in Nature.
Forster's work is pervaded by the same conviction which he
discerned in Cowper, 'that we have a humble and inalienable
heritage, country England, which no one covets, and which
nothing can take away'. This sense of inheritance is important
to Forster, and derives not only from Romanticism but from
the novelists who were Forster's immediate predecessors.
Speaking of literary influence Forster once asserted that 'the
only books that influence us are those for which we are ready,
and which have gone a little further down our particular path
than we have yet got ourselves' (TC, 214–5). This is peculiarly
apt for Meredith, with whom there may have been family
connexions, and whose presence pervades the early novels.[12]
The strenuous denigration of Meredith in *Aspects of the
Novel*, dismissing him as a fake who took the Home Counties
for the universe, reads like the apostasy of a disciple (AN, 97).
To the circle which Forster joined at Cambridge, Meredith
was a figure at which 'much of the universe and all Cambridge
trembled' (AN, 96), a writer whose 'philosophy' was seriously
debated. Speaking of Eliot in 1928 Forster noted that the
younger generation were 'inside his idiom as the young of
1900 were inside George Meredith's' (AH, 104), and his 1899
reading-list, which contains not only *The Egoist* but also *Evan*

Harrington, Richard Feverel, and 'A Reading of Earth', is eloquent testimony to this (EMF, 70). Lowes Dickinson's *A Modern Symposium* features one 'Geoffrey Vivian', whom Forster identifies as Meredith, and characterises as pouring 'new wine into the nineteenth century bottles of evolution, yet not more than they can hold' (GLD, 113). Meredith is thus seminal to Forster as an evolutionist, one who reads the evolving patterning of man and Nature. Looking back on this time, Forster testified that 'scraps from accredited authors like George Meredith and Thackeray' had 'lain about' in his mind over a period of many years (AH, 135). The agile balance between comedy and poetry which Meredith at his best achieves is also typical of Forster, and the Italian novels are the work of a writer who has learnt much from *The Ordeal of Richard Feverel* and *The Egoist.* Indeed in *A Room With a View*[13] the action is reminiscent of *The Egoist,* and it is no coincidence that Forster gives Cecil Vyse a fervent admiration for Meredith, since Vyse is an egoist trapped by his own egoism. Similarly, Rickie invests Agnes with the qualities of a Meredith heroine. After the death of Gerald 'she reminded him of a heroine of Meredith's — but a heroine at the end the book. All had written about her. She had played her mighty part, and knew that it was over'. In order to understand her, he enthuses to Ansell, it would be necessary to study, 'Beatrice, and Clara Middleton, and Brunnhilde' (LJ, VII, 75–6; LJ, IX, 87). This befuddled literary idealism tells the reader much about both Agnes and Rickie, and the roles allotted to them. The young Forster learnt from Meredith, as he makes Vyse announce, that 'the cause of Comedy and the cause of Truth are really the same' (RWV, X, 124). In the mature novels the corrective is muted, and the Meredithian Nature poetry becomes more potent: the action of *Maurice* continues the debate of 'The Woods of Westermain', and in the Marabar caves Fielding was originally depicted as reciting this very poem.[14] Forster may have rejected Meredith, but much remained in his art that was deeply Meredithian.

If Forster came to feel that he could no longer 'look up with

George Meredith to the stars, the army of unalterable law' (TC, 89), he never sloughed off a more profound debt to Hardy. The pervasiveness of Hardy is very general, as Forster revealed when he observed that 'the work of Hardy is my home and that of Meredith cannot be' (AN, 102). This presence is felt in the stress upon man's organic connexion with Nature, in the essential loneliness of the protagonists, and in the same sense of man in the grip of larger forces. Yet Hardy's portrayal of ineluctable Darwinian struggle is mitigated by Forster's comedy, and the later novelist is ultimately more lyrical and romantic in his apprehension of relationships — the causal is replaced by the casual.

The postulate that Jefferies exerted an influence is more hypothetical. The sole reference in Forster's published work is in Leonard Bast's description of his night walk; but there the discussion assumed a wide knowledge of Jefferies's writings and an understanding of his view of Nature. Forster may have associated Jefferies with Edward Carpenter. In 1885 Lowes Dickinson went to work on a socialistic farm in Surrey, and Forster recounts how in a nearby cottage was living H.S. Salt, a magnet for 'cranks and queer people' such as Shaw and the Fabians. Salt was a fervent admirer of Jefferies and Thoreau, and may have discussed their work with Lowes Dickinson, as the latter's fantasy 'Crankhill Farm' shows: two young men sit near Frensham Ponds and their talk 'drifts towards immortality, and they agree that it exists here and now, and the trouble of an hour becomes nothing' — a sense of epiphany close to *The Story of My Heart*. 'All through his life', Forster adds, 'Dickinson had this hope that, at a touch, the world of matter would be — not annihilated but transformed' (GLD, 53–4).

Forster therefore learned from an existing tradition of writing about Nature. Read in the light of this tradition, such novels as *The Longest Journey* and *Maurice* especially acquire a new signification. Forster wrote at a time when it was still possible to take Nature as a paradigm of a freer and more liberal reality. Like the boy in 'The Story of a Panic', the early work should be read as 'saluting, praising, and blessing the great forces and manifestations of Nature' (CSS, 26). Part of the power of *A Passage to India* is the new awareness that the note of *Sehnsucht* has been withdrawn from Nature and man.

III

The characteristic movement of Forster's novels is a thrust away from the enclosure of society, with its pressures of conformity, snobbery and spiritual inertia. The antithesis is direct between an enclosed safe life and one of freedom and risk. Not until *Howards End* did Forster feel capable of reconciling these antitheses. In the early novels Nature images the freeing of the psyche from imprisonment, and the struggle for freedom often has tragic results. Nature is not Forster's only symbol of awakening: Cambridge, music, friendship, all form part of the complex of ideas with which he confronts suburbia, but Nature comes to subsume these within its myriad forms and potentialities. The perception of Nature, the quality of the inner human response to landscape, helps to define the quality of the perceiving mind and heart. Nature's social lawlessness and primacy are first identified with Italy or Greece; but in the latter stages of *A Room With a View* Forster turns towards English landscape and explores its symbolic potential. *Maruice* with its impassioned vision of 'wild England' as a paradigm of human freedom fulfils this development of Forster's art. The later modernist darkening of Nature in India lies beyond the scope of this study; it may be that the nihilism of the caves had personal as well as historical philosophical roots.

Emerson once wrote, 'Man is fallen; nature is erect, and serves as a differential thermometer, detecting the presence or absence of the divine sentiment in man'. This thermometer is applied by Forster's own Emersons in *A Room With a View*, and Mr Emerson's doctrinal words are endorsed first by Italy and later by the Surrey hills. Mr Emerson becomes Lucy's spiritual tutor in Italy, enabling her to see 'the lights dancing in the Arno and the cypresses of San Miniato, and the foot-hills of the Apennines, black against the rising moon' (RWV, I, 18). ' "Do you suppose there's any difference between spring in nature and spring in man?" ' he demands. ' "But there we go, praising the one and condemning the other as improper, ashamed that the same laws work eternally through both" ' (RWV, VI, 71). It is these 'laws' which lead Lucy to the ritual kiss on the hillside, learning through the young Italian driver 'that the world was beautiful and direct', and opening herself to the 'influence of spring' (RWV, VI, 74). This is her *aufklärung*, and though the social comedy permits postponement, Nature finally triumphs at Windy Corner.

Over against the Emersons and the Italians Forster sets the 'undeveloped hearts' of convention, ranging from the Reverend Eager who finds in the thunderstorm 'something almost blasphemous in this horror of the elements' (RWV, VII, 77), to Cecil Vyse, a Meredithian who paradoxically knows nothing of Nature. Cecil mouths the platitudes of the Nature loving *littérateur*, the housebound devotee of the 'literature of the open road' so trenchantly to be dismissed in *Aspects of the Novel*. Cecil likes to animadvert upon Nature, 'simplest of topics, he thought', but the 'outdoor world was not very familiar to him, and occasionally he went wrong in a question of fact' (RWV, IX, 106–7).Lucy associates Cecil with the claustrophobia of the drawing-room 'with no view'. This is crucial and is to be a constant in Forster's imagery. Although Vyse protests that he should be connected with the open air, he is shocked when Lucy tells him how she has bathed in the woodland 'Sacred Lake' (RWV, IX, 114–5). George Emerson, on the contrary, is wholly natural. When she plays tennis with him at Windy Corner Lucy reflects on the beauty of the Weald, and concludes that 'she was noticing more things in her England' (RWV, XV, 166): the act of perception, the openness to Nature, signifies a vital development of her personality.

The seminal episode is the bathing scene (RWV, XII). This baptismal rite is a plunge below the waters of initiation into a fellowship through Nature of the type preached by Edward Carpenter. By a typical Forster irony the priest of this rite is the secular Emerson, and one of the initiates the local clergyman, Mr Beebe. Emerson assures Beebe that the Garden of Eden, biblically disposed in the past, ' "is really yet to come. We shall enter it when we no longer despise our bodies" '. ' "Today," ' he concludes, ' "I believe that we must discover Nature" '. Forster wittily undercuts this sententiousness by showing Freddy, 'appalled at the mass of philosophy that was approaching him', leading the young men out to bathe. Yet the point has been made: the fatal divorce of man from Nature of which Freud speaks is identified, and a programme of rehabilitation proposed. The ceremonial immersion, with its parallels with similar scenes in *Richard Feverel, The Dewy Morn* and *The White Peacock*, is a first step in this programme. The men strip off, George 'Michelangelesque on the flooded margin', and even for Mr Beebe the world of 'motor-cars and Rural Deans receded illimitably': 'Water, sky, evergreens, a wind — these things not even the seasons can touch'. They rotate around the pool 'after the fashion of the nymphs in Götter-dammerung', and equally in search of a lost treasure — the tap-root to Nature, which is to be realised through passion. The intervention of the ladies puts Mr Beebe to flight, but George 'bare-foot, bare-chested, radiant and personable against the shadowy woods' stands firm and bows to Lucy, drawing her psychologically away from convention into the free life of Nature, as the gamekeeper is to do for Maurice. This baptismal initiation-scene is a 'call to the blood and to the relaxed will', a 'momentary chalice for youth' which in its vital enactment transforms the participants within the sacred grove.[15]

The Longest Journey also owed its origins to an encounter with natural man. Forster recalled how he had visited the earthworks which dominate the Wiltshire section of the novel: 'I caught fire on the Rings . . . breathing the air and smelling the fields, and there was human reinforcement from the shepherds who grazed up there'. The novel circles warily round this encounter. For the first time Sawston, Cambridge and the natural world are juxtaposed in a symphonic pattern giving an effect of space which, as Forster remarked of *War and Peace*, 'is exhilarating, and leaves behind it an effect like music' (AN, 46).

The novel opens with the central issue of romanticism, perception of the outer world. Beneath the jejune Berkeleian debate on appearance and reality the nub of the matter may be discerned: does the mind merely receive, or literally create its perceptions? It is progressively shown that Rickie is incapable of perceiving reality, and solaces himself with a series of surrogates beginning with the dell, then his stories, and then, disastrously, Agnes, who immerses him in the world of Sawston School. Other characters are also limited in vision, whether like Ansell through dry intellectualism, like Gerald through mindless physicality,[16] like Mrs Failing through moral cynicism, or like the Pembrokes through dead adherence to convention. Only Stephen, nourished by his unconscious connexion with earth, sees life steady and whole. Agnes's interruption of the philosophical debate acts out the withering away of knowledge, love and friendship beneath the dead hands of Sawston. Rickie has crept 'cold and friendless and ignorant out of a great public school, preparing for a silent and solitary journey' (LJ, I, 10); ironically, the solitariness is demolished by Agnes, but Shelley's poem implies the failure of such exclusive relations, and Rickie emerges yoked forever to a partner with whom he has nothing in common. At Cambridge he expands and nourishes his secret life in a dell which becomes 'a church where indeed you could do anything you liked, but where anything you did would be transfigured' (LJ, II, 23). Rickie wishes here to find universal love, but is limited to a coterie of aesthetes. The invitation to Agnes to enter the dell represents his desire to return to a mother figure and signals his surrender to her power, a power which may have an admixture of incest-guilt. Certainly the image of the Magna Mater, all-devouring, is not far away here. The inner weakness and debility is mirrored in Rickie's stories, quasi-mythological fantasies similar to Forster's own early work.

According to Agnes's bald summary these tales take as their

theme 'getting into touch with Nature'; their vapidity is the result of an intellectualised dislocation from Nature which besets the author. Forster shows this beautifully when the sunbathing Stephen reads what appears to be a version of 'Other Kingdom' on the flat roof at Cadover: 'In touch with Nature! The girl was a tree! He lit his pipe and gazed at the radiant earth. The foreground was hidden, but there was the village with its elms, and the Roman Road, and Cadbury Rings. There, too, were those woods, and little beech copses, crowning a waste of down. Not to mention the air, or the sun, or water' (LJ, XII, 126). These allegories of Nature are an artificial failure, and Rickie seems doomed to be stifled and have life taken away from him. Yet as Rickie enters the limbo of Sawston School, Forster opens out the novel unexpectedly, so that the characters become nakedly exposed to the workings of Nature. Forster noted, 'I received, I created, I restored, and for many years the Wiltshire landscape remained haunted by my fictional ghost' (EMF, 149). Certainly his debt to Hardy is finely repaid here:

The rain tilted a little from the South-West. For the most part it fell from a grey cloud silently, but now and then the tilt increased, and a kind of sigh passed over the country as the drops lashed the walls, trees, shepherds, and other motionless objects that stood in their slanting career.

On the slopes beyond Mrs Failing and the other 'complicated people', 'stood the eternal man and the eternal dog' (LJ, X, 90), at this moment represented by Flea Thompson, whose family are all 'named out of Shakespeare' (LJ, X, 91). The effect of this dramatic shift, despite the spiky presence of Mrs Failing, who finds 'our dull stepmother' the earth 'unspeakably' boring, is remarkable. Forster lifts the veil from the social veneer of Sawston to reveal an ancient peasant life inhering in Nature. Wiltshire, with its pre-historic shrines, becomes the chief symbol of the enduring power of Nature; it is no accident that Stephen has 'knocked the bottom' out of Christianity:

Beneath these colours lurked the unconquerable chalk, and wherever the soil was poor it emerged. The grassy track, so gay with scabious and bed-straw, was snow-white at the bottom of its ruts. A dazzling amphitheatre gleamed in the flank of a distant hill, cut for some Olympian audience. And here and there, whatever the surface crop, the earth broke into little embankments, little ditches, little mounds; there had been no lack of drama to solace the gods.

(LJ, XII, 116)

The delicate symbolism, with its suggestion that the chalk ridges imply natural impulse running beneath the artifice of society, subsumes the total action.

Nature is given a number of spokesmen, two of them already dead — an idea Forster was to develop in Mrs Wilcox. The first is Mr Failing, the type of agrarian socialist beloved of Lowes Dickinson. Failing has a theory which he put into practice at Cadover, and which he propounded in his book *The True Patriot*, which Rickie reads to Mrs Failing: ' "Let us love one another. Let our children, physical and spiritual, love one another. It is all that we can do. Perhaps the earth will neglect our love. Perhaps she will confirm it, and suffer some rallying-point, spire, mound, for the new generations to cherish" '. Mrs Failing, a complex and contradictory woman, rejects this Carpenterian programme, arguing that artificiality is 'the only good thing in life' (LJ, XXXIV, 273). The sanctities of Nature counter her Wildean assertion, and the veiled presence of Failing endows the novel with a sense of instinctive wisdom. Robert, who becomes the lover of Rickie's mother, is an even more transparent presence, yet he also upholds the natural against the hermetic sterility of suburbia, a sterility which has as its *simulacrum* the flickering Dantesque horror of Sawston School. The mating of Robert and Rickie's mother, involving the resurrection of dead characters, is unsatisfactory; yet it does mark the union of two classes — an act which is crucial to Forster, and is to be repeated by Bast and Helen, Maurice and Alec, and even Aziz and Fielding. It is an act which reconciles primitive and civilised, and leads to the survival of the fittest in its issue, Stephen Wonham.

Through Stephen the boundlessness of Nature impinges upon the closed worlds of Cambridge and Sawston. His potency derives from his lack of consciousness of his role: he is part of the 'unconquerable chalk', and his lack of self-consciousness is the criterion beside which the impotent sensitivity of Rickie, the massively platitudinous Pembroke, and the stealthy intellectualism of Ansell must be judged. A cancelled chapter expands these contrasts poetically. Stephen is shown wandering unconsciously through a forest, swimming, having a comic naked encounter with a group of 'gentlefolk', and finally escaping and returning to the Rings. These images of a boy undergoing baptismal union with forest and water expertly illuminate the rigor mortis of Sawston School and Rickie's descent into unreality. When Stephen is expelled from Cadover, 'the perilous house' (LJ, XII, 116), breaking windows with a lump of the chalk from which he springs, his journey takes on the character of a quest: he wrestles with intellectualism (Ansell), demolishes suburbia (Pembroke), and tries to revive spirituality (Rickie). This quest involves both the *contretemps* at the school and the plunge into the Hades of the modern commercial world as Stephen crosses 'the black river' into London; his mind is full of images of Wiltshire (LJ, XXX, 246), images borne out by Failing's dictum that the Londoner — like Leonard Bast — is 'a country man on the road to sterility'. But there is here no accommodation with the forces of business such as Forster was to attempt in his next novel. Stephen, as Ansell divines, 'had been back somewhere — back to some table of the gods, spread in a field where there is no noise' (LJ, XXVI, 217), and in London he feels lost and disheartened. He soon retraces his steps towards the heart of England, hunting, as his affinity with Orion suggests, for the body and soul of his brother. In the poetic scene of the paper-boats flaming on the stream Rickie's blindness and adherence to empty forms is pierced, and a momentary illumination and fellowship granted.[17]

This scene, and the ensuing sacrifice, enacts Rickie's belated rejection of Agnes and of the bourgeois values which stifle natural life. Agnes had trapped him into a marriage through which he could vicariously enjoy Gerald's bullying, but Rickie's moral dereliction stems from a core of idealism. He is deluded about his mother, his wife, and his brother, and his progressive disillusionment provides the burden of the novel. As this proceeds Rickie is forced to concede 'that the love that inspired [Agnes] might be higher than his own. Yet did it not exclude them both from much that is gracious? That dream of his when he rode on the Wiltshire expanses — a curious dream: the lark silent, the earth dissolving. And he awoke from it into a valley full of men' (LJ, XIX, 179). Thus the quarrelsome horseride into Salisbury becomes in retrospect an image of potential brotherhood and fellowship in Nature, but Rickie perceives its ongoing pulsation even when, at the death of his daughter, he rails at its 'cruelty': 'our refinement and piety are but as bubbles', he realises, 'hurrying downwards on the turbid waters', carrying away the generations just as the Cadover river carries off the flame-boats: 'They break, and the stream continues' (LJ, XXIII, 195).

It is the stream of continuity, with its cycle of decay and regeneration, which Stephen embodies, and which the elemental structure of the Rings symbolises. When Rickie enters the Rings in which the family revelation is to occur, the 'whole system of the country lay spread before' him, embossed by the pre-history of Old Sarum and Stonehenge, with its substratum of chalk. Whilst he reads the Shelleyan depiction of the awfulness of the 'longest journey', with its implications for his own marriage, he simultaneously remarks the village lovers on a nearby down, and feels them 'to be nearer the truth' (LJ, XIII, 132–3).[18] Rickie's sacrificial death, with its echoes from the self-mutilation of Attis, merely acts out the implications of that moment.[19]

It is this truth — the continuity of Nature — that the final pages, with Stephen rejecting the advice of Pembroke about Rickie's manuscripts, and preparing to sleep out on the downs with his young daughter, confirm. Rickie is sacrificed in order that Stephen can continue the race. Thus read the novel becomes more than a semi-autobiographical private ritual. It is to do with the survival of the race, a survival only possible in living connexion with Nature.

The connexion which the motto of *Howards End* adjures also involves redemption and rebirth, but now Forster endeavours to bridge the gap between Sawston, whose agents, the energetic Wilcoxes, replace the narrow Pembrokes, and Bloomsbury. This reintegration is wrought through the mysterious power of Mrs Wilcox, the activity of Stephen here receding into the passive wisdom of the old lady who comes to stand for the continuity of an organic and rural life. The antitheses, and the welding of the themes, are managed with skill, but the lyrical absorption of *The Longest Journey* is sacrificed to a wider philosophical *schema*. It is again through the relation to the natural world that the characters are weighed and judged; and it is through the process of generation that racial continuity is assured.

The preoccupation as to who will take over England is an important one, as Mrs Munt accounces: ' "Of course I regard you Schlegels as English . . . to the backbone" ' (HE, II, 5). But this large concern with national identity arises naturally out of the Horatian pieties of Howards End, a place sacred to Forster's imagination since boyhood. Mrs Wilcox becomes a commentary upon Forster's remark that Crabbe 'had the great good luck to belong to a particular part of England, and to belong to it all his life' (TC, 169). The house and its attendant farm is the great good place of the novel: it acts as a yardstick against which the characters are measured. At Howards End, with its wych-elm impregnated with sacrificial pigs' teeth, 'had lived an elder race, to which we look back with disquietude. The country which we visit at weekends was really a home to it, and the graver sides of life, the deaths, the partings, the yearning for love, have their deepest expression in the heart of the fields'. It is in these English farms that 'one might see life steadily and see it whole' (HE, XXXIII, 266). The house is man's root back to the instinctual life of Nature and generation, and this wisdom is conferred upon the guardian figures, Miss Avery and Mrs Wilcox, to whom 'pictures, concerts and people are all of small and equal value' (HE, VIII, 67). Mrs Wilcox is distinguished from both the Wilcox and Schlegel clans: 'the instinctive wisdom the past can alone bestow had descended upon her' (HE, III, 19), Forster notes, adding elsewhere that in her characterisation he was interested 'in the imaginative effect of someone alive, but in a different way from other characters — living on other lives'. She represents a continuity remorselessly threatened by the modern world of discrete matter: 'London's creeping' (HE, XLIV, 337).

The permanence of the great forms of Nature which is a *donnée* of *The Longest Journey* is here questioned, and the old Forsterian distinction of 'England or Suburbia' (HE, III, 13) acquires a new urgency. England is in some sense being raped by Wilcoxian progress: 'month by month the roads smelt more strongly of petrol, and were more difficult to cross, and human beings heard each other speak with greater difficulty, breathed less of the air, and saw less of the sky. Nature withdrew: the leaves were falling by midsummer; the sun shone through dirt with an admired abscurity' (HE, XIII, 106). This sense of inexorable urbanisation points to a nomadic civilisation in which 'Trees and meadows and mountains will only be a spectacle, and the binding force that they once exercised on character must be entrusted to Love alone' (HE, XXXI, 258). Under the influence of Mrs Wilcox, Margaret begins to see London as hellish, 'the narrower streets oppressing [her] like the galleries of a mine' (HE, X, 82). Forster here draws upon the realism of Gissing and the Mark Rutherford novels, and the shadow of their lower middle-class martyrs falls upon Leonard Bast, who epitomises the struggle of the unenlightened spirit to free itself from slavery to mass production. Bast represents an indefensible result of commercial exploitation, and fights desperately against Wilcox's Social Darwinism. It is no accident that he is introduced at the Beethoven concert: culture and Nature are the modes of apprehension through which he believes he will be 'saved'. Nor is it coincidence that he is 'grandson to the shepherd or ploughboy whom civilisation had sucked into the town', one of those 'who have lost the life of the body and failed to reach the life of the spirit' (HE, XIV, 113). Bast's aspirations come home with tragic force.

The novel's proposition that 'any human being lies nearer to the unseen than any organisation' (HE, IV, 28) is given full examination in the conception of Bast, and his blind upward struggle attains a symbolic status. This struggle is conducted first in terms of music, literature and aesthetics, but most centrally in terms of a lamentably botched return to Nature. Bast is a native who can never truly return.

This episode occupies the centre of the novel. Bast, early in his career 'supposed the unknown to be books, literature, clever conversation', but gradually realises that 'walking in the dark among the suburban hills' will bring him closest to the unseen (HE, XIV, 122). In the description, both sublime and pathetic, of his adventure, Bast enacts the crucial problem for modern economic man, to go, as Margaret puts it, 'away past books and houses to the truth' (HE, XVI, 140). The 'truth' eludes Bast, and he later dies beneath a pile of books; yet it marks him off from his fellows, and holds out hope for the future. In the manuscript version Bast tells how 'he could stand it no longer' in his office and 'walked for the love of the Earth'. Though he cloaks his quest in the detritus of literary affectation, conjuring up *Richard Feverel*, Stevenson's *Prince Otto*, Jefferies, 'Borrow, Thoreau and sorrow', the genuine meaning of his experience shines authentically through: ' "But was the dawn wonderful?" asked Helen. With unforgettable sincerity he replied: "No." The word flew again like a pebble from the sling. Down toppled all that had seemed ignoble or literary in his talk, down toppled tiresome RLS and "the love of the earth" '. Although Bast attributed his motive to Jefferies, Helen perceives that it 'came from something far greater' — 'the spirit that led Jefferies to write', 'part of the eternal sunrise that shows George Borrow Stonehenge' (HE, XIV, 114–119).

The forces of capitalism express themselves in the bad advice Wilcox gives Bast, advice which destroys him; before this, however, he is 'saved' by his Shropshire encounter with Helen. In pursuing the Wilcox ménage to Shropshire Bast returns to the landscape of his ancestors, whilst Margaret realises that her own party 'had no part with the earth and its emotions. They were dust, and a stink, and cosmopolitan chatter' (HE, XXV, 212). It is at Oniton that the motifs of the novel are rehearsed, the antithesis between culture and commerce here related to the more seismic disjunction between man and Nature. The racial theme of regeneration is embodied in the night scene at Clun Castle, when Margaret calls out to the dark: ' "Saxon or Celt?" she continued, laughing in the darkness. "But it doesn't matter. Whichever you are, you will have to listen to me. I love this place. I love Shropshire. I hate London" ' (HE, XXV, 214).[20]

Charles Wilcox, the hidden representative of London, listens discomfited to this outburst. The world of telegrams and anger may disrupt Oniton, but it enjoys no life-enhancing contact with Nature, whereas Bast and Helen, in their brief union, do endow the future with a meaningful pattern. The superb close of the Oniton section, imbued with the atmosphere of Housman, subsumes these varied ideas and images:

Day and night the river flows down into England, day after day the sun retreats into the Welsh mountains, and the tower chimes 'See the Conquering Hero'. But the Wilcoxes have no part in the place, nor in any place. It is not their names that recur in the parish register. It is not their ghosts that sigh among the alders at evening. They have swept into the valley and swept out of it, leaving a little dust and a little money behind.

(HE, XXIX, 246)

The dust, Forster implies, is both the dust of conquest and a *memento mori*: the kingdom of money is built upon sand, and though its rulers are the conquering heroes they will disappear from the face of the earth without trace. That the Wilcoxes are not to inherit England is due, first, to the passive influence of Mrs Wilcox, and second, to the activity and values of the Schlegel sisters.

The sisters act out a dialectic which forces all the characters to assess their own position. Their vision of life is finally realised at Howards End; it hinges upon the centrality of Nature, defines the meaning of tradition, and articulates the distinction between themselves and the Wilcoxes who have 'moulded' England: it is a vision first realised on the Purbeck Hills:

There was a long silence, during which the tide returned into Poole harbour. 'One would lose something' murmured Helen, apparently to herself. The water crept over the mud-flats towards the gorse and the blackened heather. Branksea Island lost its immense foreshores, and became a sombre episode of trees. Frome was forced inward towards Dorchester, Stour against Wimborne, Avon towards Salisbury, and over the immense displacement the sun presided, leading it to triumph ere he sank to rest. England was alive, throbbing through all her estuaries, crying for joy through the mouths of all her gulls, and the north wind, with contrary motion, blew stronger against her rising seas.

(HE, XIX, 172).

The sisters, raised in full romantic manner high above their surroundings, gain an anthropomorphically united vision of nationhood and tradition. Helen reflects upon the 'loss' which connexion with Wilcoxes would entail, and the almost sexual imagery of joy seems to endorse her view. The rivers 'forced inwards' are drawn each to an ancient centre of English life and culture, and the sun, the principle of life, dominates the whole. Helen endorses this passionate life inhering in Nature; Margaret will attempt a compromise with the forces of the new England.

The death of Mrs Wilcox, with its Hardyesque woodcutter's commentary (HE, XI, 87), leaves Howards End vacant until the entry of the sisters and the provision of an heir. In this way a society founded in the cash-nexus is undercut by one depending on humanity and natural feeling, though the Schlegels openly admit their own dependence upon money. The virtual castration of the Wilcox empire-builders may seem, in relation to Margaret's longed-for connexion, a strange triumph. But the lyrical expansion of the closing pages reaffirms the transcendent power of Nature in human affairs. The flurry of events surrounding Bast's death and the occupation of Howards End, are meant to set the stage for a reaffirmation of the theme of *The Longest Journey*: an acknowledgement, couched in the delicate symbols of the flowers, wych-elm and hay, of the underlying pull of the earth.

'I want to love a strong young man of the lower classes and be loved by him and even hurt by him', Forster confided to his diary in 1935. 'That is my ticket, and then I have wanted to write respectable novels'.[21] Over thirty years before, as a young man, he had written: 'I'd better eat my soul for I certainly shan't have it. I'm going to be a minority [homosexual] if not a solitary, and I'd best make copy out of my position. There is nothing contemptible or cynical in this. I too have sweet waters though I shall never drink them' (EMF, 111). These two emotional outbursts may act to frame his 'unrespectable' novel, *Maurice*, the one major work in which, *sub rosa*, Forster 'made copy' out of his situation. Yet this distorts the final impact of *Maurice*: it is a work of great art and subtlety which should be read, not as a thesis novel on homosexuality, but as the quintessence of Forster's treatment of man's place in Nature. Like *Lady Chatterley's Lover*, which it resembles in its Darwinian theme of the resurrection of an atrophied upper class psyche through sexual union with the virility of the working class, *Maurice* succeeds in placing sexual matters within a wider context of industrialisation and the teeming diversity and energy of Nature. *Maurice* was conceived on a visit to Edward Carpenter, and 'belongs to an England where it was still possible to get lost. It belongs', Forster continues, 'to the last moment of the greenwood', which later 'ended catastrophically and inevitably' (M, 240). A pre-lapsarian vision thus lies at the heart of *Maurice*, as it does in *The White Peacock*. The novelist accepts Nature as a retreat into which humane values are forced by the modern world with its economic and moral pressures and conformity. The movement of the novel is thus outwards towards 'the country that is the countryside, and emerges from the unfathomable past' (TC, 243). *Maurice* attempts one answer to the questions he posed many years later in his Abinger pageant: 'Houses and bungalows, hotels, restaurants and flats, arterial roads, by-passes, petrol pumps, and pylons — are these man's final triumph? Or is there another England, green and eternal, which will outlast them?' (AH, 384).

Forster sets himself the formidable test of studying a middle-class Edwardian devoid of any unique characteristics save his sexual nature. Maurice Hall is presented as 'handsome, healthy, bodily attractive, mentally torpid, not a bad business man and rather a snob' (M, 236). The magnificent economy of the opening scene, in which Maurice's preparatory school master, Mr Ducie, attempts to instil into the boy the facts of life, adumbrates the range and power of the book. Ducie, who was 'soaked in evolution' (M, I, 4), sketches male and female organs in the sand, lectures upon them in a tangential way, and is later relieved to see them washed away by the tide. The *tendenz* is anti-Darwinian: the sexual union does not exist simply for procreation and the survival of the species. The fussy concerns of Ducie, and the cramped social world which he mirrors, are obliterated by the surging elemental sea. Returning to his soft matriarchal home in the suburbs Maruice is saddened by the absence of Ansell, the garden-boy, and is exposed to Dr Barry's querulous critique of the suburban way of life (M, II, 22). The miserable minor public school which he attends provides an ambience in which Maurice may fall harmlessly in love with a succession of older boys; he hears in a dream a voice telling him 'That is your friend'. By plodding work and unexceptionable manner Maurice gains in popularity, but the prize-giving (M, IV) articulates his nullity, with Barry chorically puncturing his aspirations.

At Cambridge Maurice is slowly released from his cage, first by the aesthetic Risley, and then by Clive Durham. The two meet first whilst listening to the 'Pathetique' Symphony, with its submerged homoerotic drama,[22] and Maurice's character gains a new strength and subtlety: 'A caution alien to his nature was at work. He had always been cautious pettily, but this was on a large scale. . . . If obliged to ask himself, "What's all this?" he would have replied, "Durham is another of those boys in whom I was interested at school" ' (M, VI, 32). In the Cambridge scenes, with their easy compression, some of the suburban constrictions fall away under Clive's questioning, a 'breath of liberty' reaches Maurice in spite of his view of unorthodoxy as 'bad form' which a man 'might have the grace' to keep to himself (M, VII, 43, 34).[23] The debate between the two friends on 'the unspeakable vice of the Greeks' (M, VII, 42) is immediately dramatized by Maurice's feral repudiation of a girl at home (M, VIII) and Clive's declaration of love (M, IX). This brings the first crisis: Maurice acknowledges his homosexuality and realises he has been 'fed upon lies' (M, X, 53). The union, which remains semi-Platonic, is consummated on the motor-bike expedition into the fens, an episode remarkable for its fidelity to the flow and recoil of feeling. Through vital movement the lovers are united in Nature:

They became a cloud of dust, a stench, and a roar to the world, but the air they breathed was pure, and all the noise they heard was the long drawn cheer of the wind. They cared for no one, they were outside humanity, and death, had it come, would only have continued their pursuit of a retreating horizon.

(M, XIII, 66–7)

After this Nature offers rest and retreat: 'They ate on a grassy embankment. Above them the waters of a dyke moved imperceptibly, and reflected interminable willow trees. Man who had created the whole landscape was nowhere to be seen' (M, XIII, 67). Maurice is sent down as a result of this exploit, but 'all the agony of separation that he went through now, instead of destroying, was to fulfil' (M, XV, 73).

The fulfilment is to be wrought through the agency of Penge, the Durhams' decaying country house in Wiltshire, which takes on something of the significance of Cadover or Wragby Hall. It stands in a thickly wooded landscape, both house and estate being marked, like Chesney Wold or Transome Court, 'not indeed with decay, but with the immobility that precedes it' (M, XVI, 77). The decay is ominous: it casts its shadow upon future developments. In this decrepit pastoral, Mrs Durham consults Maurice about Clive's future. The very notion of the future conjures up for Maurice the Darwinian ethos of Mr Ducie:

An immense sadness — he believed himself beyond such irritants — had risen up in his soul. He and the beloved would vanish utterly — would continue neither in Heaven nor on Earth. They had won past the conventions, but Nature still faced them, saying with even voice, 'Very well, you are

thus; I blame none of my children. But you must go the way of all sterility'.
(M, XVII, 87)

Ironically it is Clive, who is to submit to this law, who defiantly replies, ' "Why always children? For love to end where it begins is far more beautiful, and Nature knows it" ' (M, XVII, 88). This ramifies into the friendship between the two families, and Mrs Durham's abortive scheme to marry Clive to Maurice's sister in accordance with her theory that 'one ought to cross breeds a bit' (M, XIX, 92).

Clive, preparing for Greece, falls into a psychosomatic illness, and then in the theatre of Dionysus tells Maurice by letter that he has become normal (M, XXII). Maurice has to digest this change: 'It was nothing to him that Nature had caught up this dropped stitch in order to continue her pattern. While he had love he had kept reason' (M, XXVI, 124). From this catharsis emerges the dream which Forster makes a reality. Recognising his outlaw status Maurice reflects, 'Perhaps among those who took to the greenwood in old time there had been two men like himself — two. At times he entertained the dream. Two men can defy the world' (M, XXVI, 125). Before this may happen Maurice is to be tutored in the ways of the human heart: he must learn to accept the pagan wisdom of Mr Grace's 'new cosmogony' of solarism (M, XXVII), and to reject the surrogate religion of psychoanalysis through his visits to the hypnotist Lasker Jones (M, XXXVI, XLI). Forster's tone, one of masterly compression and understatement, expands as he describes this type of spiritual struggle as one of the 'supreme achievements of humanity' (M, XXXVIII, 132). Though Maurice is still welcome at Penge, Clive now finds him 'beyond the barrier', 'the wrong words on his lips and the wrong desires in his heart, and his arms full of air' (M, XXXIII, 152).

In a climactic chapter Maurice visits Penge and is accepted by Clive's wife. Despite the wedding the atmosphere of dilapidation has increased, the incessant rain heightening the Dantesque sense of approaching crisis: 'He didn't care for Clive, but he could suffer from him. The rain poured out of a leaden sky on to the park, the woods were silent. As twilight fell, he entered a new circle of torment' (M, XXXIV, 156). Though Maurice concludes that 'Life had proved a blind alley, with a muck heap at the end of it' (M, XXXIV, 159), his deliverance is already promised in the first glimpse of the surly young gamekeeper.[24] Returning to Penge from his first visit to the hypnotist, Maurice clashes with the rector, Mr Borenius, as to whether Alec Scudder should be confirmed prior to his intended emigration. 'Heated' by food and wine he stalks into the shrubbery, sensing that Nature is 'turning away' from him and that life is to entomb him: 'Indoors was his place and there he'd moulder, a respectable pillar of society who has never had the chance to misbehave' (M, XXXVII, 174). He bumps into Alec, and the events of the day 'began faintly to glow'. Penge acquires a complex symbolism and leads him towards a revaluation: 'There was something better in life than this rubbish, if only he could get to it — love — nobility — big spaces where passion clasped peace, spaces no science could reach, but they existed for ever, full of woods some of them, and arched with majestic sky and a friend' (M, XXXVII, 178). The friend emerges from the woods at night, and in response to Maurice's call, climbs into the bedroom.[25]

This intricate moment brings together civilised and natural man, and allows the union to cohere into a universal statement. Its analogue in the cricket match in which the two are ranged against society (M, XXXIX), with its resultant stress, leads Maurice into a collapse. When Lasker Jones tells him that homosexuality was once a capital offence Maurice appeals to his myth of Nature: ' "England wasn't all built over and policed. Men of my sort could take to the greenwood" ' (M, XLI, 196). The woods beckon, not as a Pre-Raphaelite land of lost content, but as a vital and organic antithesis to the world of commerce: all Forster's work has tended towards this moment. The intensity of the response to sex, art or Nature differentiates those experiences from the society in which they are experienced.

Thus Maurice fails increasingly to relate to the closed world of Edwardian England; seeing the king and queen 'he despised them the moment he bared his head. It was as if the barrier that kept him from his fellows had taken another aspect. He was not afraid or ashamed any more. After all, the forests and the night were on his side, not theirs; they, not he, were inside a ring fence' (M, XLII, 199). In *Howards End* Forster deliberately remained within the ring fence, and allowed his characters to bring about the desired changes. In *Maurice*, and even more in *A Passage to India*, the tone has darkened, and the possibilities of change are denied to those who, like Maurice's office companions, desire 'shelter everywhere and always, until the existence of earth and sky is forgotten' (M, XLII, 202–3).

In the Shavian interview at the British Museum, with the unexpected interpolation of Mr Ducie restating conventional Darwinism, Forster delicately portrays a duel between two views of life. A similar duel is fought out at the dockside between Maurice and Mr Borenius over the young keeper. When Maurice finally realises that Maurice will stay in England Nature reasserts her power over humanity; the claims of freedom, of passion and love, and indeed of the unconscious are to be acknowledged in Forster's conclusion: 'White clouds sailed over the golden waters and woods. . . . How negligible they had all become, beside the beautiful weather and fresh air'. The ship to Argentina becomes a death ship, whilst the lovers inherit the earth:

They must live outside class, without relations or money; they must work and stick to each other till death. But England belonged to them. That, besides companionship, was their reward. Her air and sky were theirs, not the timorous millions' who own stuffy little boxes, but never their own souls.
(M, XLV, 223)

Forster was determined that 'in fiction anyway two men should fall in love and remain in it, for the ever and ever that fiction allows' (M, 236). He had indeed noted as early as 1905 that 'the prevalence of sad endings is a sign both of conscientiousness and incompetence: the first because artists now realise that marriage, the old full stop, is not an end at all, the second, because it would be finer to end happily, and they cannot. It doesn't mean that they are pessimistic in life, but that they are too clumsy to be optimistic in art' (EMF, 132). Forster, on the contrary, ends with beautiful tact and poetry. Because the social world breeds hypocrisy and unreality, he releases his protagonists into the woods which have been beckoning since the middle of the novel. It is an ending which works on the level of myth.

Forster appropriately named his novel 'Whitmannic' in its vision of ideal democratic brotherhood. 'It is to the development, identification, and general prevalence of that fervid comradeship', Whitman announced, 'that I look for the counterbalance and offset of our materialistic and vulgar American democracy, and for the spiritualisation thereof'.[26] To become *déclassé*, as in *Lady Chatterley's Lover*, is a first step in the reconstitution of society through passion. Forster does not go so far as Lawrence, the taboos are too great for him; but the open ending of *Maurice*, its endorsement of clandestine passion which will undermine the structures of ordered society, its poetic realisation of the tow of the unconscious underlying rationality, points to a consummation fuller and more satisfactory than in any of his earlier novels. In the ghostly close, with its final dismissal of Clive Durham, Nature and spontaneity win out over convention and repression; the claims of society have been examined and found wanting. Forster's coherently realised lyricism transcends the problems of the subject-matter, and the long search for a return to Nature is at an end.

IV

Forster shared with Lawrence a literary inheritance: the authors who were crucial to Forster were also vital to the young Lawrence a few years later. Both authors drew upon a tradition of the novel which centres upon the contrast between Nature and civilisation, and develops the theme of the primacy of emotion and the instinctual in human behaviour. It was his constant return to this theme which gave Lawrence what

Forster identified as his 'rapt bardic quality', 'irradiating nature from within'. Referring to Birkin's stone-throwing, Forster acknowledged Lawrence's potency: 'It is the prophet back where he started from, back where the rest of us are waiting by the edge of the pool, but with a power of re-creation and evocation we shall never possess' (AN, 146–7).

This illuminates the affinities and divergences of the two men. Lawrence rejected Forster's passivity: 'A man of strong soul has too much honour for the other body — man or woman — to use it as a means of masturbation. So he remains neutral, inactive. That is Forster', he told Bertrand Russell. Yet he also recognised Forster as working in the same tradition and espousing the same fundamental values as himself: 'there is something real in him, if he will cause it not to die. He is *much* more than his dummy-sucking, clever little habits allow him to be'. T.E. Lawrence's contrast between Forster's 'neatly layered' world which never strays beyond 'trim privet hedges' and Lawrence's turbulent world of 'hussies and bounders' hits upon a central truth. Yet even before the publication of *Maurice* the links between the two writers, their sense of anguish at the deathliness of modern society, and their commitment to the positives of Nature and passion, were clearly apparent. *Maurice*, Forster's most Lawrencean work, relates closely to the world of *The White Peacock* and *Sons and Lovers*, Forster's favourite Lawrence novels. In the work of both novelists, the Nature theme introduced by Hardy and Meredith is reworked within a dynamic new context to yield fresh and exciting fictional insights.

Notes

1 E.M. Forster, *Abinger Harvest* (1936) (Harmondsworth, Penguin Books, 1967, hereafter cited as AH), p. 99.
2 E.M. Forster, *Goldworthy Lowes Dickinson* (1934) (London, Arnold, 1934, hereafter cited as GLD), p. 193.
3 E.M. Forster, *Two Cheers for Democracy* (1951) (London, Arnold, Abinger edn., 1972, hereafter cited as TC), p. 54.
4 E.M. Forster, *A Passage to India* (1924) (Harmondsworth, Penguin

Books, 1966, hereafter cited as PI).

5 E.M. Forster, *The Longest Journey* (1907) (Harmondsworth, Penguin Books, 1967, hereafter cited as LJ).

6 E.M. Forster, *Maurice* (1971) (London, Arnold, hereafter cited as M).

7 E.M. Forster, *Aspects of the Novel* (1927) (Harmondsworth, Penguin Books, 1966, hereafter cited as AN), p. 170.

8 P.N. Furbank, *E.M. Forster: A Life, Vol. I* (London, Secker & Warburg, 1977, hereafter cited as EMF), p. 47.

9 E.M. Forster, *Collected Short Stories* (1947) (Harmondsworth, Penguin Books, 1965, hereafter cited as CSS), p. 117.

10 E.M. Forster, *Howards End* (1910) (London, Arnold, Abinger edn., 1972, hereafter cited as HE).

11 E.M. Forster, *Where Angels Fear to Tread* (1905) (Harmondsworth, Penguin Books, 1968, hereafter cited as AFT).

12 Forster's aunt, Laura Forster, settled in Abinger in 1878 and struck up an acquaintance with Meredith (EMF, 45–6).

13 E.M. Forster, *A Room With a View* (1908) (Harmondsworth, Penguin Books, 1966, hereafter cited as RWV).

14 See S.P. Rosenbaum, 'E.M. Forster and George Meredith', PMLA, LXXXVI (1971), pp. 1037–8; and J. Perry Levine, *Creation and Criticism, A Passage to India* (Chatto & Windus, 1971), pp. 85–6. For a detailed analysis of the relationship see M.Y. Shaheen, 'Forster on Meredith', *Review of English Studies*, n.s., XXIV (1973), pp. 185–91.

15 See J.G. Frazer, *The Golden Bough* (London, Macmillan, 1936; abridged edn.), pp. 110–35. The sacred grove, with its initiatory role in a cycle of regeneration, reappears in 'Other Kingdom', 'The Road from Colonus', in Rickie's dell, and most extensively in the woodlands of *Maurice*.

16 Gerald's death may be read as an ironic Forsterian reply to Housman's 'To an Athlete Dying Young'.

17 In view of the title from *Epipsychidion* this scene may recall the delight of Shelley and Peacock in launching paper-boats. However, the incident also appears highly Meredithian. Forster knew 'The Thrust in February' well (AN, 96), and it contains lines which pre-figure Forster's moment of communion:

The sighting brain her good decree
Accepts; obeys those guides, in faith,
By reason hourly fed, that she,
To some the clod, to some the wraith.

Is more, no mask; a flame, a stream,
Flame, stream, are we, in mid career
From torrent source, delirious dream
To heaven-reflecting current clear.

Meredith's theme here might be endorsed by Stephen: 'For love we Earth, then serve we all;/Her mystic secret then is ours'. Forster may also, in this scene, be remoulding the game which Irene and Rubek play beside the mountain stream in *When We Dead Awaken*, a play Forster deeply admired (see 'Ibsen the Romantic', AH, 95–101).

18 The atmosphere of the Wiltshire section is close to W.H. Hudson's sketches in *A Shepherd's Life*, which describe the 'high downs' with 'the memorials of antiquity carved on their smooth surfaces . . . and the vast green earthworks crowning their summit' (Chapter XIII). Though Hudson's book appeared after *The Longest Journey*, his first version, 'A Shepherd of the Downs', had appeared in *Longman's Magazine* in 1902, and may well have contributed to the portrayal of Stephen and his ambience. The presence of Housman may also be felt here: 'Across the glittering pastures/And empty upland still/And solitude of shepherds/High in the folded hill' ('The Merry Guide').

19 The Attis rituals were connected with a sacred tree, just as Rickie's great test takes place within the Rings, with the solitary tree at the centre (*The Golden Bough*, pp. 374 ff.).

20 The language here, and the underlying theme of racial continuity, suggests the influence of Meredith's last novel, *Celt and Saxon*. This appeared in the *Fortnightly Review* from January to August 1910, and was published in July in book form. *Howards End* was published in October.

21 E.M. Forster, *The Life to Come* (1972) (London, Arnold, Abinger edn., 1972, hereafter cited as LC), p. xiv.

22 Later Maurice is to hear the 'Pathetique' and to study Tschaikowsky's life as clue to his own behaviour (M, XXXII).

23 Possibly a punning reference to Mr Grace with his unorthodox sun-religion. Maurice's situation pre-figures that described by T.E. Lawrence in *Seven Pillars of Wisdom*: 'There was a craving to be liked — so strong and nervous that never could I open myself friendly to another. The terror of failure in an effort so important made me shrink from trying; besides, there was the standard; for intimacy seemed shameful, unless the other could make the perfect reply in the same language, after the same method, for the same reasons'. In his copy A.E. Housman wrote against this confession, 'This is me'.

24 'Not much can be premised about him', Forster wrote of Alec Scudder. 'He must loom out of nothing until he is everything'. Forster's erroneous claim that Alec is 'senior in date to the prickly gamekeepers of D.H. Lawrence', and 'had not the advantage of their disquisitions', is odd in view of his admiration for *The White Peacock*, which had been published in 1911.

25 The encounter with Alec may owe something to Forster's visit to Henry James at Rye in 1908. Escaping from the over-refined atmosphere of the

Master's drawing-room Forster glimpsed a young labourer smoking in the shadows. It was a crucial moment of self-definition, and led to a poem:

> when I left the room
> Where culture unto culture knelt
> Something just darker than the gloom
> Waited — it might be you I felt.
> It was not you; you pace no night
> No youthful flesh weighs down your youth.
> You are eternal, infinite,
> You are the unknown, and the truth.
> Yet each must seek reality:
> For those within the room, high talk,
> Subtle experience — for me
> The spark, the darkness, on the walk.

(Quoted in EMF, 165)

26 W. Whitman, *Democratic Vistas* (Routledge & Kegan Paul, 1906), pp. 72–3. Forster quotes Whitman on Nature in *The Longest Journey*.

8 D.H. Lawrence and the nature tradition

I

There is a striking scene towards the end of *The Rainbow*, when Anna has begun her studies at the college in Nottingham. After the purgatory of her school-teaching experience she at first feels a sense of 'joy', almost of 'ecstasy' at being allowed to study under the lecturers, 'black-gowned priests of knowledge, serving for ever in a remote, hushed temple'. Soon comes inevitable disillusionment as she realises that the college is a 'sham store, a sham warehouse, with a single motive of material gain, and no productivity', and that the 'religious virtue of knowledge was become a flunkey to the god of material success'. The section has an autobiographical feeling; Ursula here, to all intents and purposes, is the young Lawrence. The one strand of college life which pierces through her 'inertia' is her study of botany: she is 'fascinated by the strange laws of the vegetable world', the microscope giving her access to 'something working entirely apart from the purpose of the human world'. As she gazes raptly at the 'plant-animal lying shadowy in a boundless light' she frets over a conversation she has had with Dr Frankstone, a lecturer in Physics. Dr Frankstone is a thoroughgoing materialist. ' "I don't see why we should attribute some special mystery to life — do you?" ' she demands of Ursula. ' "May it not be that life consists in a complexity of physical and chemical activities, of the same order as the activities we already know in science? I don't see really, why we should imagine there is a special order of life, and life alone —" '. Thus Ursula begins to ponder, 'what was the purpose':

Electricity had no soul, light and heat had no soul. Was she herself an impersonal force, or conjunction of forces, like one of these? She looked still at the unicellular shadow that lay within the field of light, under her microscope. . . . What then was its will? If it was a conjunction of forces, physical and chemical, what held these forces unified, and for what purpose were they unified?

As her gaze intensifies, Ursula experiences a species of revelation which nullifies Dr Frankstone's materialism:

Suddenly in her mind the world gleamed strangely, with an intense light, like the nucleus of the creature under the microscope. Suddenly she had passed away into an intensely-gleaming light of knowledge. She could not understand what it all was. She only knew that it was not limited mechanical energy, nor mere purpose of self-preservation and self-assertion. It was a consummation, a being infinite. Self was a oneness with the infinite. To be oneself was a supreme, gleaming triumph of infinity.

After this she feels a 'great craving to depart', a dread of the material world and of her own 'transfiguration': 'She wanted to run to meet Skrebensky — the new life, the reality'. This new life is expressed in Ursula's sensual awareness released by her reconciliation with her lover. Watching her fellow-citizens in the tram or the train she sees 'beneath their pale, wooden pretence of composure and civic purposefulness, the dark stream that contained them all. They were like little paper ships in their motion'. But deep down 'each one was a dark, blind, eager wave urging blindly forward, dark with the same homogeneous desire' (TR, XV, 431 ff.).

This seminal sequence lays bare the crux at the heart of Lawrence's conception of Nature, the constant clash between materialism and pantheism here encapsulated in the debate between Dr Frankstone and Ursula. In his finest imaginative work Lawrence reconciles causal evolution with Nature mysticism; the sources of his evolutionary reading of the universe have already been examined; it now remains to examine the opposing tradition of Nature mysticism as it was fed into Lawrence's being.

II

Lawrence's early work is insistently concerned with man's place in Nature. The stress in these books, and indeed in all his best work, falls upon what he calls 'a great background, vital and vivid, which matters more than the people who move upon it'. The 'immorality of nature', Lawrence maintained, 'surrounds us in its eternal incomprehensibility, and in its midst goes on the little human morality play'. Hardy, he argues, shares with Shakespeare, Tolstoy or Sophocles this 'setting behind the small action of his protagonists the terrific action of unfathomed nature' (STH, 31) — an accurate description of the world of *The White Peacock*, or *The Tres-passer*.[1] This sense of connexion between man and his environment grows first out of Lawrence's sensuous and scientific awareness of Nature, and secondly out of the work of his precursors, from each of whom, with the priority of genius, he extracted the essentials for his own art.

The formative influences were various: the pressures of home life; the tradition and authority of chapel worship; the economy and ritual of a mining community, and the more ancient underlying patterns of agricultural England. Lawrence had a superb sense of what all this meant. Of the peculiarly moulding experience of family life much has been written; of the early intellectual and literary milieu much remains to be explored. In addition to the philosophical influence of such 'sages' as Carlyle, Ruskin, Schopenhauer, and Edward Carpenter, the transmission and synthesis of fictional tradition in Lawrence repays the closest evaluation. Lawrence may rightly be seen as heir to a number of 'lines' including American, Russian and French fiction. The crucial line where the origins of his imaginative art are in question is, however, the Nature novel, with its stress on the creative potential of man and the natural world. Lawrence's imagination was, in his early years, vitally shaped by the concepts of Nature and man which he found, not only in Hardy, but also in Meredith, Hale White and Jefferies. Lawrence responded to tradition in drawing upon a body of work concerned with response to and thought about Nature, a tradition going back two artistic generations and having its roots in the Romantic movement. That Lawrence 'emerges' from Hardy and Meredith has long been acknowledged; but he does not outgrow this tradition with World

War I; on the contrary it remained deeply buried within him and was, subject to that constant psychic revaluation and transformation which marks his art, an informing principle in *The Rainbow*. Towards the end of his career, after all the foreign quests for 'blood consciousness', such works as 'The Virgin and the Gipsy' and *Lady Chatterley's Lover* mark an imaginative return to this tradition. Lawrence's boyhood exploration of the woods and fields around Eastwood, and his sense of the interpenetration locally of Nature and industrialisation, was inextricably linked with his response to literature, and most potently to the literature of Nature which he discovered in the Transcendentalists, in Borrow, and in the fiction of Meredith, Hardy and Jefferies. The 'country of my heart' was both topographical and literary.

III

Lawrence's early work, in poetry and prose, had its origin in a specific social and literary milieu. The Lawrences' domestic entanglement, entrenched Congregational nonconformity, the rationalist debates of the Eastwood Pagans, each facet of Lawrence's early life, seen against the antithesis between Eastwood and Haggs Farm, is brought to fruition in *The White Peacock, The Trespasser* and *Sons and Lovers*. To trace Lawrence's debts to the tradition of Meredith and Hardy is not to reveal Lawrence as plagiarist; on the contrary such a study shows the transformation of tradition at the hands of a great writer. It is in Lawrence that the novel of Nature culminates.

Jessie Chambers's memoir deals interestingly with Lawrence's literary formation. It is the record of a broad spectrum of interests, in which certain patterns may be discerned — concern with French or Russian fiction, for instance. The self-education which Lawrence and Jessie undertook, partially documented in *Sons and Lovers*, was based upon the twin sources of the local chapel and the Eastwood Mechanics' Institute Library. The chapel, Jessie recalled, 'became the centre of our social life. There was a Literary Society, and we all paid our shilling for a membership card'. Here the Pagans 'talked about books and writers, and about life, gropingly, trying to find the hidden reality behind the appearance of things' (ET, 53, 58). This exploration was fuelled by the volumes borrowed from the Institute Library, and Jessie Chambers's memories here are especially relevant:

the visit to the library was at that time the outstanding event of the week . . . I always went if possible, though Lawrence inevitably did most of the choosing. He would take possession of my list and pounce on the book he was looking for; he always seemed to know just where to look for it. We were both excited by this hunting among books.

Jessie added that Lawrence 'seemed to be acquainted with nearly everything in the little library', though this may be hyperbole, since the collection ran to over 3000 volumes (ET, 92–3).[2] A complete catalogue was made in 1895, and this reveals the wealth of reading in books and periodicals available to the young Lawrence.[3] Taken together with recent research into Lawrence's reading,[4] the catalogue provides a fairly complete picture of his literary and intellectual formation in these crucial years. Lawrence's reading habits must be a classic instance of creative reading, and nowhere more so than in relation to his closest literary forerunners.

Lawrence's conception of Nature was a living force, capable of transmutation. But it had its roots in the Romantic movement, and the Transcendentalists, whose image of the integration of the mind with Nature held a fascination for him. Although later in his career he was to dismiss a visitor as 'rather a tiresome New Englander of the ethical mystical-transcendentalist sort' (SCAL, 154),[5] and to hold that 'the cosmos and humanity were too much manufactured in New England' (SE, 37), Lawrence's early years were imbued with Transcendental influence. Indeed, it could be said of Lawrence as he remarked of Thoreau, that he 'isolated his own bit of locality and put it under a lens, to examine it'. The Transcendentalists, he recognised, were engaged by the 'moral issue' of man's place in Nature (SCAL, 120, 180), and he admired their direct simplicity of utterance.

Jessie Chambers notes that Lawrence 'read and liked' Emerson's *Essays*,[6] which he knew as early as 1905 (ET, 101). The *Essays* sound a Lawrencean note at many points. Emerson, for example, holds that the principle of duality is central to human life: 'Polarity, or action and reaction, we meet in every part of nature; in darkness and light; in heat and cold; in the ebb and flow of waters; in male and female; in the inspiration and expiration of plants and animals' (*Essays*, 67). Man is 'a bundle of relations, a knot of roots, whose flower and fruitage is the world', yet 'Whoso would be a man must be a nonconformist' (*Essays*, 26, 34). The thesis of the *Essays* is the transcendence of Nature, a thesis presented as a peculiarly New England variety of pantheism: 'The true doctrine of omnipresence is, that God reappears with all his parts in every moss and cobweb. The value of the universe contrives to throw itself into every point' (*Essays*, 71). This vision of man and universe conjoined is ultimately a religious one:

> that great nature in which we rest, as the earth lies in the soft arms of the atmosphere; that Unity, that Over-Soul, within which every man's particular being is contained and made one with all other; that common heart, of which all sincere conversation is the worship, to which all right action is submission;   (*Essays*, 187)

The stress upon 'right action' is important; Emerson shares with Haeckel that concept of man's emergence which is so crucial in *The White Peacock*: 'nature has a higher end, in the production of new individuals, than security, namely, *ascension*, or the passage of the soul into higher forms' (*Essays*, 275).[7]

Lawrence perhaps reserved his highest admiration for Thoreau. Jessie recalled his becoming 'wildly enthusiastic' over *Walden*, especially 'The Ponds'. She recounts how Lawrence accompanied her brother to the Greasley fields, 'telling us meanwhile how Thoreau built himself a hut in the woods and lived beside the pond' (ET, 101). Thoreau's cool presence may be detected in the spiritualised landscapes of *The White Peacock* and the early poems, helping Lawrence to focus more concretely his romantic afflatus, and to define the role of man in the new industrial world.

Meredith was undoubtedly a more heady influence, strikingly discernible in the early work, but still present in later years. Thus in 1922, expressing his dislike of contemporary literature, Lawrence argued that 'false in part though they be', Hardy, Dickens, Maupassant and Meredith 'are still looking on life with their own eyes' (SE, 278). Even later, in 1927, in the course of his attack on Galsworthy's characterisation, he was to cite Sir Willoughby Patterne as an example of a human being 'in the same category as ourselves' (SE, 218), and in the first version of *Lady Chatterley* he made Lady Eva proclaim her desire for 'romantic love, and politics, something in the George Meredith line' (FLC, 32).[8] It is, however, in the early work that Meredith's presence is inescapable, marking both the Nature mysticism of *The White Peacock* and the rhapsodic eroticism of *The Trespasser*, as well as many of the early poems.[9] The intense emotional links between man and the landscape which predominate in Lawrence at this period owe a great deal to Meredith. 'You mustn't try to put too much thought into verse, as I often try, and — presumptuous contiguity — Meredith does', Lawrence instructed Louie Burrows, a girl he associated with Meredith's heroines.[10] 'Do you know Meredith's poetry', he went on, ' "Love in [the] Valley" — and "Woods of Westermain" and "Modern Love": very fine indeed. "Love in [the] Valley" is a bag of jewels, rare, precious as can be, and beautiful"'. This 'bag of jewels', which Jessie Chambers acknowledged 'had a special significance for him', together with *Richard Feverel* holds the key to the atmosphere of *The White Peacock*:

> Lovely are the curves of the white owl sweeping
> Wavy in the dusk lit by one large star.
> Lone on the fir-branch, his rattle-note unvaried,
> Brooding o'er the gloom, spins the brown eve-jar.
> Darker grows the valley, more and more forgetting:
> So were it with me if forgetting could be willed.
> Tell the grassy hollow that holds the bubbling well-spring,
> Tell it to forget the source that keeps it filled.

Meredith's spirit of affirmation, his celebration of the rhythms of Nature, and his acute interest in female psychology, all this reappears in Lawrence with a new and modern perspective.[12] It is significant that during the gestation of *The Insurrection of Miss Houghton* (later to become *The Lost Girl*) Lawrence told Garnett that his novel 'might find a good public amongst the Meredithy public' (L, 183).[13] *The Rainbow*, in its grasp of the full implications of the emergence from an agrarian to an industrial society, goes far beyond Meredith; but the sense of the struggle and fecundity of the Brangwens in the early chapters may justifiably be called Meredithian.

By contrast, Lawrence's debt to Hardy is amply recognised. Jessie Chambers records that 'Hardy's name had been familiar in our house since childhood days' (ET, 110), and much of Lawrence's work may be read as a continuation of themes which predominate in the Wessex novels. Hale White, on the other hand, has received nothing like his due in this respect. With his clarity of utterance, his sense of nonconformist tradition, his delineation of passionate heroines, his intense moral gaze, and his overall view of man within a Spinozan Universe, Hale White exerted a peculiar attraction upon the young Lawrence. He had read the *Autobiography* and *Clara Hopgood* as early as 1906, and 'admired with reservations' (ET, 110). However, even these reservations seem to have been swept away when at the end of 1912 Lawrence re-read the *Autobiography* and read *The Revolution in Tanner's Lane*, finding himself 'fearfully fond' of Hale White. 'I used to think him dull', Lawrence recalled, 'but now I see he is so just and plucky and sound' (L, 164). Hale White's influence is perhaps less clearly discernible than that of Meredith or Hardy. But the tone of strenuous earnestness, and the depiction of human struggle and deliverance through Nature, clearly impresses Lawrence deeply. The Spinozan debate in *The White Peacock*, and more centrally, the delineation of Ursula and Gudrun, may be indebted to *Clara Hopgood*; in a general sense Hale White offered, therefore, a growing-point to the young Lawrence.

In 1895 the Institute Library contained three important works by Jefferies, and many of his essays.[14] The fact that Lawrence had access to *Hodge and His Masters, Round About a Great Estate*, and *Wild Life in a Southern County* suggests that his literary origins may have been as deeply rooted in Jefferies as in Hardy. The relationship may be traced in various ways, but it can most easily be divided into three areas: Lawrence's specific references to Jefferies; correspondences in theme and incident; and analogous philosophical positions.

Lawrence's direct comments upon Jefferies are sparse, and relate mainly to *The Story of My Heart*. Yet when Louie Burrows sent him a copy of *The Open Air* for his birthday in 1909 he remarked significantly, 'I am very fond of Jefferies, and the pieces in *The Open Air* are so many of them down here' — that is to say, in the South London suburbs.[15] This implies that Lawrence had a fair knowledge of the Nature writer with whom he may have felt a unique affinity. This affinity emerges strongly in his ambiguous remarks about *The Story of My Heart*, the work of Jefferies which struck most deeply into Lawrence's sensibility, and which he had in mind whilst writing *The Trespasser*. In 1911, referring to *The Trespasser* as 'a work too *chargé*, too emotional', Lawrence confessed to Garnett, 'I shrink from it rather. I wonder whether Jefferies used to wince away from *The Story of My Heart*' (L, 88). *The Trespasser*, begun in March 1910 as *The Saga of Siegmund*, was rewritten in the early part of 1912, the same year in which Garnett had Duckworth's reissue *The Story of My Heart*, and it is likely that the two men discussed Jefferies's autobiography. In January 1912 Lawrence wrote to Garnett, 'I loathe the book, because it will betray me to a parcel of fools. Which is what any deeply personal or lyrical writer feels, I guess. I often think Stendhal must have writhed in torture every time he remembered *Le Rouge et le Noir* was public property: and Jefferies at *The Story of My Heart*. I don't like *The Story of My Heart*' (L, 94). Despite this last assertion, Lawrence's statement reveals how he associated himself with Jefferies as a 'lyrical writer', imbuing Nature with his own philosophical passion. The confessional intensity of Jefferies's spiritual autobiography was to be fictionalised by Lawrence in *The Trespasser* and elsewhere; but even his critical writing, he felt, was part of the overall pattern. Thus when he came to write his study of Hardy he described it as 'A sort of "Story of My Heart" ' (L, 298).

Lawrence's involvement with Jefferies illuminates many features of his work. Indeed it reveals in the fullest sense the meaning of tradition, both in the sense of specific indebtedness and in the wider sense of one artist learning from and developing upon the work of another. Within the framework of the concept the man and Nature, many elements are discernible which may have derived from Jefferies.

One such element is Lawrence's use of the figure of the gamekeeper as archetypal outsider. Jessie Chambers found that Lawrence's 'extraordinary obsession with gamekeepers is difficult to account for'; throughout their life together she could recall only one encounter with a keeper, though she concedes that they 'must have often seen us' (ET, 117–8, 33). In this encounter, Jessie's sister remarked, the Pagans 'were pulled up by the keeper to learn of the rights of others', and at other times they were often observed by the keepers, who had a hut in the local woods.[16] In the depiction of his gamekeepers Lawrence may have drawn upon this episode; but he must also have derived something of his conception from the Jefferies volumes in the Library, especially *Round About a Great Estate* and *Wild Life in a Southern County*, and from other Jefferies works, notably *The Gamekeeper at Home* and *The Amateur Poacher. The Gamekeeper at Home* portrays Keeper Haylock in words which find a curious transmutation in the figures of Annable and Mellors, and indeed in Alec Scudder. Jefferies notes that 'freedom and constant contact with nature have made him every inch a man; and here in this nineteenth century of civilised effeminacy may be seen some relic of what men were in the old feudal days when they dwelt practically in the woods'. The characterisation of Annable, Parkin and Mellors might also recall Jefferies's adverting to a proposal 'that gentlemen who had met with misfortune or were unable to obtain congenial employment should take service as gamekeepers' (GAH, 12, 34).

The White Peacock emerges directly out of the world of Jefferies.[17] The very opening with its evocation of the past of the mill, echoes Jefferies's chapter on 'The Water Mill' in *Round About a Great Estate*. 'There is something peculiarly human in a mill', Jefferies writes, 'something that carries the mind backwards into the past, the days of crossbow and lance and armour' (RGE, 104).[18] In the population surrounding the mill, and especially in the presentation of George, the presence of Jefferies may be suspected. *Round About a Great Estate* gives a trenchant account of the decline into alcoholism of Aaron, a young farmworker, 'one of the best of his class — a great, powerful fellow, but good-natured, willing, and pleasant to speak to', whose 'vice was drink', a vice which leads him to the Sun Inn, where like George at the Ram, 'he pottered round the inn of an evening' (RGE, 40, 51). In *The Open Air*, which Lawrence received from Louie Burrows, he would have read a more grimly realistic account of agricultural drinking, in the story of Roger in 'One of the New Voters'. Whilst Lawrence had no need of literary reminders of the evils of drink, Jefferies may have furnished him with authentication of its effects upon an agricultural physiology. Annable's growth from Jefferies's keepers seems clear; one of his quirks, the ability to switch from educated speech into dialect — an idiosyncrasy carried further by Mellors — might owe something to Farmer Iden, who possesses the faculty of 'quite altering his pronunciation from that of the country folk and labourers amongst whom he dwelt to the correct accent of education' (AF, 7).[19]

It is, however, in the climactic scenes of *The White Peacock* that the influence of Jefferies may most interestingly be sensed. These correspondences and analogues argue no simple borrowing; rather, they exemplify the ways in which the Nature tradition could be renewed. The churchyard ambience of *The White Peacock*, for instance, where Annable unburdens himself to Cyril, though based upon Annesley church, also resembles Jefferies's description of Essant Hill church. This isolated and empty edifice, Jefferies notes, is 'simply the mausoleum of the Dessant family', whose park it overlooks. Jefferies describes the 'much-decayed' yew-trees, the multitudinous tombs, and the air of dilapidation: 'the old church slumbered in the midst of the meadows, the hedges, and woods, day after day, year after year'. As Jefferies watches the funereal scene, pheasants, which he notes elsewhere are 'often called peacocks' (FH, 201), get into the churchyard from the surrounding park. This scene, redolent with decay, may have lodged in Lawrence's imagination and provided him with the core of his churchyard confessional (AP, 274–5).

Jefferies, in planning the reconciliation of his hero and heroine in *The Dewy Morn*, made this outline: 'Her swim to him; her beauty. Her impersonification of flower and leaf and tree. Poem of love' (NB, 145). Excepting the adventitious change of sex this is an apt resumé of Lawrence's 'Poem of Friendship' chapter: both scenes enact rites of love and initiation in Nature. As Felise swims in the woodland lake she discerns 'something almost sacred to her in the limpid water, in the sweet air, and the light of day. The flower in the grass was not only colour, it was alive. The water was not merely a smooth surface, the air not merely an invisible current, the light not merely illumination. As if they had been living powers, so they influenced her' (DM, XI, 65, XIV, 92).[20] Full of the 'great powers of nature', she reclines on the bank; there follows a long and passionate description of the human form, explaining how 'the human heart yearns towards that which is rounded, smooth, shapely', 'an instinct in the depth of our nature', an instinct which Cyril knows when he admires the 'noble, white fruitfulness' of George's form. Martial, hidden in the bushes, 'could have bared his forehead in the grass, in the purest worship of beauty'. Both scenes are absolutely characteristic, in their enraptured commingling of pantheism and hedonist sensuality.

In the succeeding chapter of *The White Peacock*, 'Pastorals and Peonies', Cyril's friends picnic in the hay-fields, quoting classical mythology, romancing and condescending to George; a 'giddy little pastoral', as one of them remarks. The interplay of comedy and poetry here closely approaches the tone of 'The Wooden Bottle' chapter of *Greene Ferne Farm*, in which the middle-class group, Valentine, Geoffrey, Felix St Bees, undertake the hay-making for Mrs Estcourt, whose workers are on strike. Geoffrey and Valentine, rivals for Margaret Estcourt's hand, vie with one another in the vigour of their hay-making.[21] As the party relaxes over a bottle, St Bees reads a nature poem, and Valentine a 'Bacchic meditation' satirising Jabez, Mrs Estcourt's shepherd. St Bees dilates upon versification, but his learned discourse is interrupted by the farm labourers, shamefacedly resuming work. The sense of unresolved tensions, centring upon Lettie, is stronger in *The White Peacock*; but Lawrence's scene recalls Jefferies's handling of scene and dialogue.

The climactic sequence of *The Trespasser*, furthermore, is exceptionally close to the central chapters of *Greene Ferne Farm* — a scene to which Lawrence was to return in *The Rainbow*. In each novel a pair of lovers wanders lost over the downs, in a scene which dramatizes the ecstasy and pain of love, and the renewing power of Nature. In Lawrence, however, this communion with earth signifies the break-up of the personal relationship, to be replaced by something larger and more universal.

Beneath a 'silver-greyness of stars', with above 'the velvet blackness of the night and the sea', Siegmund and Helena become full of 'mystery and magic': ' "gorse and the stars and the sea and the trees, are all kissing" ', she tells him. They lie upon the earth and Siegmund greets her as an earth-mother. He feels 'deathly', but the moon delivers him:

Then Siegmund forgot. He opened his eyes and saw the night about him. The moon had escaped from the cloud-pack, and was radiant behind a fine veil which glistened to her rays, and which was broidered with a lustrous halo, very large indeed, the largest halo Siegmund had ever seen.

(T, XI, 73; XII, 77)

Passing by the Catholic graveyard they head for the security of home. In *Greene Ferne Farm* Margaret and Geoffrey, marooned for the night on top of the downs, pass the night in a dolmen, 'the sepulchre of an ancient king — of a nameless hero', elated by the rise of the moon, a 'distorted gibbous disk', 'weird and magical'. In the dawn Geoffrey experiences a mystical sense of transcendence as 'his heart went out towards the beauty and glory of it':

The East flamed out at last. Pencilled streaks of cloud high in the dome shone red. An orange light rose up and spread about the horizon, then turned crimson, and the upper edge of the sun's disk lifted itself over the hill. A swift beam of light shot like an arrow towards him, and the hawthorn bush obeyed with instant shadow: it passed beyond him over the green plain, up the ridge and away. The great orb, quivering with golden flames, looked forth upon the world.

Margaret wakes up and the lovers descend to the world of agrarian reality (GFF, VI, 116, 119, VII, 131). Lawrence's poem on *The Trespasser* episode reveals psychological and verbal links with *Greene Ferne Farm*:

> A gibbous moon hangs out of the twilight,
>   Star-spiders, spinning their thread,
> Drop a little lower, withouten respite
>   Watching us overhead.
>
> Come then under this tree, where the tent-cloths
>   Curtain us in so dark
> That here we're safe from even the ermine moth's
>   Twitching remark.
>   ('The Yew-Tree on the Downs')

In *The Rainbow*, even more decisively than in *The Trespasser*, the night episode on the downs and the resultant communion with the circumambient world of Nature signals the withering away of purely personal relations. Once again the analogy with Jefferies is striking. The 'developing germ of death' in the affair between Ursula and Skrebensky comes to a head when they stay in a cottage in Sussex, and Ursula, like Felise, takes to roaming alone over the downs, 'a high, smooth land under heaven, acknowledging only the heavens in their great, sun-glowing strength'. Sitting on 'an old prehistoric earth-work' she weeps at the tiny train down in the Weald, with its 'blind, pathetic courage', and the downs, 'in magnificent indifference, bearing limbs and body of the sun'. The train, mechanistically working to destroy the vital plenitude of Nature, symbolises that 'corruption' of the earth by industrialism which Ursula sees in her final vision of Beldover. Overwhelmed, like Jefferies at the opening of *The Story of My Heart*, she turns to the earth: 'she lay face downwards on the downs, that were so strong, that cared only for their intercourse with the everlasting skies, and she wished she could become a strong mound smooth under the sky, bosom and limbs bared to all winds and clouds and bursts of sunshine.' Ursula now hates houses and beds, longing for the vital touch of Nature's rhythm; she and Skrebensky therefore spend their nights out on top of the downs, running naked across the 'smooth, moonless turf'. They watch the dawn from the top of 'an earth-work of the stone-age man', and the ecstatically pantheist experience surely echoes the scene in *Greene Ferne Farm*:

The light grew stronger, gushing up against the dark sapphire of the transparent night. The light grew stronger, whiter, then over it hovered a flush of rose. A flush of rose, and then yellow, pale, new-created yellow, the whole quivering and poising momentarily over the fountain on the sky's rim. . . . The sun was coming. There was a quivering, a powerful, terrifying swim of molten light. Then the molten source itself surged forth, revealing itself. The sun was in the sky, too powerful to look at.

Even Skrebensky, locked within his blind animal passion at this stage, comprehends the significance of this moment of transfiguration: 'He too realised what England would be in a few hours' time — a blind, sordid, strenuous activity, all for nothing, fuming with dirty smoke and running trains and groping in the bowels of the earth, all for nothing. A ghastliness came over him.' As the lovers prepare to return to the Midlands, Skrebensky is 'overcome by a cruel ineffectuality' (TR, XV, 463–66).[22]

The stresses of meaning and implication fall differently in

the two authors. But the correspondence in situation, feeling and imagery is indisputably close. In each sequence Nature offers a mode of transcendence; but Lawrence, with his profound awareness of the processes of industrialism, recognises that such a rebirth must first involve the withering away of urban civilisation and consciousness.

In its articulation of man's passionate relation with the natural world *The Trespasser* may be read as a fictionalised version of *The Story of My Heart*. At the critical point of their relationship, for instance, Siegmund and Helena walk along the downs in the twilight. The intensification accompanying their love-idyll has told upon their psychic reserves, and Helena comes to see Siegmund as 'a stooping man, past the buoyancy of youth'. She sobs wildly, and shelters near an ancient tumulus. Siegmund's reaction is hypnotically strange: 'He lay down flat on the ground, pressing his face into the wiry turf, trying to hide. Quite stunned, with a death taking place in his soul, he lay still, pressed against the earth'. Afterwards he glimpses the sea and stars, and acknowledges that 'it was all sacred' (T, XV, 100 ff.). This mysterious enactment of arcane pantheist ritual which recurs at Lawrencean moments of climax closely parallels the famous opening of *The Story of My Heart*, where Jefferies climbs up to the tumulus on the downs, and stretches himself out on the earth: 'I turned my face to the grass and thyme, placing my hands at each side of my face so as to shut out everything and hide myself . . . I now became lost, and absorbed into the being or existence of the universe' (SH, 23). In this posture, as Jefferies wrote elsewhere, 'the strange and marvellous inner sight of the mind penetrates the solid earth' (HV, 291). This 'inner sight' frees Jefferies from the shackles of time, as the lovers seek, through their own passion, to be free:

now is the immortal life. Here this moment, by this tumulus, on earth, now; I exist in it. The years, the centuries, the cycles are absolutely nothing; it is only a moment since this tumulus was raised; in a thousand years more it will still be only a moment. To the soul there is no past and no future; all is and will be ever, in now.　　　　　　　　　　　　　　　　　　(SH, 41)

Landscapes of Lawrence and Jefferies blend uncannily here. *The Open Air*, for instance, prefigures much of the night imagery of *The Trespasser*: 'The sliding meteors go silently over the gleaming surface; silently the planets rise; silently the earth moves to the unfolding east. Sometimes a lunar rainbow appears; a strange scene at midnight, arching over almost from the zenith down into the dark hollow of the valley' (OA, 173).

Jefferies's constant invocation of 'sun-life' recurs like a motto-theme in *The Trespasser*, and often in Lawrence's work up to 'Sun',[23] with such insistence that he might justly be called Jefferies's greatest disciple:

> With the great sun burning over the foam-flaked sea, roofed with heaven, — aware of myself, a consciousness forced on me by these things — I feel that thought must yet grow larger and correspond in magnitude of conception to these . . . I burn life like a torch. The hot light shot back from the sea scorches my cheek — my life is burning in me. The soul throbs like the sea for a larger life. No thought which I have ever had has satisfied my soul.
>
> (SH, 80)[24]

It is this yearning for a larger life, which also moves Ursula, which finally kills Siegmund. He fails because, unlike Jefferies, he has not got the resource of a truly creative personality, and because he is divided against himself.

Jefferies's philosophy of Nature is thus transmitted directly to Lawrence. The 'commonest form of matter', Jefferies held, 'excites the highest form of spirit': 'Inhaling this deep feeling, the soul, perforce, must pray' (HV, 278–9). The separateness of matter and human perception is acknowledged by both writers, yet both as it were strive to obliterate this gap. Although in 'Hours of Spring' Jefferies asserted that matter and spirit 'are distinctively two, utterly separate, and shall never come together' (FH, 7), and in *The Story of My Heart* declared that 'All nature, all the universe that we can see, is absolutely indifferent to us' (SH, 52), the burden of his writing is to disprove this postulate. Indeed in his most famous essay, 'Hours of Spring', Jefferies writes in mystical terms which anticipate Lawrence's dreams of renewal and resurrection: 'Under the Night of winter — under the power of dark Ahriman, the evil spirit of destruction — lay bud and germ in bondage, waiting for the coming of Ormuzd, the Sun of Light and Summer' (FH, 14). This resurrection is to be effected by the sloughing-off of civilisation and all the old forms of knowledge — a programme which strikingly anticipates Lawrence:[25]

Full well aware that all has failed, yet, side by side with the sadness of that knowledge, there lives on in me an unquenchable belief, thought burning like the sun, that there is yet something to be found, something real, something to give each separate personality sunshine and flowers in its own existence now. . . . It must be dragged forth by might of thought from the immense forces of the universe . . . all the learning and lore of so many eras must be erased. . . . Go straight to the sun, the immense forces of the universe, to the Entity unknown; go higher than a god; deeper than prayer; and open a new day.

(SH, 74)

A burning away of the living death of convention, Jefferies proposes, involves the reawakening of what Lawrence was to designate 'blood consciousness': 'I believe all manner of asceticism to be the vilest blasphemy — blasphemy towards the whole of the human race. I believe in the flesh and the body, which is worthy of worship' (SH, 84). *The Story of My Heart*, indeed, propounds doctrine which it was to be Lawrence's life-work to elaborate in the context of the modern world: 'The world would be the gainer if a Nile flood of new thought arose and swept away the past, concentrating the effort of all the races of the earth upon man's body, that it might reach an ideal of shape, and health, and happiness' (SH, 90).

Lawrence's own discovery of Jefferies was undoubtedly given new impetus when he came into contact with Edward Garnett and his circle. Garnett, who was a committed advocate of Jefferies, joined Duckworth's in 1901. Between then and World War I reprints of Jefferies figured prominently in Duckworth's catalogue; in addition, Garnett commissioned the collection of Jefferies's essays known as *The Hills and the Vale* from Edward Thomas, and encouraged Thomas to write his study of Jefferies.[26] Through Garnett, Lawrence came to read another major contributor to the Nature tradition, W.H. Hudson, who was also deeply indebted to the example of Jefferies. Lawrence was reading *Nature in Downland* (1900) at the end of 1911, whilst preparing to rewrite *The Trespasser*, and described it as 'very delightful', not returning the copy to Garnett until the New Year (L, 87, 89, 91). In this volume, as Garnett remarked, the spirit of the South Downs, 'its soil, plant and bird life, human story and changing atmosphere' are caught 'with exquisite freshness and ease'.[27] At the outset Hudson reflects on the paucity of writers on Sussex, and argues that Jefferies's powers, if not cut short by death, would now have attained 'their fullest maturity'. Like Lawrence, Hudson has strictures to make about the 'strain of intense unnatural feeling' which 'touches the borders of insanity' in *The Story of My Heart* — strictures to which Garnett took exception. Nonetheless, Hudson, after a weird encounter with Jefferies's 'double', reverts to Jefferies's supremacy as a celebrator of the natural world, 'lamenting again that he was prematurely torn away from this living green world he worshipped'.[28]

In Hudson, as in Jefferies, Lawrence discovered a writer who, in Garnett's words, can 'make us penetrate into that vast archipelago of nature's life where man's being and doing appear as merely one more of phenomena, as the human speck in the universal ocean of life'. Hudson, in common with all the writers of this tradition, and with Lawrence supremely, is marked by 'his refusal to divide man's life off from nature's life'.[29] Thus, standing on the ruins of Calleva at Silchester, Hudson responds vitally to the sense of organic interaction:

The very soil and wet carpet of moss on which [Roman] feet were set, the standing trees and leaves, green or yellow, the rain-drops, the air they breathed, the sunshine in their eyes and hearts, was part of them, not a garment, but of their very substance and spirit. Feeling this, death becomes an illusion; and the illusion that the continuous life of the species (its immortality) and the individual life are one and the same is the reality and truth.[30]

The essential meaning of Hudson, notwithstanding his more

laconic style,[31] is identical with that of Jefferies:

The blue sky, the brown soil beneath, the grass, the trees, the animals, the wind, and rain, and sun, and stars are never strange to me; for I am in and of and am one with them; and my flesh and the soil are one, and the heat in my blood and in the sunshine are one, and winds and tempests and my passions are one.[32]

Lawrence had also read some of Hudson's South American books (ET, 122; SCAL, 33), but *Nature in Downland* and possibly *A Shepherd's Life* (1910), with their discursive reflections upon an immemorial agrarian community, may have decisively influenced Lawrence.[33] This influence appears in *The Trespasser*, both in Siegmund's implausible dream of farming life, and in the valedictory closing scene where Helena and Byrne, walking on the North Downs, watch the sheep and the hay-making (T, XXI).

But the deepest significance of Jefferies, Hudson and the whole line of Nature writers was still to reveal itself in Lawrence's work. Whilst composing *Sons and Lovers*, Lawrence dismissively referred to his first two novels as 'a florid prose poem' and 'a decorated idyll running to seed in realism' (L, 66–7). This was unjust; but in any case it in no way devalues the potency of this tradition in relation to Lawrence's imaginative art. Without the germination of this tradition within him *The Rainbow* would never have been written.

IV

Lawrence's work centres upon the clash between the rationalist-materialist reading of the Universe expounded by Darwinism and the transcendental-vitalist reading of the Romantic Nature tradition. The Romantic tradition, discovering in the external world a mode of spiritual transcendence and sense of the ineffable creative mystery, necessarily rejected scientific determinism.

Jefferies gave exemplary expression of this viewpoint in *The Story of My Heart*, which Lawrence read so keenly. The 'intense concentration of the mind on mechanical effects', Jefferies observes, 'appears often to render it incapable of perceiving anything that is not mechanical' (SH, 123) — in essence, Ursula's riposte to Dr Frankstone. The belief that the human mind was evolved 'in the process of unnumbered years, from a fragment of palpitating slime through a thousand gradations, is a modern superstition'. 'Nothing is evolved, no evolution takes place', Jefferies asserts, on the grounds that it is never *seen* to take place: 'There is no evolution any more than there is any design in nature':

> There is no inherent necessity for a first cause, or that the world and the universe was created, or that it was shaped of existing matter, or that it evolved itself and its inhabitants, or that the cosmos has existed in varying forms for ever. There may be other alternatives altogether. The only idea I can give is the idea that there is another idea.

The creative potency of man lies elsewhere than in a causal universe of objects. Jefferies, from 'standing face to face so long with the real earth, the real sun, and the real sea' is convinced that 'there is an immense range of thought quite unknown to us yet'. He argues that the narrowness of human capacities and conceptions has blinkered man to the infinite possibilities of existence. The alternatives of extinction or immortality may not be the only ones: 'There may be something else, more wonderful than immortality, and far beyond and above that idea'. The mind and imagination, the essential self mystically transcending the merely physical, — this is the key to Jefferies and to much in Lawrence: 'there is a vast immensity of thought, of existence, and of other things beyond even immortal existence' (SH, 90–95). In Jefferies, as in Lawrence, there is a constant sense that 'there is still a limitless beyond' (SH, 117) of which Nature signals to man, and which issues in Jefferies's insistent demand for more 'soul-life'. By acknowledging the soul, the inner-self, 'we can proceed to shape things yet further, and to see deeper, and penetrate the mystery' (SH, 122) — to discover what Jefferies designates the 'Fourth Idea', and what Lawrence was to refer to as the 'Fourth dimension'.

The mystery underlying the emergence of mind, even in accordance with the laws of natural selection, the sense of infinity both outer and inner, and the vital spark of creativity, this is reconciled with the inexorable wave-like progress of all evolutionary forms in Lawrence. He had read in Spencer's *First Principles* that the nature of the universe is ultimately unknowable and inscrutable, and that therefore all law of cause and effect was relative. His work seeks to resolve the clashes and tensions between the two world-views. Lawrence's sense of phoenix-like renewal in man and Nature, the creative mystery at the heart of things, represents a synthesis of his intellectual and literary antecedents, a synthesis not merely doctrinal but transmuted into the sensuous immediacy of great art. The apocalyptic moment of Ursula's vision of the rainbow, now read with the full weight of these traditions behind it, may stand as a moving epitome of Lawrence's reconciliation of scientific and romantic apprehensions of Nature upon the anvil of his creative will:

And the rainbow stood on the earth. She knew that the sordid people who crept hard-scaled and separate on the face of the world's corruption were living still, that the rainbow was arched in their blood and would quiver to life in their spirit, that they would cast off their horny covering of disintegration, that new, clean, naked bodies would issue to a new germination, a new growth, rising to the light and the wind and the clean rain of heaven. She saw in the rainbow the earth's new architecture, the old, brittle corruption of houses and factories swept away, the world built up in a living fabric of Truth, fitting to the over-arching heaven.

(TR, XVI, 495–6)

Notes

1 Lawrence goes on to criticise Hardy for taking as his theme the idea that 'transgression against the social code' brings disaster, 'as though the social code worked our irrevocable fate' (STH, 32).

2 The Eastwood and Greasley Mechanics' Hall was erected in 1863. In addition to the library it held a news room, a hall, and billiard tables.

3 A *Catalogue of Books Belonging to the Library of the Eastwood and Greasley Artisans' and Mechanics' Institution* (Eastwood, W. Townsend, 1895). Subsequently referred to as *Eastwood Catalogue*. Consulted by kind permission of the Notts. County Librarian.

4 R.M. Burwell, 'A catalogue of D.H. Lawrence's reading from early childhood', *D.H. Lawrence Review*, III (1970), pp. 193–324.

5 D.H. Lawrence, *Studies in Classic American Literature* (New York, Doubleday, 1951, hereafter cited as SCAL).

6 R. Emerson, *Essays* (London, Oxford University Press, Worlds Classics edn., 1927, hereafter cited as *Essays*). The phrase 'sons and lovers' occurs in Emerson's *Essays*: see R. Dimaggio, 'A note on *Sons and Lovers* and Emerson's "Experience"', *D.H. Lawrence Review*, VI (1973), pp. 214–16.

7 Lawrence may also be recalling Emerson in 'The Cathedral' chapter of *The Rainbow*: 'The Gothic cathedral is a blossoming in stone subdued by the insatiable demand of harmony in man. The mountain of granite blooms into an eternal flower' ('History', *Essays*, 14).

8 Earlier, in *Women in Love*, Alexander Roddice is likened to 'a Meredith hero who remembers Disraeli' (WL, VIII, 94).

9 Lawrence may have read *Diana of the Crossways* and 'Love in the Valley' as early as 1908; he refers to *Richard Feverel* and *Rhoda Fleming* in 1910, 'Modern Love', 'The Woods of Westermain', and the 'wonderfully clever' *Tragic Comedians* in 1911, and to *The Egoist* in 1927. (Burwell, *op.cit.*, 207, 210, 220, 221, 282). Lawrence's admiration for *The Tragic Comedians* is particularly significant, since after *Richard Feverel* it is the most 'Lawrencean' of the novels. Meredith's portrayal of the effete aristocratic male (Patterne, Dudley Sowerby, Lord Fleetwood) is certainly picked up by Lawrence; but the neo-Darwinian reversal of this situation in the personalities of the dynamic Alvan and the wavering Clothilde, a representative of an obsolescent social class, was peculiarly calculated to appeal to Lawrence.

10 He compared Louie Burrows with Rhoda Fleming, and wrote 'I have not the beautiful pristine fervour of a young Feverel to meet you with' (Moore, *The Priest of Love*, 124, *Lawrence in Love*, 73).

11 Letter of 27 March 1911 (*Lawrence in Love*, 85). But see a later reference to 'Modern Love' as 'nauseous' (WL, XIX, 299).

12 Interestingly, referring to the first version of the novel, Lawrence held that Letitia 'is *not* romantic — she is not Meredithian' (Letter of 13 May 1908, L, 11).

13 Ursula, in this novel, being regarded as an advanced young woman, is presented with poems of Swinburne and Meredith by Mr Harby (TR, XIV, 424).

14 *Eastwood Catalogue*, items 1050, 1051, 1052. The Library held a number of journals containing contributions by Jefferies:

(i) *Cassell's Family Magazine*
'How to read books', August 1876; 'Let me think', October 1876; 'Which is the way?', December 1876 (item 2066); 'Some triumphs of poor men', April 1877; 'The story of furniture', June 1877; 'The

Queen's new subjects', August 1877 (item 2067); 'The average servant', January 1878; 'Training school for servants', March 1878 (item 2068); ' "Autonomy" and what it means', February 1887; 'Entered at Stationer's Hall', October 1887 (item 2078).

(ii) *Chambers' Journal*

'A king of acres', 5 and 12 January 1884; 'Birds of Spring', 1 March 1884; 'Nature on the Roof', 21 June 1884; 'Under the acorns', 18 October 1884 (item 2173); 'Outside London', 17 January and 21 February 1885 (item 2174); 'Winds of heaven', 7 August 1886; 'Just before winter', 18 December 1886 (item 2175); 'The makers of summer', 28 May 1887 (item 2187).

(iii) *Good Words*

'Out of doors in February', February 1882 and May 1883; 'Haunts of the lapwing', January and March 1883; 'The green corn', May 1883 (items 2363 and 2364).

15 This was probably the Chatto & Windus edition of 1908. The girl who succeeded Louie Burrows in Lawrence's affections, Helen Corke, was also a disciple of Jefferies before she had met Lawrence. She described having 'discovered Richard Jefferies' Open Air philosophy and read his books' in the early years of the century. See *In Our Infancy*, p. 127.

16 May Chambers Holbrook, in E. Nehls, *D.H. Lawrence: A Composite Biography*, Vol. III (Madison, Wis., University of Wisconsin Press, 1959), pp. 595 ff.

17 This is not to deny other rural novels some influence. About the time of composing *The White Peacock* Lawrence was reading something by James Prior. This may well have been *Forest Folk* (1901), a novel of rick-burning set on the Notts-Derby border, which depicts the conflict between the passionate roughness of the Rideout family at Low Farmhouse and their neighbours. Anthony Rideout might have sat for George Saxton: 'He had developed into a young man of superb physique, a keen sportsman ... a careless acquirer and spender.... Sometimes he worked, it is true ... but the larger share of his time was divided between his more active pastimes and mere idling at the pothouse or in the open air'. Despite talent and intelligence, the events of the novel cause his gradual disintegration. Anthony has a sister named Letitia, and their grandmother lives at a cottage in 'The Bottoms'. 'What a curious man James Prior is!' Lawrence exclaimed to Garnett. 'I did not know him, and he is so near home. I was very much interested. But what curious, highly flavoured stuff!' A few weeks later he was telling Garnett how the whole Croydon household had 'devoured' Prior's book, and wondering why Heinemann had described him as a failed author (letters of 13 December 1911 and 3 January 1912, L, 87, 91).

18 The depredations of the rabbits over the estate which finally oust Mr Saxton from his farm reflect a topic frequently adverted to by Jefferies.

See, for example, *Chronicles of the Hedges*, p. 157, and *Field and Farm*, pp. 41, and 93.

19 This sociologically fascinating trait is also found in *Adam Bede* and *Tess*. It epitomises something engrained in Lawrence's experience. His sister recalled that Mrs Lawrence 'could never speak the local dialect, and we children were careful about it when we were with her, even though we let fling among ourselves' (Ada Clarke and S. Gelder, *Early Life of D.H. Lawrence* (London, Secker, 1932), p. 21). Jessie's sister, remembering conversations in dialect, added that 'Bert was very good and gave us samples new to us' (quoted in Nehls, *op.cit.*, p. 579). Many of Lawrence's characters share this dichotomy of speech, which reflects the ambivalence of his feelings about his parents. Thus Aaron, with his 'intelligent, almost sophisticated mind', 'had repudiated education. On purpose he kept the Midlands accent in his speech' (AR, VII, 82). This speech atavism runs through Lawrence's work like a motif, from Tom Renshaw in *The White Peacock* who 'spoke to his father in dialect, but to Emily in good English' (WP, iii, VIII, 412–13) right up to Mellors.

20 Many other episodes in *The Dewy Morn*, such as Martial's horseback meeting with Felise, or his struggles in the mill-dam, are prescient of Lawrence in their potency of unconscious suggestion and symbolism.

21 This rivalry may have suggested a starting-point for Lawrence's tale based on a similar situation, 'Love Among the Haystacks', although the story also relates to the Chambers's farm (see *Lawrence in Love*, 11).

22 *Amaryllis at the Fair*, in its account of the growth to consciousness of a young girl living on a farm, pre-figures *The Rainbow*. The scene where Will, 'his old trousers tucked into his boots', carefully sets his potatoes and unconsciously imprisons Ursula in her play-world (TR, VIII, 221 ff.), appears to echo Iden's expert potato planting when, clad in 'the raggedest coat ever seen on a respectable back', he ignores Amaryllis's importunities to look at the daffodils (AF, I, 4 ff.).

23 See the Brangwen women who 'lived full and surcharged, their senses full fed, their faces always turned to the heat of the blood, staring into the sun, dazed with looking towards the source of generation' (TR, I, 9).

24 See Lawrence's statement in *Apocalypse*: 'What we want is to destroy our false inorganic connexions, especially those related to money, and re-establish the living organic connexions, with the cosmos, the sun and earth, with mankind and nation and family. Start with the sun, and the rest will slowly, slowly happen' (A, 126). His essay on 'Aristocracy' also sounds a note familiar to the student of Jefferies. Man's life, Lawrence argues, 'consists in a relation with all things' but his 'greatest and final relation is with the sun, the sun of suns' (PH II, 481–2). Jefferies reiterates, in *The Story of My Heart* and elsewhere, his impassioned desire for more life: 'Fullness of physical life causes a deeper desire of soul-life' (SH, 83), and Lawrence repeatedly takes up this cry: 'More life! More *vivid* life! . . . He who gets nearer the sun is leader' (PH II, 483).

Elsewhere he declares: 'When I can strip myself of the trash of personal feelings and ideas, and get down to my naked sun-self, then the sun and I can commune by the hour, the blazing interchange, and he gives me life, sun-life, and I send him a little new brightness from the world of the bright blood' (A, 28). 'What is our petty little love of nature — Nature!! —' Lawrence exclaims, 'compared to the ancient magnificent living with the cosmos, and being honoured by the cosmos' (A, 27). In similar vein Constance Chatterley repudiates the industrial milieu of Wragby, with its 'eternal sunlessness': 'The next world, the electric world, would be short and sharp, and would lead back into the sun again. Back into the sun!' (JT, XIV, 316–7).

25 The sloughing-off process is classically explored in 'Snake', a poem which is adumbrated in Jefferies's thought: 'suddenly there is a rustle like a faint hiss in the grass, and a green snake glides over the bank. The breath in the chest seems to lose its vitality; for an instant the nerves refuse to transmit the force of life. The gliding yellow-streaked worm is so utterly opposed to the ever-present Idea in the mind. Custom may reduce the horror, but no long pondering can ever bring that creature within the pale of the human Idea' (SH, 53).

26 Duckworth's Jefferies reprints were: *After London*, 1905, 1908; *Amaryllis at the Fair*, 1904, 1908, 1911 (with an introduction by Garnett); *The Hills and the Vale*, 1909, 1911; *The Story of My Heart*, 1912; *Bevis*, 1904, 1908, 1913 (with an introduction by E.V. Lucas).

27 W.H. Hudson, *Nature in Downland* (London, Dent, 1951), Introduction, p. ix.

28 *Ibid.*, pp. 13 and 15.

29 E. Garnett, *Friday Nights* (London, Cape, 1922), p. 17.

30 W. H. Hudson, *Afoot in England* (London, Dent, n.d., The Wayfarer's Library), p. 96. Edward Thomas described Hudson's style aptly; 'a combination as curious as it is ripe and profound, of the eloquent and the colloquial, now the one, now the other, predominating in a variety of shades which make it wonderfully expressive' (E. Thomas, *In Pursuit of Spring* (London, Nelson, 1914), pp. 249–50.

32 W.H. Hudson, *Hampshire Days* (London, Dent, 1923), p. 47.

33 Lawrence's admiration for Hudson was not reciprocated. Hudson disliked Lawrence's 'insistence' on the 'hotness', 'colour' and 'curves' of the flesh, which he felt to be 'an obsession, a madness' which disfigured even a 'very good book' like *Sons and Lovers*. He finally dismissed Lawrence as a 'small minor poet', *Letters from W.H. Hudson to Edward Garnett* (London, Dent, 1925), pp. 127, 130, 144 and 160).

Index